Institutional Diversity in Self-Governing Societies

Institutional Diversity in Self-Governing Societies

The Bloomington School and Beyond

Edited by
Filippo Sabetti and Dario Castiglione

LEXINGTON BOOKS
Lanham • Boulder • New York • London

Published by Lexington Books
An imprint of The Rowman & Littlefield Publishing Group, Inc.
4501 Forbes Boulevard, Suite 200, Lanham, Maryland 20706
www.rowman.com

Unit A, Whitacre Mews, 26-34 Stannary Street, London SE11 4AB

British Library Cataloguing in Publication Information Available

Library of Congress Cataloging-in-Publication Data Available

ISBN 978-1-4985-2767-5 (cloth : alk. paper)
ISBN 978-1-4985-2768-2 (electronic)

∞™ The paper used in this publication meets the minimum requirements of American National Standard for Information Sciences—Permanence of Paper for Printed Library Materials, ANSI/NISO Z39.48-1992.

Printed in the United States of America

To Barbara Allen, Daniel H. Cole and Michael D. McGinnis
in gratitude for their energy and skill
in bringing together the writings of Vincent and Elinor Ostrom
to readers on every continent

Contents

List of Figures and Tables

FIGURES

TABLES

Acknowledgments

This book would not have been possible without the thoughtful challenges, hard work and insightful analyses of colleagues who actively participated in the research efforts described herein. We hope that this volume can illuminate and inspire the way we think of institutional diversity in self-governing societies and point to new directions in the long intellectual polycentric journey of the Workshop and the Ostroms' research program to understand human affairs. We would like to extend our thanks to the wonderful community of the Ostroms' Bloomington Workshop scattered in all parts of the world.

We wish to acknowledge the support of Dr Marios Filis in the final editorial preparation of the Manuscript and the Department of Politics of the University of Exeter for a contribution toward it. One of the editors, Dario Castiglione, wishes to acknowledge the steadfast and collegiate way in which Filippo Sabetti managed to push all of us along, keeping the project afloat and making sure that it would reach its natural conclusion in good time. Both editors agree that the collaboration has been a thoroughly positive experience for both of us, suggesting fruitful lines of future inquiry. On his part, Filippo Sabetti wishes to acknowledge support for his work on this project by the Social Sciences and Humanities Research Council of Canada (SSHRC 410-2011-0698) and to thank McGill University of a generous Sabbatical Leave (2015–2016) that allowed him to devote his full attention to the success of this project. At Lexington Books, Joseph C. Parry and Emily Roderick were most supportive, help which we also wish to acknowledge.

Dario Castiglione and Filippo Sabetti
August 2016

Introduction

Creativity, Diversity and Governance—Extending the Ostroms' Research Program

Dario Castiglione and Filippo Sabetti

Efforts to present a comprehensive overview of the Bloomington School of Political Economy received new impetus with the award of the Nobel Memorial Prize in Economic Science to Elinor Ostrom in 2009. Since then, renewed efforts have been made to map the contributions that Lin and Vincent Ostrom made to theories of governance, multiple methods of analysis, applied institutional analysis, and in-depth comparative case studies of human artisanship involved in taking hold of social and ecological systems, common pool resources, public economies, and metropolitan reform (e.g., Aligica 2014; Cole and McGinnis 2015, Aligica and Sabetti 2014). But the open-ended and multiform nature of the Ostrom program defies a single comprehensive overview. At the same time, its very place in social science is secure, as the significance of four decades of research activity of students, visiting scholars and other colleagues of the Workshop in Political Theory and Policy Analysis, now renamed the Ostrom Workshop, is recognized world-wide. All this work highlights both creativity in research alongside the recognition of the fallibility as well as the creative capacity of human beings, when given the opportunity, to partly shape and renew the world in which they live. What sets this volume apart is that it brings together theory and practice, models and work on the ground, design and creativity, empirics and norms, to outline the significance of the Ostrom research program for the future while remaining true to some of the basic concerns of this community of scholars—how fallible human beings can achieve and sustain self-governance in the face of a complex and ever-changing social and physical world.

Each contribution takes the Ostromian perspective as the point of departure, amplifies it and prepares the ground for future work by engaging with other approaches and areas of research with which the Bloomington School has some affinities. This way of testing and extending the ideas and methods of the Ostroms by engaging with other approaches and bodies of knowledge is particularly appropriate since the research program the Ostroms initiated and nurtured through the Workshop, has always been in-between different fields and sub-fields in the social sciences (political science, economics, public administration, law, history, anthropology), cultivating a strong interdisciplinary way of doing research, and exploiting the virtuous circle between theory, analysis, model building, and empirical research. Such in-betweeness with regard to the object of study, and the critical, often creatively "marginal" way (Castiglione 2014) in which the research program and the Bloomington school has interacted with other approaches and programs (public choice, rational choice, neo-institutionalism, social capital, federal and constitutional theory), set the context for and highlight the scope of this volume. A confrontation and creative dialogue with ideas and methods of other research programs is a way of sharpening one's analytic tools, while renovating one's own vision of social research. It is an exercise of thinking through and beyond the Bloomington School. We hope that this volume will contribute to such a task. In organizing the various contributions, we have divided them in three Parts. The chapters in Part I explore ways that extend theoretical and analytical creativity in social inquiry. Those in Part II engage these ideas with other approaches and research areas pointing to new directions. Finally, those in Part III offer examples of governance case studies with theoretical insights for future research.

THEORETICAL AND ANALYTICAL EXPLORATIONS

As far back as the early 1960s, well before the creation of the Workshop in 1973, Vincent Ostrom was developing new ways to approach the study politics. But the first more or less formal presentation of the framework of analysis of what later became known as the Institutional Analysis and Development (IAD) framework was in 1982 with a chapter by Larry Kiser and Elinor Ostrom on "the three world of action: a metatheoretical synthesis of institutional approaches" in a volume on strategies of political inquiry edited by Lin Ostrom. The contributions here draw attention to the persistent and evolving theoretical and analytical explorations that have both led the consolidation of the Ostroms' program and kept it at the evolving frontline of social science research (e.g., E. Ostrom 1982; Poteete et al., 2010).

The contribution by Albert Weale focuses on the distinction between rationality and reasoning in political choice. He reconstructs the logical foundations of the Ostroms' theory of public choice to show how and why it differs from standard public choice. To understand the centrality of language as a distinctive features of the Ostroms' notion of rationality, Weale contrasts it with standard expected utility theory grounded in the ordinalist theory of choice. Standard expected utility theory is behaviorist, and therefore has no need to impute language skills to agents. The reason why language is important in understanding public choice is that language is "a vehicle for creating bodies of common knowledge, mutual understanding, social accountability, and patterns of trust" (V. Ostrom 2014 [1993], 164). Two important consequences follow from this conception of agents as language users. The first is that language provides the basis for common knowledge, and therefore the possibility of agents having their actions guided by norms and rules. The second consequence is that it provides an understanding of the role of learning in social interaction, in contrast with the individuals assumed in standard expected utility theory, since we are urged to think of individuals as "fallible learners" and as capable of considering "their personal commitment to keeping promises and honoring forms of reciprocity extended to them" (Ostrom and Ostrom 2014 [2004], 118). Language does not just give voice to preferences, but it extends their range, enabling individuals to cooperate to mutual advantage, while providing them with the capacity for self-reflection. This is a reflective type of rationality not captured simply by consistency conditions on choices (Weale 2013, 101–11).

Against this backdrop, Weale suggests ways of expanding the Bloomington program by, for instance, exploring the distinction between regularities in behavior and rule-governed behavior, as outlined in the cited work of the legal philosopher H.L.A. Hart, which may help explaining important features of common property resource regimes. A language-based and non-monotonic conception of rationality can also offer, according to Weale, a more robust defense of institutional polycentricity by questioning close world assumptions. In a more critical vein, Weale notices a certain tension between Vincent Ostrom's bottom-up localism in polycentricity, and his characterization of constitutional choice as the product of deliberation and reflection. Such a tension suggests two differing conceptions of social order, which can be partially reconciled by making the distinction between "choice of constitutions" and "choice within constitutions" less sharp, partly reconciling two views of institutions as the result of either evolution or design, reducing their difference to a largely empirical question. Even though they are not operating in a closed world, those deciding constructively may hit upon solutions to collective action problems that through deliberation anticipate a wide range of cases. Even when an institution is the product of human action but not of human design, it may equally be recognized as a solution to a collective action problem.

The second contribution in this section is a reconsideration of a paper that Polski and Ostrom wrote in 1999, on how to use the IAD to do policy analysis and design. Polski elaborates on the linkages between the IAD and other approaches and areas of research in decision analysis, operations research, new institutional economics, social cognitive neuroscience and the complexity sciences. A chief merit of this update by Polski is to show the value of incorporating advances in science and technology that Lin and she did not consider in 1999 (Polski and Ostrom forthcoming [1999]), and to consider the implications of these developments for identifying and analyzing governing dilemmas. In the process, Polski invites us to broaden the definition of institution as a signaling device to encompass a broader array of mechanisms for understanding and conceptualizing social order that go beyond language-based constructs and expand the scope of our analyses and intellectual collaborations.

The third contribution is by Paul Dragos Aligica and Ion Sterpan. They reflect on various applications of the IAD framework and point to new "theoretical scenarios." They suggest that the framework can be applied to assess a classical theme in political philosophy and constitutional political economy: the state of nature and state of nature thought experiments. The core idea developed in the chapter is that the IAD framework enables us to detect a variety of unarticulated assumptions at work in different state of nature models. The authors illustrate how the framework can be used to identify such assumptions in state of nature thought experiments, to redraw the scope of their conclusion and carefully limit their claim.

NEW WAYS TO UNDERSTAND HETEROGENEITY AND SELF-GOVERNANCE

Recognition that we live in a multi-constitutional world helped Vincent Ostrom to develop in 1961 what remains his single most important legacy, the core concept of polycentricity. As we have seen from the previous section, the Ostroms then worked to develop a framework of analysis for tracing the different configurations of rules that apply to multiple levels and diverse types of organizations drawn from the public, private and community-based voluntary sectors. The result was an appreciation of the overlapping realms of responsibility and functional capacities of local undertakings and the centrality of citizens as cocreators of that world (Aligica's and Sterpan's chapter; and Sołtan 2014).

Ronald J. Oakerson's contribution focuses on the role of citizens as co-creators by expanding on Vincent Ostrom's institutional theory of democratic governance and his criticism of the standard understanding of representation as an instrument of democracy. In the process, Oakerson extends Ostrom's ideas to deal with contemporary problems in the American political system. Mainstream democratic theory regards representation—and the electoral process on which it depends—as the institutional core of modern democracy. Vincent Ostrom disagreed with such a conclusion and Oakerson discusses why.

Common to both Madison and Ostrom is a sense that electoral representation has critical limits as an institution of self-governance. It becomes important to specify both its limiting conditions and its possibilities. Founding republicans saw the need for multiple channels of representation as a countervailing factor to the limits of a single channel. Traditionally, republicans conceived of the separation of power and bicameralism as multiple vehicles of representation, while Madison and Hamilton considered federal institutions as capable of greatly amplifying this capability. Traditional republicans also thought that certain individual freedoms were of fundamental importance in the design of republics, strengthened by the addition of a "bill of rights" to an enforceable constitution. Ostrom would pick up on this complex of ideas as the basis for what he called an "open public realm," the arena of public liberty in which citizens are free to associate with one another and deliberate openly on the requirements of the public good. The open public realm is, in Ostrom's thinking, the core of a republican system of governance, sustained in considerable part by multiple channels of representation. The principle of multiple-agency, is complemented by the "anyone rule" as a way for individual persons to exercise their constitutional "authority" through the courts. Where multiple-agency serve to prescribe law, the anyone rule serves to invoke law in what Ostrom considered a *democratic* republic.

Following similar principles, Oakerson analyzes what he regards as two cases of institutional failure in the present American political system and suggests some possible reforms. One regards possible ways of counteracting oligarchical tendencies currently prevailing in the internal operations of Congress, especially in the House of Representatives, resulting in legislative deadlock. This diminishes, if not nullifies, the culture of inquiry-based deliberation, which, according to Ostrom, treats policies as hypothesis, and should characterize legislative assemblies. The other case concerns ways of constraining the police so to avoid abuses against individual citizens, like those that have come recently to the public attention in the United States, often involving brutal and unrestrained violence against African-Americans. Oakerson suggests that in order to enhance police accountability, a possible remedy lies in treating police officers as "representatives" of the discrete communities they serve. In this way, the main source of accountability is horizontal rather than vertical, lying in direct interaction with the public realm, organized through civic associations, rather than through the intermediation of the apparatuses of politics, administration or the law, which may lack place-based knowledge and cannot easily produce the empathy and mutual respect that is required for police accountability.

In his contribution, Anas Malik explores the potentials for polycentric governance in Islamic contexts and in the process raises the question of "does polycentric order require a particular culture of covenant resting on specific metaphysical foundations?" His answer is a qualified yes: the culture of covenant, covenant-like understandings, and covenantal behaviors should be defined expansively, beyond the narrow Jewish and Christian contexts. Further, the scholarly exploration of covenant has been hampered by an academic cultural legacy arguably traceable to the Enlightenment. This legacy is manifested in such divides as the split between humanities and social sciences. Covenant has both empirical and nonempirical dimensions, and the prevailing social scientific culture tends to treat both religion and metaphysical claims through empiricist lenses, distorting and limiting inquiry. This extends especially to the crucial activity of artisanship in covenanted associational forms, and a more integrative approach that considers exemplary causes may improve our insights. Malik advances his analysis by drawing on his interactions with the Ostroms and other Workshop scholars, and on his own research on polycentricity in Islamic contexts and interreligious collective action.

Dario Castiglione's chapter deals with the issue of political order and associational life from a different, though in many points related, perspective, by exploring how questions of contextuality and social meaning play a central role in the way in which the Ostroms considered politics not only as a problem-solving activities, but also as something that contributes to transform both the self-understanding of the social agents and the situations in which they operate. The complexities they injected in the analysis of the way in which people engage in collective action and how communities come together makes their institutional analysis distinctive. Looking in particular at Elinor Ostrom's work, Castiglione emphasizes the importance of social learning in the way in which individuals act together and engage in more stable and cooperative enterprises. Such ability to learn in social context and to engage with others offer a view of agency that goes beyond economic rationality and that helps agents to transform themselves at the same time as overcoming social traps and solving collective action problems. A similar process of transformation from a more isolated *homo economicus* to a more socially and culturally embedded *homo sapiens* is typical of Vincent Ostrom's conception of constitutionalism. Castiglione identifies the core of his conception in a "covenantal" conception understood through the socially sophisticated social psychology of Tocqueville, and on the principle of self-governing associations as an alternative to more centralized and monocratic conception of sovereign power. One of the key elements of this conception is the importance that intersubjectivity and shared meaning in the constitution of political society, which offers a thoughtful balance between individualistic and more communitarian forms of social organization.

The contributions by Oakerson, Malik and Castiglione point to the importance that Ostrom attached to the science of citizenship at work in society and how human beings can draw on different conceptions and systems of ideas to fashion different social realities that give meaning to particular configurations of political associations. In his chapter, Karol Sołtan builds specifically on this science of citizenship by treating the Bloomington School as part of an emerging interdisciplinary discipline in civic studies situated in a broad renewal of the republican tradition. From this perspective, theories of collective action and constitutional choice can help us to understand how a public science of civics can emerge from the practice of self-governance.

The form of civic theory Sołtan outlines, like the Bloomington School, has its roots in rational choice institutionalism, and its concern with polycentricity. But as an alternative to rational choice institutionalism, Sołtan proposes a civic account of human minds in interaction, with room for incentives, ideas and institutions. And as a foundation for a normative theory he proposes a reformulation of the republican tradition, including a civic and polycentric form of natural law. Sołtan's reformulation requires both a framework for the empirical exploration of human action and a program for the transformation of the social world, including an account of both institutions and ideals. At the center of the empirical framework there is the idea of fields of power, providing the context, including incentives, for purposive human action. But human minds are in turn capable of both creating and changing such fields of power, responding and modifying the incentives provided by the field of power. The more normative and programmatic part of Sołtan's reformulation is based on such an idea of human beings as creative (*homo creativus*), as well as on a fundamental opposition to arbitrariness.

As both an empirical and a normative project, civic theory aims to establish the conditions for a res publica, as a field of power, where power is exercised not in an arbitrary way, while serving the common good and supporting justice. Law, the modern state, and organizations in general, need to be organized in a polycentric manner for the reduction of arbitrariness. Markets, in so far as they are structured as incubators of entrepreneurial creativity, can also contribute to a polycentric society aimed at the reduction of arbitrariness. Sołtan further embeds this ideal of polycentric reduction of arbitrary power within a larger project of moderation, which consists of three pillars: first, a commitment to a realistic appraisal of human cognitive and moral capacities, and the shape of their limits; second, a commitment to balance, equilibrium and harmony, expressed in the ideals of unity in diversity, elaborating the idea of polycentric cocreation; and finally, a commitment against the influence of human destructiveness.

FROM STUDIES OF GOVERNANCE TO THEORY BUILDING

The final Part of the volume offers three examples of governance studies with a theoretical message. What would happen if we started the search for productive orders by not limiting ourselves to a conception of order derived from the stylized models of Adam Smith's market and Hobbes's state? This was the question that Vincent Ostrom often asked and that animated the Ostroms' program and produced, among others, Elinor Ostrom's *Governing the Commons*. There is plenty of evidence in support of the standard model of European history which sees centralized monarchies as creating the conditions for social, political and economic development. But that does not mean that other kinds of orders were inferior in fostering self-governance and economic development. Vincent Ostrom's fascination with the Holy Roman Empire as an early polycentric order on a large scale has found support in Peter H. Wilson's recent account of how the Holy Roman Empire worked for centuries (Wilson 2016).

The first contribution in this section by Sabetti and Candela adds to the insight suggested by Ostrom and the empirical analysis by Peter H. Wilson. Sabetti and Candela show that there is more to Sicilian history than individualist behavior, oligarchic tendencies and institutional weakness and failure, if we are willing to free ourselves of the conventional wisdom and not limit ourselves to conceptions of order derived from Adam Smith and Hobbes (E. Ostrom 2014 [1998]). Manifestations of productive orders can indeed be found in Sicily's past even though they often could not be sustained over many centuries or extended periods of time The net result is a more accurate, if more complex, understanding of the Sicilian past. A chief value of their analysis if that it allows to remove the shadows and false lights that have for a long time obscured an appreciation of the struggle of successive generations of people to constitute and sustain productive orders in Sicily and to open the way for more in-depth accounts.

The second contribution by Michael Fotos III is a diagnosis of counter-intentional policy outcomes to help us understand why often things do not work as agents intend. He starts by examining the logic of classification that informs the Ostroms' typology of goods. He suggests that such typology contains elements of an encompassing theory for explaining policy outcomes. When situated with reference to the IAD framework, the conceptual logic of the typology can be shown to account for coproduction, rule-writing that anticipates implementation scenarios, and the occurrence and consequences of rent-seeking. When policy problems are reformulated with reference to the attributes of public goods, non-exclusion and joint use, the conceptual logic of the Ostroms' typology, can be re-worked in order to take into account counterintentional policy outcomes. Examination of counterintentionality leads to a strong argument for using shared intentionality, rather than axiomatic standards such as efficiency or equity, as the primary criterion for testing and developing policy theory.

The final chapter by Abigail Sullivan, Abigail York and Scott Yabiku, which is centered on ways to move toward sustainability, builds upon new institutional scholarship examining community forestry governance and common pool resource management (see E. Ostrom 2005). The chapter emphasizes the importance of understanding the connection between sustainable policy and arrangements and social equity, an issue less studied than the relationship between sustainability, on the one hand, and environmental protection and economic development, on the other. Within the literature, there is a recognition that the first step in understanding equity for sustainable resource management is an assessment of who has the rights to access (E. Ostrom 2005), yet there is a dearth of literature that actually examines this question empirically. In this chapter, the authors develop a multi-level model that explores access rights to natural resources by unpacking the factors that influence community forest membership in Chitwan, Nepal. The case study of community forestry in Chitwan examines the sustainability of community forest governance and the differential impacts on minority groups (intra-generational equity) as well as the implications current management decisions have for future generations (intergenerational equity). According to the authors, these new ways of conceptualizing and studying the results of this particular case study offer a means for scholars to more completely integrate equity in the institutional analysis of sustainability so as to have a fuller understanding of its prerequisites and policy implications.

In fine, the collection of essays may be viewed as an exercise in thinking through and beyond the Bloomington School. The collection shows the considerable empirical and theoretical progress that has been made in responding to its basic concern: how fallible human beings can achieve and sustain self-governance in the face of a complex and ever-changing social and physical world. But it equally shows new ways to refine and extend the significance of the Ostrom research program for the future. The challenge of how to understand why so many diverse institutions are created and the consequences they engender in diverse ecological, social and economic settings remains.

REFERENCES

Aligica, Paul Dragos. 2014. *Institutional Diversity and Political Economy. The Ostroms and Beyond.* New York: Oxford University Press.

Aligica, Paul D. and F. Sabetti. 2014. "The Ostrom's Research Program for the Study of Institutions and Governance. Theoretical and Epistemic Foundations," in Elinor Ostrom and Vincent Ostrom. *Choice, Rules and Collective Action: The Ostroms on the Study of Institutions and Governance*, edited by F. Sabetti and P. D. Aligica. Colcester, UK: ECPR Press, 1–19.

Castiglione, Dario. 2014. "Foreword," in Elinor Ostrom and Vincent Ostrom. *Choice, Rules and Collective Action: The Ostroms on the Study of Institutions and Governance*, edited by F. Sabetti and P. D. Aligica. Colcester, UK: ECPR Press, xi–xvii.

Cole, Daniel H. and Michael D. McGinnis, eds., 2015. *Elinor Ostrom and the Bloomington School of Political Economy.* vol 1. Lanham, MD: Lexington Books.

Kiser, Larry L. and Elinor Ostrom 1982. "The Three Worlds of Action. A Metatheoretical Synthesis of Institutional Approaches," in E. Ostrom, ed., 1982. *Strategies of Political Inquiry.* Beverly Hills, CA: Sage Publications, 179–222.

Ostrom, Elinor. [1998] 2014. "A Behavioral Approach to the Rational Choice Theory of Collective Action," in F. Sabetti and P. Aligica, eds., *Choice, Rules and Collective Action. The Ostroms on the Study of Institutions and Governance.* Colchester: ECPR Press, 121–66.

Ostrom, Elinor. (2005). *Understanding Institutional Diversity.* Princeton: Princeton University Press.

Ostrom, Vincent. [1993] 2014. "Epistemic Choice and Public Choice," reprinted in F. Sabetti and Paul D. Aligica, eds., *Choice, Rules and Collective Action. The Ostroms on the Study of Institutions and Governance.* Colchester: ECPR Press, 45–60.

Ostrom, Elinor and Vincent Ostrom. [2004] 2014. "The Quest for Meaning in Public Choice," in *ibid. Choice, Rules and Collective Action. The Ostroms on the Study of Institutions and Governance*, edited by F. Sabetti and P. Aligica. Colcester, UK: ECPR Press, 61–93.

Polski, Margaret and Elinor Ostrom. Forthcoming [1999]. "An Institutional Framework for Policy Analysis and Design," in Daniel H. Cole and Michael D. McGinnis eds. *Elinor Ostrom and the Bloomington School of Political Economy:* Volume 3, *Frameworks and Methods of Institutional Analysis.* Lanham, MD: Lexington Books, forthcoming [2017].

Poteete, Amy R., Marco A. Janssen, and Elinor Ostrom. 2010. *Working Together. Collective Action, the Commons and Multiple Methods in Practice.* Princeton: Princeton University Press.

Sołtan, Karol E. 2014. "The Emerging Field of a New Civics," in Peter Levine and Karol E. Sołtan, eds., *Civic Studies.* Washington, DC: Bringing Theory to Practice.

Weale, Albert. 2013. *Democratic Justice and the Social Contract.* Oxford: Oxford University Press.

Wilson, Peter H. 2016. *The Holy Roman Empire. A Thousand Years of European History.* Cambridge: Harvard University Press.

Part I

THEORETICAL AND EPISTEMIC FRAMEWORKS

Chapter 1

Rationality and Reasoning in Public Choice

Albert Weale

In *Governing the Commons* Elinor Ostrom denied that the tragedy of the commons was an iron law of social organization.[1] Given a shared interest in conserving the pool of resources from which they derived their livelihood, individuals could craft institutions for successfully managing the rate at which they harvested resources. The separate interest of each in as large a harvest as possible could be reconciled with the joint interest of all in maintaining the long-term sustainability of the common resource pool from which the harvest came (E. Ostrom 1990, 31). Constructing institutions to protect common pool resources requires an agreed understanding of the character of the problem that individuals commonly face if the otherwise seemingly inevitable tragedy of the commons is to be avoided. It is a matter of historical fact that there are communities, examples of which were presented in *Governing the Commons*, that have managed to avoid the over-exploitation of common pool resources. It is a matter for social science theory to construct the required conception of rational choice that would make such an achievement possible.

Much of Vincent Ostrom's work was devoted to analyzing and articulating a conception of rational choice rendering intelligible the ability of individuals to craft institutions to their mutual benefit. Through his concept of "epistemic choice" Ostrom aimed to provide the logical foundations for the understanding of the institutions of public choice. This concept is clearly articulated in his paper "Epistemic Choice and Public Choice," in which he advocates a theory of choice and an associated theory of rationality that incorporates language, perception and what he called the "artifactual" character of social life which "transforms the material conditions of nature into a habitat shaped by human knowledge" (V. Ostrom 1993, 167). These logical foundations are rearticulated with Elinor Ostrom in their joint paper "The Quest for Meaning in Public Choice." In that paper the Ostroms give a central role to the use of language in understanding human social institutions, noting that the term "action" refers to those forms of behavior to which individuals attach subjective and instrumental meaning (Ostrom and Ostrom 2004, 108 and 117).

Vincent Ostrom's (1993, 163) distinction between a narrow economic reasoning defined by the standard expected utility theory of rational choice and his own epistemic account of choice suggests that the switch in the conception of rationality that is needed is substantial, if we are to understand the logic of social cooperation to protect public goods. The Ostroms' critique of the predominant account of rationality in public choice theory has a number of distinct elements. It includes the need to pay attention to the bounds of rationality, the role of experience and hence learning in any rational calculation, as well as the ability to craft institutions to reinforce the rational interest that individuals have in the production of public goods. However, all these elements presuppose the centrality of language in social cooperation, and therefore the need for social science to understand what effects language—the mother of all public goods—has in the ability of individuals to participate in institutions to their mutual advantage.

Focusing primarily on the work of Vincent Ostrom, this chapter seeks to reconstruct the logical foundations of the Ostroms' theory of public choice, and in particular the claim that language use is central to any conception of rationality adequate to account for the construction of sustainable common pool resource regimes. I shall suggest that we can begin to understand the distinctive features of the required notion of rationality, if we contrast it with standard expected utility theory grounded in the ordinalist theory of choice. Moreover, Vincent Ostrom's notion of epistemic choice can be complemented with an influential strand of Wittgensteinian thinking that rests upon a distinction between rules and regularities. Ostrom (2012, 15) himself alludes to this line of thinking in his references to the work of Searle (1969), but there is a much larger body of work and argumentation that is also relevant. The Ostroms open wide the doors of social science perception.

ECONOMISTIC RATIONALITY

In both their empirical and methodological works the Ostroms were writing primarily for readers whom they could reasonably expect would be familiar with standard choice-theoretic account of decision making and utility. It was probably for this reason that they did not spend time reconstructing the foundational logic of that theory. However, properly to understand the depth and scope of their critique, it will be helpful to provide a brief intellectual history of standard expected utility theory by way of introduction to the alternative theory that Vincent Ostrom advanced.

Standard expected utility theory, as it came to be formulated in the mid-twentieth century, is a product of the ordinalist revolution of the 1930s. The achievement of the ordinalist revolution was to show how it was possible to formulate a theory of choice dispensing with a notion of utility understood as a motive force of human action. Bentham famously claimed at the beginning of *An Introduction to the Principles of Morals and Legislation*: "Nature has placed mankind under the governance of two sovereign masters, *pain* and *pleasure*. It is for them alone to point out what we ought to do, as well as to determine what we shall do." (Bentham 1780, 11). Subsequent utilitarians developed and modified this idea, but kept the notion that utility was a stream of experienced pleasure and pains, varying in intensity and duration, and arising from human choice in the natural and social environment. Thus, in the seventh edition of *The Methods of Ethics*, published in 1907, Sidgwick devoted the whole of Book II to the study of hedonism as a method of ethics, assuming "that in ordinary practical reasoning, at any rate, the assumption is implicitly made that all the pleasures and pains that man can experience bear a finite ratio to each other in respect of pleasantness and its opposite" (Sidgwick 1907, 124). Although Sidgwick concluded that there was no reliable method by which either individual agents or analysts of human action could establish what circumstances and choices gave rise to greater net pleasures, his discussion was conducted on the assumption that it was meaningful to suppose that individuals sought to maximize the net balance of pleasure over pain when making a choice. In this respect, Sidgwick accurately reflected an intellectual tradition in which the idea of utility was conceived in terms of pleasures and pains having substance in their own right.

The ordinalists dispensed entirely with this notion of utility. They kept the *word* but they meant something quite different. Rather than referring to a substance that could in principle be measured in and of itself, the term utility was reserved to denote a mathematical representation of the choices of individuals, when those choices satisfied certain requirements of consistency (Luce and Raiffa 1957, Chapter 2). In particular, choosing individuals were assumed to have coherent rank-orderings over alternative states of affairs, where coherence was understood in terms of transitivity. If state A was ranked higher than state B, and state B higher than state C, then state A would be ranked higher than state C if the rank-ordering was to be consistent. With such a rank-ordering forming the basis of an individual's preferences, it is possible to show that choices could be represented by a mathematical function that was unique up to positive linear transformation. Adding to the function or multiplying it by a constant would not alter the prediction about how someone would choose. Ordinalists claimed that observed individual behavior could be understood as though individuals were seeking to maximize this mathematical function. So, when someone sought to climb to the top of a hill, an ordinalist could say that the person aimed to maximize his or her height above sea level, subject to the constraint of the hills available in the locality. Moreover, it would not matter whether the mathematical representation of this maximizing behavior was measured in feet or meters. Since a meter equals approximately 3.1 feet, a meter measurement is simply a linear transformation of the imperial measure, giving no less or no more information. An ordinalist could also say that someone was intending to maximize his or her height above sea level, even if the climber had no such thought in mind, but was simply intent on reaching an attractive looking peak. In climbing the hill, the climber was behaving as though he or she was maximizing the height attained.

Ordinalists also provided an account of choice under uncertainty, although they transformed the problem into one of choice under risk. In standard expected utility theory individuals might not know what future events would occur, and in that sense they were subject to uncertainty. However, they do know the range of events that could occur and in that sense they are logically omniscient. Suppose that you are betting on the outcome of a throw of a dice. You do not know which of the six faces will show on top, but you do know that it will be one of the six. If you think that the dice is a fair one, you know that there is a one in six chance of any one of the faces showing on top. On that basis you can make a decision as to what bet you would be prepared to stake when the prize depended on the outcome of a throw of the dice. Of course, ordinalists recognized that not all choice situations were of this type, but they assimilated choice under uncertainty to choice under risk by supposing that coherent individual choice in the face of uncertainty could be understood *as though individuals assigned a subjective probability* assessment to the range of possibilities (Savage 1954). Individuals might be disappointed by an outcome, but they could never be completely surprised, for rational individuals will anticipate that sometimes even low probability events will occur. Shackle (1969, 291) once noted that an expected utility theorist inhabited a "games of chance universe," a nice phrase that captures the logical form of the theory.

Against this background theory of choice modern utility theorists developed the dilemmas of collective choice, including the most famous of all, the prisoner's dilemma. The prisoner's dilemma poses an especially tough challenge for social cooperation, because it is written in such a way that neither prisoner need calculate the probability that the other will confess. From the individual point of view, it is *unconditionally* better to confess, because confession is the dominant strategy. Whether your fellow prisoner confesses or not, it is still better for you to confess. Since this is true for each player, mutual defection is the equilibrium outcome of the rational strategies of each actor. Neither is better off changing their behavior, whatever the behavior of the other. The pay-off matrix is constructed so that this is so, the cell entries being a way of representing all that matters to the individuals (Binmore 1993). Even if you were playing your twin, you still ought to defect, because the numbers in the cells represent all that is important to you, including the weight of brotherly love (presumably discounted for sibling rivalry). If rational choice is the coherent rank-ordering of the outcome with which you are confronted, then you should act as though you maximize the utility numbers in the pay-off matrix.

Standard expected utility theory is behaviorist, and therefore has no need to impute language skills to agents. All that matters is consistent choice behavior. The simplest way to appreciate this point is to note that expected utility models have been applied by evolutionary biologists to nonhuman species. For example, John Maynard Smith (1979) discussed the application of what he termed the "hawk-dove" game, a version of the chicken game, to the evolution of species in which the propensity of individuals to reproduce is a function of the strategy that they play in games in which they encounter one another in competitive situations. In particular, Maynard Smith sought to identify the strategies that would be stable in evolutionary terms, that is to say strategies that if played by individuals in fights with one another would lead to the reproduction of those individuals in proportion to their best returns given the strategies that other individuals play. He shows, for example, that, in the hawk/dove game, neither the pure strategy of playing "hawk" nor the pure strategy of playing "dove" would be evolutionarily stable, and so in symmetric contests individual strategies would always be mixed. He suggests that this pattern is exhibited by species as different as male dung beetles, Harris sparrows and digger wasps.

EPISTEMIC CHOICE

What is the alternative conception of rationality to be found in the work of the Ostroms? Its most important element is the centrality they ascribe to language in the understanding of public choice. As Vincent Ostrom puts it toward the end of "Epistemic Choice and Public Choice": "Language and its place in the articulation of knowledge is the most fundamental source of productive potentials in human societies." (V. Ostrom 1993, 175). Language is important in understanding public choice because it is "a vehicle for creating bodies of common knowledge, mutual understanding, social accountability, and patterns of trust" (V. Ostrom 1993, 164), the most fundamental sources of capital upon which people can draw in their productive relations. Languages then are "means for constituting knowledge, organizing thought, arraying alternatives, ordering choices, and taking actions in arranging present means in appropriate ways to realize future apparent goods." (V. Ostrom 1993, 166).

Given that standard expected utility theory can be applied in the context of nonhuman animal behavior, it is unsurprising to find Ostrom contrasting the explanation of nonhuman animal behavior, in which he assumes language does not play a role, with the explanation of human behavior, in which reference to language is essential. He suggests that Hobbes's (1651) state of nature is a hypothetical thought experiment in which humans are devoid of speech "and thus comparable to animals like lions, bears, and wolves" (V. Ostrom 1993, 166). From this claim a substantial difference is said to follow:

> Working out the conditions for gaining a livelihood and dealing with the intergenerational cycles of life is quite different in human societies than among lions, bears, and wolves. The production, exchange, and consumption of goods and services viewed as an economic order occurs in the context of an epistemic order concerned with the generation, transmission, and use of knowledge, and a political order concerned with the formulation, use, monitoring, adjudication, and enforcement of mutual expectations about rule-ordered relationships. (V. Ostrom 1993, 167).

Epistemic choice thus gives a central place to understanding what actors themselves understand as the meaning of their behavior. To echo the title of an important joint article by the Ostroms, there is always "a quest for meaning in public choice" (Ostrom and Ostrom 2004).

There are at least two important consequences that follow from this conception of agents as language-users. The first is that language provides the basis for common knowledge, and therefore the possibility of agents' actions being guided by norms and rules. Words by themselves do not convey meanings but "they depend upon communities of shared understanding among members of speech communities" (V. Ostrom 1993, 174). In such circumstances the reasoning of individuals can be guided by the golden rule of not doing to others what they would not have done to themselves. Moreover, institutions, like rule by assembly, in which the members of a community come together to determine a common course of action, are not possible unless there is a shared understanding among the members of a community about the rules of assembly (Ostrom and Ostrom 2004, 108). Thus, language is at the base of an institutional analysis of public choice, because an institution is a shared set of norms and rules conveyed by language.

The second consequence of this reorientation of the concept rationality toward language is that it provides an understanding of the role of learning in social interaction. By contrast with the individuals conceptualized in standard expected utility theory, we are urged to think of individuals as "fallible learners who vary in terms of the number of other persons whose perceived benefits and costs are important to them and in terms of their personal commitment to keeping promises and honoring forms of reciprocity extended to them" (Ostrom and Ostrom 2004, 118). Where individuals have incomplete knowledge of all possible alternatives and their likely consequences, we have to accept that they will make mistakes in their choice of strategies, but we should also note that different social and institutional contexts will provide different incentives for learning. For these reasons we need to work with a concept of bounded rationality rather than the assumption of perfect information and utility maximization used axiomatic social choice theory (Ostrom and Ostrom 2004, 118–19).

Language thus makes possible shared understanding among the members of a community and provides the capacity for social and individual learning. One way of understanding the methodological implications of these twin claims is to consider the type of rationality that must be presupposed in Elinor Ostrom's (1990) account of the crafting of institutions for the management of common pool resources. Consider, in this context, the classificatory function of language, in other words the ability of language to make distinctions that "relate to classificatory schema that identify sets and subsets in patterns of associated relationships" (V. Ostrom 1993, 165). Language becomes the means by which agents individually and collectively come to classify and understand their common situation and so come to reflect on possible solutions for the problems with which they are confronted. Language does not just give voice to preference. It extends the range of preferences that agents can have. If they can craft a set of norms and rules that enable them to cooperate to mutual advantage, then they can reclassify their joint situation in terms other than the iron logic of the tragedy of the commons. Language provides the capacity for self-reflection, that is to say the capacity to conceive, classify and construct an understanding of the bases of their choices and the collective outcome of those choices.

Whether a collective action problem, like over-fishing, is seen in a community of shared understanding as a prisoner's dilemma or as an assurance game is not something that is given purely by the material circumstances in which agents find themselves. In a prisoner's dilemma it is always unconditionally better to defect. That is how the game is defined in standard utility theory. In an assurance game, provided agents credibly believe that others will cooperate, they will cooperate. However, which of these two perceptions—that agents are playing a prisoner's dilemma or an assurance game—will prevail cannot be inferred solely by the returns measured in material products that each player secures in the game. Whether the chance of my gaining positional advantage over you by landing more fish yields a higher utility or not depends upon how that relative advantage is conceived. Given that the utility numbers are supposed to capture all that is relevant to the choosing agent, maximizing my catch by breaking agreed rules may yield lower utility than gaining the positional advantage. So, if the collective action problem is seen by participants who need to cooperate to conserve common pool resources as one of assurance, in which the willingness of agents to keep the rules is conditional upon their believing that others will keep the rules, it will transform the logic of unconditional defection. In such a game, if one can be assured that other players will cooperate, then it is better to cooperate. Which game the agents are playing, then, will depend upon the set of normative assumptions each player brings to the game. A set of circumstances in which there is normatively unrestrained competition for a limited resource will be a prisoner's dilemma. A set of circumstances in which there are agreed norms and rules about how the resource is to be shared transforms the game from a prisoner's dilemma to an assurance game. In either case the inference to utility depends upon a reconstruction of the beliefs of the relevant agents.

In some of the common pool resource regimes studied by Elinor Ostrom, a transition could be observed between a prior "state of nature" in which individuals were appropriating resources in unconstrained ways, and a "post-contractual" state in which agents were limiting their appropriation of resources in line with agreed norms and rules. A clear example of this transition was to be found in Alanya in Turkey, where, following the depletion of fish stocks arising from the unrestrained fishing of over-capitalized boats, a regime was instituted in which rotational access was secured to each party to the contract (see Ostrom 1990, 18–22 and Berkes 1986). The social contract that emerges in such a situation is a conscious social construction in the face of a common problem, rather than the emergence of an evolutionary stable strategy through repeated interaction. The ability to construct a social contract of this type requires a reflective type of rationality that is not captured simply by consistency conditions on choices (Weale 2013, 101–11).

In an article cited by Vincent Ostrom (V. Ostrom 1993, 163), Amartya Sen (1977) once identified individuals in standard expected utility theory as "rational fools" precisely because those individuals would lack the second-order mental capacities to reflect upon and modify their first-order choices. Lacking such second-order capacities, they would lack the capacity for normative self-direction that was an important part of Ostrom's own broader political philosophy. Thus, when he wrote that people "who fail to invest in themselves in fashioning bonds of family, kinship, friendship, collegiality, neighborhood, and other associations are likely to become the helpless ones who cannot cope with the difficulties in life" (V. Ostrom 1991, 288–89) he was linking his insistence that the theory of agency had to contain an interpretative second-order capacity to an account of social order in which common rules were essential. The shift from rationality as utility to rationality as epistemic is conceptually fundamental.

ANALYSIS

The methodological discussions of the Ostroms arose from their work as practicing social scientists. The Workshop in Political Theory and Policy Analysis at Bloomington is a text-book example of a Lakatosian progressive research programme (Lakatos 1970; compare Aligica and Sabetti 2014, 5). It provided a core set of assumptions around which fruitful empirical work could be organized, allowing for the interpretation of both confirming and discrepant observational findings as well as generating puzzles that initiated forms of intellectual advance for participants. One should always pay attention to the methodological manifestos of accomplished practicing social scientists. I share Vincent Ostrom's high valuation of the importance of artisanship in human affairs. Communities cannot live without such intelligent artisanship (V. Ostrom 1991, 267). The same is true of intellectual communities. Better to have reflection on decades of accumulated experience than the proclamation of abstract manifestos of method by those who lack such experience.

However, this does not mean that we can take for granted Vincent Ostrom's account of the logical foundations of the Bloomington programme. Even when one thinks that a sound position is being advanced, it is important to scrutinize the grounds of the claims being made. In particular, to accept that there is a clear logical distinction between a standard expected utility theory of rational choice and an epistemic theory of rational choice does not imply that one is superior to the other, even if well-placed practicing social scientists say so. Moreover, Vincent Ostrom did not rely solely for his claims on the fruits of experience; he also sought to support his position by conceptual and methodological arguments. So, the question inevitably arises as to how far those arguments stand on their own two feet.

To see why, consider just one example. As I have already noted, Vincent Ostrom draws a distinction between the world of nonhuman animals without language and the language using world of humans. Yet, that distinction is rather more complicated than his portrayal suggests. Animals that live in groups or hunt in packs often need to signal to one another for various joint purposes. Jonathan Bennett once wrote a fascinating and entertaining study of rationality which turned precisely on the point at which signaling turned into language, taking the signaling of bees studied by Karl von Frisch as his starting point (Bennett 1964). A solitary bee that has found food will return to the hive and perform a dance that signals the distance, direction and sugar concentration of the food source. The members of the hive will then fly off to the indicated place without the original bee. Apiologists account for this behavior by reference to a stimulus-response model (the energy content of the food found stimulates certain types of bee flight). Bennett develops an extensive thought experiment in which actual bee behavior is modified in successive stages to identify the points at which we can say that a creature has intelligence, rationality and language, treating these as distinct items. Much in his analysis turns on the distinction between regularities and rules and the associated ability of one creature to deny the claims of another. Even if, in the successive stages of this thought experiment, we find clear qualitative differences of ability, rather than gradations of a common kind, the exact demarcation of reasoning capacities is not simple. What this suggests is that in order to provide the foundations for the concept of epistemic choice, we need to look carefully at the logical characteristics of linguistically and normatively governed behavior. The Ostrom programme needs a clear account of the distinction between rules and regularities.

That distinction was an important element in the analyses of the logic of human action that followed Wittgenstein's *Philosophical Investigations* (Wittgenstein 1953). Bennett's account obviously relied on the distinction, as did Searle's (1969, 50–53) differentiation of brute from institutional facts, to which Vincent Ostrom referred. It was also important in Hart's *The Concept of Law* (Hart 1994), where the distinction between regularities in behaviour and rule-governed behavior is seen to have three important aspects. First, in institutional interactions rules are needed to define what is required in order for human action to count as an institutional fact, for example, a rule defining what is to count as off-side in football, the valid signing of a will or any other institutional performance. Second, participants in the institution should take the rule as a generally valid guide to their own behavior. Third, the rules can be taken by participants to be reasons for criticizing others if their behavior fails to conform to the rule (see Hart 1994, 55–56). None of these features are exhibited in behavior merely conforming to a regularity.

To see the force of the distinction, consider the case of a purported statistical regularity of a type sometimes advanced by political scientists, namely the association between economic prosperity and the popularity of the government of the day. Suppose it to be the case that increases in prosperity are associated with increases in the popularity of the government, controlling for relevant confounding variables. This is a regularity of behavior. There is nothing in the association that gives a citizen a reason for increasing their support for the government, any more than that the popularity of a film gives someone a reason for going to see it. To be sure, someone might take the popularity in both cases to be evidence that there is reason for support ("A government that makes people prosperous cannot be that bad, despite their other faults" or "A film that is so popular must have something of interest, despite all appearances to the contrary"). However, unless the economic policy of the government or the character of the film relates to someone's interests, opinions, tastes or ideals, no one has a reason for supporting the government or going to the film. No one could be criticized for failure to conform to the regular patterns of others' behavior. By contrast, if someone makes false tax declarations, fails to turn up for jury service, ignores rules imposing limits on water use in a drought, pollutes local waters, drives dangerously, marries bigamously, fails to care for their children or behaves disrespectfully at a funeral, then they will open themselves up to criticism, and the criticism will be taken as justified. Failure to conform to a regularity may be odd; failure to conform to a legitimate rule is wrong.

Given that the distinction between rules and regularities turns on liability to criticism, it is not surprising that the logic of excuses is so central to understanding institutional practices. As J. L. Austin (1970, 176) once pointed out, excuses come in two kinds. One kind takes the form of justification, in which we accept responsibility for our actions, but deny that those actions were bad. The second kind are excuses in the proper sense, in which we accept that what we did was bad, but deny responsibility. So in justification those who have breached a rule admit what they did, but claim that in the circumstances it was the right thing to do. Examples are familiar. The hospital canceled appointments for non-urgent surgery because it had to attend to the victims of an accident, or the government refused to pay the ransom for hostages to avoid creating an incentive for terrorist action. Excuses proper take a different form. Pollution was discharged onto the beach, but as a result of a sudden storm surge that could not have been reasonably foreseen, or the review of the case was delayed, because the responsible administrative officer fell ill. In these cases a wrong is admitted, but is associated with a claim that the circumstance of action made the wrong inevitable, and so worthy of excuse. Both justifications and excuses are routine features of personal and administrative behavior, because rule-governed behavior is distinguished from mere regularity by its forming the potential for criticism in cases of breaches of the rules.

Rule-conformity, justification and excuses explicate one central aspect of the logic of the Ostrom programme, explaining why Elinor Ostrom (1990, 94–100) identified a regime of *graduated* sanctions as one of the elements of a success common pool resource regime. Sanctions need to be graduated because departures from rules come in different shapes and sizes and must allow for the seriousness of the breach, given the possibility of justification and excuses. The moral meaning of any particular failure needs to be judged by someone in the circumstances in which it occurs. This insight generalizes to issues of regulatory enforcement more widely. Regulatory activity is carried out by street-level bureaucrats, for example, environmental inspectors. Empirical studies confirm that enforcement is not a matter of the mechanical application of rules, but of the interpretation of the moral meanings involved (Hawkins 1984). If someone is in breach of a pollution discharge level, the inspector has to make a series of judgments about intention, culpability, the likelihood of recurrence and so on. Such inspectors may be as much concerned with negotiating future compliance as in enforcing penalties for broken rules (Hawkins and Thomas 1984). These complexities of administrative enforcement behavior have been observed across policy sectors and in different jurisdictions, suggesting that there is some basic psychological feature of the interpersonal interaction of street-level enforcement that is coming into play (Weale 1992). Such phenomena are unintelligible if we simply use the standard expected utility theory of rationality.

POLYCENTRICITY AND RATIONALITY

In their political theory the Ostroms gave a central place to polycentricity, the idea that a well-functioning polity would be made up of a multiplicity of centers of decision making without those different centers being integrated into a single hierarchy of power and authority. A polycentric political system would therefore be composed of many autonomous units choosing to act in ways that take account of one another through various forms of coordination including cooperation, competition, conflict and conflict resolution (Ostrom and Ostrom 2014, 46). Polycentricity allows for diversity of local experience and conditions, as well as for diversity in the range of agreements and understandings negotiated among existing authorities and agents.

There is a direct connection, largely unexplored by the Ostroms, between their critique of the standard expected utility model of rationality and their defense of polycentricity. The standard expected utility model of decision making rests upon a synoptic account of rationality. In the "games of chance" universe of standard expected utility theory, all logically possible outcomes are known, and in this sense decision makers operate in a closed world. Moreover, all aspects of all alternatives are known to decision makers, a feature well captured in Kenneth Arrow's (1963, 17) definition of a social state over which social choices are made, as "a complete description" of each type of commodity held by individuals, the amount of each type of productive resource invested in each type of commodity and the various amounts of collective activity. Complete descriptions preclude decision makers being confronted by the unknown outside a given closed world.

Once granted, a closed world assumption makes it possible to suppose that the calculus of decision making is deductive. If reasoning has a deductive structure, the conclusion is "contained" in the premise, rather as the yolk is contained in the egg. It is a well-known logical feature of deductive reasoning that it is monotonic. That is to say, adding extra premises to the reasoning will not alter the conclusion, given that the conclusion is contained in the premise. Extra premises may augment but can never overturn an established conclusion. One standard example in the literature says that, given the conclusion that Socrates is mortal follows from the true assumption that all men are mortal, there is nothing one could learn about Socrates that would overturn the conclusion that he was mortal, even for example seeing him jump over the Parthenon (Ginsberg 1994, 3). This is the significance of the logical omniscience of those making a decision in the face of risk in standard expected utility theory. The decision tree encompasses all that is possible in the situation, and there is no information that anyone could discover that would change the shape of the decision tree. Genuine surprises cannot happen.

Schemes for the rationalization of public administration, of the sort against which Vincent Ostrom (2008a, 100–8) inveighed implicitly rely upon a closed world assumption and an associated deductive notion of rationality. Were central policy makers able to acquire sufficient information to plan in a deductive way, then the sort of concentrated public administration that Vincent Ostrom associated with Woodrow Wilson would be feasible. If the planning of high-level policy makers could encompass all the variety of circumstances in which their policies were to be implemented, then they could decide deductively and they could successfully coordinate across the range of public policy. However, circumstances matter, and a policy design that works for some local contexts will not work for others. The assumptions of policy makers as to the ways in which the policy will work may be defeated by those circumstances, which is one of the reasons for being against proposals to reduce local governments in the United States by 80 percent, eliminating overlapping jurisdictions.

Ostrom's skepticism about the rationality of top-down centralized solutions can be bolstered by the experience of planned economies. In his summary of the lessons to be learned from the experience of Soviet planning, Alec Nove (1983, 97) once pointed out that "Soviet experience underlines the importance of prices. . ." as a decentralized method of allocating resources. The chief reason is that administrative planners can only feasibly substitute their judgment about the priorities for production when they are aware of the social value of *each* product, that is to say the cost in forgone production in one line of activity that is incurred by production in another line of activity. This does not simply mean that they have to be aware of the costs of producing certain types of goods *in general*, for example, that of footwear or of agricultural machinery, but rather they must know the costs of production associated *with specific kinds* of shoes or of plow (Nove 1983, 101–102). The information requirements for such calculations are overwhelming in practice, even if they can be addressed in theory. Central administrators are unable to identify and calculate the value that different consumers will place on different goods, it will be impossible for those administrators to write the orders in such a way that some goods are not left on the shelf and other goods rendered unobtainable, and this is so particularly when people are unable to trade to mutual advantage.

In giving up on rational central planning, we are also giving up on the deductive account of rationality. Even if central planners could acquire all the relevant information to make coherent decisions at a particular time, knowing the complete descriptions of current social states, they would also have to assume that there was no further information that they could conceivably learn that would overturn their conclusions. However, defeated premises are a routine and regular feature of practical reasoning and decision making. I intend to travel at a certain time, but then realize that, because of a special event on that day, the train will be crowded and so I decide to take an earlier one. I plan to build a house in a particular place, but the survey unexpectedly reveals the likelihood of subsidence. A government department negotiates an agreement with a foreign government, only for elections to overturn the incumbents. These examples are typical not deviant or extreme cases, and they undermine the extent to which any form of practical reasoning can be deductive. Instead, it is always defeasible. (There is a line of argument that asserts that all reasoning, including theoretical reasoning about empirical matters, is defeasible (see Brandom 2000, 87–89), but the present argument does not have to take sides on that issue—though it is my position.)

It is this non-monotonic feature of practical rationality that underscores the case for polycentricity. If public choices could be conceived of as being orderings over complete descriptions of social states, then practical rationality could be deductive. Of course, such a conception of public choice would have to confront Arrow's (1963) impossibility theorem, given that there is no social welfare function that is simultaneously responsive to the full diversity of individual preferences and sufficiently coherent to be represented by an ordering. However, the problem of cycling in public choice may not be a problem if there are grounds for supposing that the alternatives over which cycling takes place are confined to a relatively small and central set of the space of alternatives within the region of the uncovered set (McGann 2006). What will be a problem is that the alternatives from which public choices are made will always be incompletely described.

The above line of argument echoes the Austrian critique of state planning with its stress upon the limits of the knowable for central decision makers (Hayek 1950). The Ostroms' willingness to embrace untidy and locally negotiated institutional arrangements in the supply of public goods is of a piece with this critique, as is their willingness to embrace the idea of the evolution of a social order. However, this bottom-up localism is at odds with another equally central aspect of their thought, namely the characterization of constitutional choice as the product of deliberation and reflection. Between these differing conceptions of social order there appears to be an irreconcilable tension that I will consider in the next section.

DELIBERATE OR EVOLUTIONARY CHOICE?

The Ostroms offer their political theory as a theory of constitutional choice. However, there is an unresolved tension in their work that follows directly from the above account of practical rationality. Simplifying greatly, it is possible to identify two traditions of constitutional thinking in political theory. The first is the tradition nicely expressed by Alexander Hamilton at the opening of the *Federalist Papers* in a passage quoted more than once by Vincent Ostrom (2008b, 27; 2012, 541):

> It has frequently been remarked, that it seems to have been reserved to the people of this country, by their conduct and example, to decide the important question, whether societies of men are really capable or not, of establishing good government from reflection and choice, or whether they are forever destined to depend, for their political constitutions, on accident and force. (Hamilton 1787, 1).

On this account constitutional choices can be made consciously in the light of reflection. The second tradition contrasts with this account. Instead of deliberate design arising from conscious reflection, it stresses the importance of evolutionary processes in the development of social institutions. This view was cogently expressed by Hayek as the view:

> [That] the orderliness of society which greatly increased the effectiveness of individual action was not due solely to institutions and practices which had been invented or designed for that purpose, but was largely due to a process first described as "growth" and later as "evolution," a process in which practices which had first been adopted for other reasons, or even purely accidentally, were preserved because they enabled the group in which they had arisen to prevail over others. (Hayek 1973, 9).

Hayek (1973, 20) summarizes this position in the words of Adam Ferguson as institutions being "the result of human action but not of human design." He thinks that those who ascribe social institutions to conscious design are caught in a fallacious constructivist conception of rationality.

With their emphasis upon the adaptive, the specific and the local as integral elements of institutional choice, the Ostroms look as though they ought to favor Hayek against Hamilton, spontaneous order against designed institutions and evolutionary rationality against constructivist rationality. However, this is not so. Vincent Ostrom (2014, 46–47) explicitly confronted this issue in his discussion of Michael Polanyi's (1951) use of the term "polycentricity" which is of course cut from the same cloth of Austrian thinking about economy and the social order as Hayek's views. In that discussion, Ostrom denies that we should use the term "spontaneous" in connection with social orders, arguing that "a great deal of deliberateness may be required to establish a federal system of governance where power is used to check power amid opposite and rival interests." He admits that the views of Polanyi and Hayek have some merit. Yet he leaves the tension unresolved. Does this open him to a Hayekian charge that although deliberate and conscious choice plays a role in human affairs, the emergence of advantageous institutions can seldom be ascribed to such conscious choice?

This is a difficult question to answer, not least because Hayek himself was ambiguous on the question of how far a constitutional order can be expected to emerge from the decentralized interaction of many people through evolutionary processes. At one crucial point, at least, Hayek himself displayed a constructivist approach in his discussion in the third volume of *Law, Legislation and Liberty* (Hayek 1979, Chapter Seventeen) where he looks at issues concerned with institutional design in the political constitution of a free people. In that discussion, Hayek employs David Hume's notion of a perfect commonwealth, and even speaks of constructing a political order. Much of the book as a whole, as well as this chapter in particular, is taken up with specifying the rules and institutions for a constitution of liberty in a seemingly constructivist way.

One possible way of reconciling these conflicting accounts of rationality with their associated conflicting accounts of the character of social order is by making a sharp distinction between constitutional choices, which can be the product of rational deliberation, and choices within a set of constitutional arrangements, which take the form of evolutionary development. This distinction was crucial to Buchanan and Tullock's (1962) theory of the calculus of consent to constitutional choices in which the uncertainty facing those seeking an arrangement for the supply of public goods induced consensus and agreement on voting rules. Buchanan and Tullock's discussion was a significant theoretical innovation for the Ostroms. A similar distinction between the choice of constitutions and the choice of legislation within constitutions was also made by Rawls (2005, 232), with his idea that the body of citizens at the constitutional stage of political organization will fix "once and for all" certain constitutional essentials through the exercise of its constituent power.

How far does the distinction between the choice of constitutions and choice within constitutions help to reconcile the tension between thinking of institutions as the product of design and thinking of institutions as the product of evolution? There is clearly a distinction between decisions on a framework of rules on the one hand and decision making within a framework of rules on the other. Constitutional decision making typically focuses on rights as powers and immunities whereas within constitution decision making focuses on rights as claims and freedoms. However, constitutional choices do not always emerge as the product of a specific constitutional moment and to suppose otherwise is to overgeneralize from the experience of the processes leading to the adoption of the US constitution. Bagehot (1867, 59) once said of the English constitution that it was like an old man who still wore the fashions of his youth: what you see on the outside is the same, but underneath all is utterly changed. Ostrom thought that Bagehot's account of the centralization of political power within the constitution echoed the mistaken idea that the natural tendency of political power was to hierarchy and centralization. However, one can recognize Bagehot's account of the process of change within the English constitution without committing oneself to any further generalization about the tendencies of political power. What makes for constitutional change in a specific situation is one thing; whether what makes for change in that situation exhibits a more general logic is something else.

That members of a community sometimes experience constitutional moments in which they institutionalize joint responses to collective action dilemmas is an important political and social fact. Given his interest in the role of deliberate choice in the construction of institutions, it is not surprising that Vincent Ostrom's political theory drew heavily on the experience of the 1787 constitutional convention in Philadelphia. Similarly, the work that the Ostroms conducted on the establishment of institutions for resource use and conservation illustrate how important deliberated collective responses can be. However, if we make too sharp a distinction between constitutional choice and choice within a constitution, we risk obscuring our understanding of the collective deliberative capacity to manage collective action problems. It is like focusing on Kuhnian paradigm change without paying attention to the processes by which normal science is developed and refined (Kuhn 1970). Just as normal science is not merely replication of existing findings but a set of creative processes within a paradigm, so intra-constitutional decision making requires deliberative skill in the application of paradigmatic concepts to particular situations and recurrent problems. For example, a fisheries regime may establish the basic principles of a maximum allowable catch, but fluctuations in fish stocks occurring naturally or the discovery of new scientific evidence may require elaboration and modification in the operationalization of the concept (maximum allowable catch within different periods of time, with different types of equipment, by boats of a certain size and so on).

Because much of the Ostroms' theory was drawn from the experience of regimes for environmental protection, the relative novelty of those regimes may be the reason why they focus so much on the constructivist element in institutional analysis. Prior to the establishment of a collective regime environmental protection, resource use follows the logic of Hohfeldian liberties (Hohfeld 1923). A regime of Hohfeldian liberties exists when everyone is in competition for a resource and, although no one is under an obligation to allow others to use the resource first, they are under an obligation to allow others to use resources once they have established a use. For example, no one in a system of Hohfeldian liberties is under an obligation to refrain from fishing in an area when no one else is, but they are under an obligation to refraining from interfering with someone who is fishing in an area already. The potential crowding effects of such a regime are obvious, and regimes of environmental protection typically replace such open systems with more highly defined claim rights and corresponding obligations (Weale 2013, 73–76). Many of the empirical examples that the Ostroms discuss are effectively concerned with moves from regimes of Hohfeldian liberties to regimes of claim rights. However, if one focuses on the development of environmental protection in the twentieth century, there is going to be selection bias in the choice of institutional developments. Were one to take, say, the regime of German social health insurance from 1883 onward, one would observe an institution whose basic principle has remained the same, but where the paradigm was extensively developed in response to developments in modern medicine. The transformation of the institution does not come about as a result of a deliberate reconceptualization at a particular point in time in the set of rules determining claim rights, but as a consequence of the incremental development of an already existing body of rights and obligations. Quantitative differences have passed into qualitative differences.

If this is so, then there is no easy demarcation to be made between understanding by reference to conscious design and understanding by reference to evolutionary processes. In particular, the distinction cannot be explicated by reference to the difference between constitutional choice and within constitutional choice. The instability of the distinction has implications in turn for the status of the idea of polycentricity. Ostrom used that idea to resist the claims of rationalist or managerially inspired reforms that sought to model public administration in accordance with a few explicit organizational principles. However, unless one can draw a sharp distinction between those domains of choice that are properly a matter for the exercise of reflective deliberation and those domains of choice in which the decentralized processes of political evolution should hold sway, then polycentric orders will be in principle open to "rationalizing" reforms.

CONCLUSION

In this chapter, I have argued that the logical foundations of the Ostroms' programme provided by the work of Vincent Ostrom has much to be said in its favor. It provides an account of human action in which meaningful distinctions of different types of social interaction are recognized, in particular the distinction between a prisoner's dilemma and an assurance game. This is particularly important in relation to the possibility of avoiding what is sometimes claimed to be the inevitable tragedy of the commons. The program gains strength by its being complemented by a post-Wittgensteinian account of human action, of the sort developed by Hart, in which the distinction between rules and regularities was central. It can be further strengthened by a theory of non-monotonic rationality in which the defeasible character of practical reasoning is recognized. From there it is a short step to polycentricity. These suggestions are offered by way of friendly amendment to the Ostroms' programme.

The unresolved issue is whether the implied account of epistemic choice fits an evolutionary or constructivist model of understanding. Here the role that the study of the Philadelphia constitution as well as the creation of common property resource regimes plays in the background of the thinking of the Ostroms leads them to a constructivist bias in their theory of institutional innovation. However, while constitutional choices may be deliberate and explicit, their consequences are not always the product of that deliberate reflection. The most telling example in this context is the US Civil War some seventy years after the Philadelphia convention. In the *Federalist Papers* John Jay explicitly argued for the federal constitution as a safeguard of peace among the states. Experience was to show that there was no shared understanding of that constitution to prevent war as westward expansion and a changing economy put a strain in the interstate bargain over slavery. Conversely, not all constitutional change arises from the sort of deliberate rationality associated with Philadelphia. Piecemeal constitutional adaptation, taking the form of new wine in old bottles, as Bagehot pointed out in relation to the English constitution, may be better able to adapt to unforeseeable developments.

Do the advocates of a social theory need to make an a priori choice between an evolutionary and a constructivist account of rationality? I think not. Whether constitutional and institutional developments are characterized by incremental or constructivist processes of rationality seems to be a complex matter of judgment that brings together considerations of empirical assessment and theoretical heuristics. Even though they are not operating in a closed world, those deciding constructively may hit upon solutions to collective action problems that through deliberation anticipate a wide range of cases. Even when an institution is the product of human action but not of human design, it may equally be recognized as a solution to a collective action problem. The Bloomington research programme would be expanded, not restricted, by incorporating such questions prompted by these contrasting accounts of rationality into its core.

NOTE

1. I should like to thank Dario Castiglione and Filippo Sabetti for the invitation to contribute to this book, as well as for their supportive comments on an earlier draft. Needless to say, all remaining errors are my own.

REFERENCES

Aligica, P. D. and Sabetti, F. 2014. "The Ostroms' Research Program for the Study of Institutions and Governance: Theoretical and Epistemic Foundations," in *Choice, Rules and Collective Action*. E. Ostrom and V. Ostrom, edited by F. Sabetti and P. D. Aligica, 1–19. Colchester: ECPR Press.

Arrow, K. J. 1963. *Social Choice and Individual Values*. Second edition. New Haven and London: Yale University Press.

Austin, J. L. 1970. *Philosophical Papers*, edited by J. O. Urmson and G. J. Warnock. Oxford: Oxford University Press.

Bagehot, W. [1867] 1963. *The English Constitution*, with an Introduction by R. H. S. Crossman. London: Fontana.

Bennett, J. 1964. *Rationality*. London: Routledge & Kegan Paul.

Bentham, J. [1780] 1970. *An Introduction to the Principles of Morals and Legislation*, edited by J. H. Burns and H. L. A. Hart. London: The Athlone Press.

Berkes, F. 1986. "Local-level Management and the Commons Problem: A Comparative Study of Turkish Fisheries." *Marine Policy* 10: 215–29.

Binmore, K. 1993. "Bargaining and Morality," in *Rationality, Justice and the Social Contract: Themes from Morals by Agreement*, edited by D. Gauthier and R. Sugden 131–56. New York: Havester-Wheatsheaf.

Brandom, R. B. 2000. *Making It Explicit*. Cambridge, Mass.: Harvard University Press.

Buchanan, J. M. and Tullock, G. 1962. *The Calculus of Consent*. Ann Arbor: University of Michigan Press.

Ginsberg, M. L. 1994. "AI and Nonmonotonic Reasoning," in *Handbook of Logic in Artificial Intelligence and Logic Programming*, Volume 3, *Nonmontonic Reasoning and Uncertain Reasoning*, edited by D. M. Gabbay, C. J. Hogger, J. A. Robinson and D. Nute 1–33. Oxford: Clarendon Press.

Hamilton, A. [1787] 2003. "The Federalist No. 1," in *The Federalist with Letters of "Brutus,"* edited by T. Ball. Cambridge: Cambridge University Press.

Hart, H. L. A. 1994. *The Concept of Law*. Second edition. Oxford: Clarendon Press.

Hawkins, K. 1984. *Environment and Enforcement*. Oxford: Clarendon.

Hawkins, K. and Thomas, J. M. eds. 1984. *Enforcing Regulation*. Boston and The Hague: Kluwer-Nijhoff.

Hayek, F. A. ed. 1950. *Collectivist Economic Planning*. London: Routledge & Kegan Paul.

Hayek, F. A. 1973. *Law, Legislation and Liberty, Volume I, Rules and Order*. London: Routledge.

Hayek, F. A. 1979. *Law, Legislation and Liberty, Volume III, The Political Order of a Free People*. London: Routledge.
Hobbes, T. [1651] 1946. *Leviathan*. Edited with an Introduction by Michael Oakeshott. Oxford: Basil Blackwell.
Hohfeld, W. N. 1923. *Fundamental Legal Conceptions*. New Haven: Yale University Press.
Kuhn, T. S. 1970. *The Structure of Scientific Revolutions*. Second edition. Chicago: University of Chicago Press.
Lakatos, I. 1970. "Falsification and the Methodology of Scientific Research Programmes," in *Criticism and the Growth of Knowledge*, edited by I. Lakatos and A. Musgrave, 91–196. Cambridge: Cambridge University Press.
Luce, R. D. and Raiffa, H. 1957. *Games and Decisions*. New York: John Wiley Sons, Inc.
Maynard Smith, J. 1979. "Game Theory and the Evolution of Behaviour." *Proceedings of the Royal Society of London, Series B, Biological Sciences*, 205: 475–88.
McGann, A. 2006. *The Logic of Democracy: Reconciling Equality, Minority Protection and Deliberation*. Michigan: University of Michigan Press.
Nove, A. 1983. *The Economics of Feasible Socialism*. London: George Allen & Unwin.
Ostrom, E. 1990. *Governing the Commons: The Evolution of Institutions for Collective Action*. Cambridge: Cambridge University Press.
Ostrom, E. and Ostrom, V. 2004. "The Quest for Meaning in Public Choice." *American Journal of Economics and Sociology* 63: 105–47. Reprinted in: E. Ostrom and V. Ostrom, *Choice, Rules and Collective Action*. Edited by F. Sabetti and P. D. Aligica, 61–93. Colchester: ECPR Press, 2014. Citations from original.
Ostrom, V. 1991. "Some Ontological and Epistemological Puzzles in Policy Analysis," in V. Ostrom, *The Quest to Understand Human Affairs: Essays on Collective, Constitutional and Epistemic Choice*. Edited by Barbara Allen, 253–96. Lanham: Lexington Books, 2012.
Ostrom, V. 1993. "Epistemic Choice and Public Choice." *Public Choice* 77: 163–76. Reprinted in E. Ostrom and V. Ostrom, *Choice, Rules and Collective Action*. Edited by F. Sabetti and P. D. Aligica, 243–69. Colchester: ECPR Press, 2014. Citations from Original.
Ostrom, V. 2008a. *The Intellectual Crisis in American Public Administration*. Third Edition. Tuscaloosa, AL: University of Alabama Press.
Ostrom V. 2008b. *The Political Theory of a Compound Republic: Designing the American Experiment*. Third Edition. Lanham: Lexington Books.
Ostrom, V. 2012. *The Quest to Understand Human Affairs: Essays on Collective, Constitutional and Epistemic Choice*. Edited by Barbara Allen. Lanham: Lexington Books.
Ostrom, V. 2014. "Polycentricity: The Structural Basis of Self-Governing Systems," in E. Ostrom, and V. Ostrom, *Choice, Rules and Collective Action*. Edited by F. Sabetti and P. D. Aligica, 45–60. Colchester: ECPR Press.
Polanyi, M. 1951. *The Logic of Liberty: Reflections and Rejoinders*. Chicago: Chicago University Press.
Rawls, J. 2005. *Political Liberalism: Expanded Edition*. New York: Columbia University Press.

Savage, L. J. 1954. *The Foundations of Statistics*. New York: John Wiley & Sons, Inc.

Searle, J. R. 1969. *Speech Acts: An Essay in the Philosophy of Language*. Cambridge: Cambridge University Press.

Sen, A. 1977. "Rational Fools: A Critique of the Behavioral Foundations of Economic Theory." *Philosophy and Public Affairs* 6: 317–44.

Shackle, G. L. S. 1969. *Decision Order and Time in Human Affairs*. Cambridge: Cambridge University Press.

Sidgwick, H. [1907] 1981. *The Methods of Ethics*. Foreword by John Rawls. Indianapolis and Cambridge: Hackett Publishing Company.

Weale, A. 1992. "Implementation Failure: A Suitable Case for Review?" in *Achieving Environmental Goals*, edited by E. Lykke, 43–63. London and Florida: Belhaven Press.

Weale, A. 2013. *Democratic Justice and the Social Contract.* Oxford: Oxford University Press.

Wittgenstein, L. Third Edition [1953] 1967. *Philosophical Investigations*. Translated by G.E.M. Anscombe. Oxford: Basil Blackwell.

Chapter 2

Extending the Institutional Analysis and Development Framework to Policy Analysis and Design

Margaret M. Polski

After observing students and visiting scholars wrestle with applying the Institutional Analysis and Development (IAD) framework to their practical concerns, Elinor (Lin) Ostrom and I wrote a paper on how to use the IAD for policy analysis and design (Polski and Ostrom Forthcoming [1999]).[1] Previous descriptions of the IAD framework had focused on using it for scholarly research. But as interest in institutional analysis grew, many analysts wanted to understand how they could apply it to better understand and solve public problems. So Lin and I set out to describe how the IAD could be used as a tool for policy analysis, that is, to evaluate policy, strategy, or program effectiveness, initiate reform, or design new policies, strategies, or programs. We aimed to write simply and avoid jargon so that we could reach a broad audience.

Policy analysis methods have continued to evolve since 1999 and Lin and I shared a keen interest in these developments. Lin was an avid methodologist and she studied and applied new analytic tools in her research until the day she died. For example, late in life, her collaboration with colleagues in the computational social sciences gave her a chance to more rigorously explore behavior in complex social and physical systems using insights from the complexity sciences and agent-based modeling approaches.[2] Lin and Vincent Ostrom also enthusiastically supported my interest in applying emerging work in cognitive neuroscience to better understand the biological underpinnings of decision behaviors, and they patiently considered my early ruminations about the potential implications for the IAD framework (Polski 2009).[3]

The Ostroms and I also shared an interest in and concern for how social systems evolve, and the implications of changes that policy makers make that alter the patterns of order that have been crafted over time. One of the primary lessons that I learned from studying and contending with both of the Ostroms was the importance of taking time to develop a detailed understanding of the logic of the visible and invisible infrastructure that facilitates social behavior. In my experience, this approach can help us achieve better results in both research, where the necessity is fairly obvious, and policy making, where it less obvious.

For example, in basic research, we use commonly accepted principles of scientific inquiry to patiently accumulate evidence in a never-ending search for truth. The scholarly community is trained to appreciate that truth requires a firm foundation in extensive knowledge that is accumulated and vetted over time. Basic research communities tolerate and often encourage highly focused analyses from a single disciplinary perspective.

However, everyday public problem-solving takes place in complex systems and structures. Policy makers typically confront problems that require multi-disciplinary expertise to cut paths in areas where the research findings are ambiguous, or that basic researchers may not have explored. And more often than not, policy constituents have different understandings of accumulated evidence about potential choices. Rather than searching for truth, policy analysis, design, and development involves searching for a range of logically related and politically acceptable alternative courses of action with and without respect for disciplinary or scientific convention.

In this chapter I revisit and extend the paper that Lin and I wrote in 1999 based on my research and policy analysis experience over the past decade and a half. This experience spans a wide range of policy problems and systems including banking and financial systems, innovation "ecosystems," the organization and use of biological materials, economic development, and political-military operations. I have strived to put new empirical foundations under old assumptions, and consider the theoretical and practical implications of extending the IAD. The first section of the chapter, which forms the starting point for reconsidering the IAD framework as a tool for policy analysis, provides an overview of the IAD framework as Lin and I extended it in our 1999 paper. I also consider the implications of conceptualizing policy making as decision making and the IAD as a tool to support decision analysis—something that Lin and I did not explicitly articulate in 1999. In the second section of the chapter I further extend the IAD to capture the implications of what we are learning from advances in the cognitive neurosciences and the complexity sciences. In the third section I speculate about future challenges for institutionally oriented policy analysis, and in the final section I summarize.

THE IAD FRAMEWORK CIRCA 1999

In an essay on the foundations of institutional analysis and development, Vincent (1988) argued that the focus of institutional analysis is on how rule-ordered relationships are crafted in human societies. Analysts, developers, and designers have distinct but interrelated roles. Analysts are concerned with understanding and explanation. What Vincent calls "developers" and I call "designers" are concerned with how structures of rule-ordered relationships are conceptualized, modified, and changed. Implementers, or what I understand Vincent to mean by the term "organizers" are concerned with implementing, maintaining, and revising rules.

In our 1999 paper, Lin and I argued that the IAD could be used in policy analysis and design to guide thinking about behavior in policy systems in a rigorous way (Polski and Ostrom Forthcoming [1999]). We believed that the framework could provide a means to account for contextual variables, visible and invisible situational dynamics, patterns of interaction, and the outcomes associated with policy problems. And because it is a framework rather than a theory or a method, we felt that the IAD would be compatible with the very wide range of specialized analytic assumptions and techniques that are used to address many policy problems. We estimated that if analysts rigorously employ the IAD framework, they would have a better chance of producing useful analyses and effective policies.

Figure 2.1 depicts the IAD framework as Lin and I conceptualized it in 1999. Like the original IAD framework, this version guides an analyst to carefully specify the physical, historical, and social context of the policy "action arena." As we thought about it at the time, the action arena is a policy-relevant process. Behavior in the action arena may be related to patterns of interaction and outcomes. However, the behavior in any given policy arena is potentially enabled or constrained by the physical and community attributes associated with the policy problem, and the rules-in-use that govern the process in the action arena.[4]

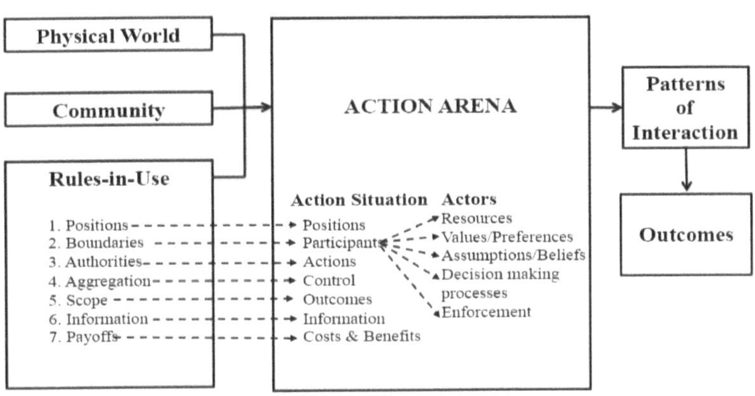

Figure 2.1 The IAD Framework for Policy Analysis and Design Circa 1999. *Source*: Created by author.

While Lin and I preserved the original structure of the IAD in our conceptualization, we extended the framework to explicitly recognize that policy making involves uncertainty and strategic behavior. Borrowing from specification practices in game theory, experimental economics, and Lin's experience working with Roy Gardner and Jimmy Walker (Ostrom et al. 1994), we added a typology of rules-in-use and we defined the action arena to include a typology of institutional characteristics of the policy-relevant environment (Action Situation) and a typology of decision-relevant characteristics of the actors in the arena (Actors). We felt that these additions would help analysts better understand and more clearly specify the potential relationships between the attributes of the rules-in-use and the elements of a policy action arena.

Institutions and Organizations

Another contribution that Lin and I made in the 1999 paper was to differentiate between the terms "institution" and "organization." Following Crawford and Ostrom (1995), we defined an institution as "a widely understood rule, norm, or strategy that creates incentives for behavior in repetitive situations." We observed that institutions may be formally described in writing in the form of a law, policy, or procedure, or they may emerge informally as norms, standard operating practices, or habits. By contrast, we argued that an organization could be thought of as a set of institutional arrangements and participants who have a common set of goals and purposes, and who must interact across multiple action situations at different levels of activity. Organizations may be formally or informally structured. Examples of organizations include legislatures, government agencies, multilateral organizations like the United Nations or the World Bank, nongovernmental organizations, colleges and universities, business enterprises, cooperatives, religious groups, clubs, social networks, clans, tribes, and families.

Another point that Lin and I made in our 1999 paper was that participants in organizations make policy and are subject to policy. Indeed, many organizations have formal and informal rules about how policies are made and who may participate in policymaking activities. Moreover, in addition to nested levels of rules about activities in the action arena, any given arena may include individuals, organizations, and unorganized groups of individuals. Hence the policy analyst must take into account the possibility that there are contending rules-in-use in a policy arena that may be only loosely related to the substantive nature of the policy matter, and find a way to account for these dynamics.

The IAD as a Tool for Decision Analysis and Support

As I reconsider the work that Lin and I did in 1999 and the way that I have used the IAD framework, it seems to me that there were a number of linkages with other areas of theory and research that we understood at the time but failed to explicitly acknowledge. For example, we were each in our own way influenced by the work of Herbert Simon. Originally trained as a Political Scientist under Harold Lasswell and Charles Merriam at the University of Chicago in the late 1930s and early 1940s, Simon was renowned for his multidisciplinary work and was awarded the Nobel Prize in Economics in 1978. Simon argued that theories of public administration are really theories of human decision making behavior. His own quest to understand human decision making led him to embrace work in cognitive psychology, sociology, economics, and the emerging fields of computer science and artificial intelligence.

Simon's profoundly simple insight has important implications for basic research on complex questions such as the behavior of resource systems or human societies over time, and for applied work that is focused on analyzing and addressing policy problems. If we follow Simon's lead and broadly construe policy analysis as decision analysis, it drives us to do everything we can to objectively specify a policy problem as a decision making problem. It is then easy to see why we might wish to focus on the logic of decision making by identifying the decisions that are being made, who has the right to participate in making them, who is actually making them, how they are making them, what experience, capacity, and bias that they bring to decision making, and aspects of the policy context that constrain participant's choices or processes, or provide opportunities to innovate. As Lin discovered, both game theory and experimental economics have well-developed frameworks for this type of specification that we can borrow from to enrich the IAD framework.

Rationality Assumptions

Another important assumption that Lin and I did not explicitly articulate in our paper had to do with the extent to which policy choices are or can be construed to be "rational." We assumed that focusing on the logic of decision making and aiming to objectively specify this logic is not the same thing as assuming that decision making is strictly rational. To be clear: the IAD framework is not a rational choice theory nor is it *per se* based on rational choice theory. Those who studied with Lin and took her Micro course in the Workshop will remember being asked to identify the set of assumptions that underpin rational choice theories, and then to enumerate potential threats to these assumptions.

Influenced by Simon and our own intellectual endeavors, Lin and I both felt that methods used by rational choice theorists are useful for specifying the logic of decision making but believed that the rationality of decision making must be demonstrated empirically rather than assumed. As I recall, at the time, we were both inclined to speculate that the evidence on any given instance of policy decision making would more closely support Simon's theories of bounded rationality and satisficing than strict theories of rational choice. For my part, I continue to view strict rationality as a rebuttable assumption.

As the first drafter on the 1999 paper, I also brought other areas of theory and research to the project that I don't remember specifically discussing with Lin in connection with that paper. In the years before I entered my doctoral program under Lin's supervision, I both studied and practiced in the areas of management science—particularly organizational analysis, design, and development—bargaining/negotiation, and decision analysis.[5] I understood from my previous education and experience that real-world problem-solving is not like solving an optimization problem: finding and implementing the "best" solution is ultimately a normative and subjective process rather than a positive and objective process, it is very hard, and it is common to make mistakes. While my experience taught me that one could strive to improve decision making processes to make them more "rational" in the sense of being data-driven and evidence-based, one could never completely remove bias or uncertainty, prevent corruption, distortions, or other unintended consequences, or foreclose the potential that participants will change the rules while engaged in the process of making decisions about them.

For example, as a young professional, I learned to work with a team to tackle a complex problem using situation analysis techniques that were then common in operations research. As I migrated toward designing negotiation and facilitated dispute resolution processes, I drew on work by Howard Raiffa (1970 [1968]), who explored decision making under uncertainty; Thomas Schelling (1980 [1960]), who explored interdependent decision making involving uncertainty and conflict; and Robert Axelrod (1984) who explored how cooperative decision making develops.

While I can and probably did at the time find similar influences in Lin's previous work and her field research data, I do not remember that we specifically discussed these influences and apart from the references that are contained in the 1999 paper, we did not attempt to directly apply them in the way that we extended the IAD framework. However, I can be sure that standard Workshop assumptions about methodological individualism, human fallibility, and the role of contestation in policy making informed our thinking and writing even if we did not specifically discuss these issues in the paper.

FURTHER EXTENDING THE IAD FRAMEWORK TO POLICY ANALYSIS

One of the first extensions of the IAD framework to policy analysis that I pursued was when I began to grapple with advances in the cognitive neurosciences to identify the biological basis of human decision making. By this point I was explicitly conceptualizing policy making as decision making. Following the Workshop convention of methodological individualism, this conceptualization led me to think of the formal and informal institutions and organizations that institutional analysts had been studying as second-order effects of human biological processes. In other words, I began to see our unique biological make up as first-order rules-in-use. I believe that this line of inquiry, which the Ostroms enthusiastically followed, has important implications for how we think about and use the IAD framework.

A Biological Perspective on Institutional Analysis and Design

Despite the fulsome and ancient debate in the research and philosophy literature about the nature of human nature and our decision making capacities, contemporary policy analysts often assume that humans are akin to dispassionate, unbiased optimization machines that aim to make decisions that will minimize costs and maximize benefits. However, the evidence from work in the cognitive neurosciences strongly contradicts this conceptualization.

Human decision makers are more like massively complex "smart" sensors with action potential than either rational or even boundedly rational optimization machines (Polski 2008). In general, decision making processes involve comprehension, prediction, and response. As Figure 2.2 illustrates, human decision making processes are fundamentally shaped by biological sensing

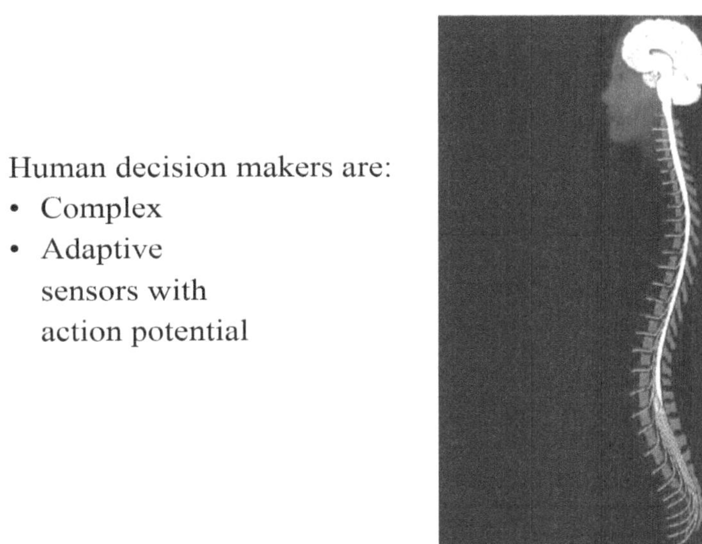

Figure 2.2 Decision Makers as Smart Sensors. *Source*: Created by author.

capacities and pattern recognition processes. To comprehend, predict, and respond to events, we rely on cells in our bodies to capture cues from our environment and communicate about them across networks and systems in the body and the brain. Biological information capture and communication processes are partly autonomic and partly intentional.[6]

The research on the sensory and pattern recognition processes associated with human cognition and decision making is still in its infancy. However it currently appears that as long as we are alive, we are constantly collecting and processing signals using our sensory capacities, albeit in more and less attentive states. In a fully attentive state, we sense the need to decide and act based on the "loudest" integrated pattern of signals that emerge from a polycentric system of internal and external cues. From this sensory screaming frenzy a state of mind or "mental model" emerges and we act before we "know" what we have decided to do. These patterns or mental models allow us to comprehend what is happening in our environment, what could happen, and what we should do in response.[7]

Our cognitive processes are governed by rules that are fixed based on heredity, routinized based on experience, and fundamentally biased. At the biological level, human decision making is governed by polycentric, multilevel sets of rules that govern signaling behavior at cellular, network, subsystem, and system levels.[8] Governing rules are partly hardwired by genetics, and partly wired by experience and training. For example, assuming that we have not been disabled by injury or disease, our ability to see the color of the sky and estimate whether it will rain or snow is shaped by genetically-determined rules that structure the process of converting light into images: we either are able to process light signals in such a way that we "see" colors or we are not able to do so.

However, we are also affected by what is happening in the environment in which our body is situated, as well as the experience that we have previously had operating in similar environments. Continuing with our example, we would have no reason to decide that the sky is blue and that it probably won't rain or snow unless we have had the experience of seeing a blue sky and associating this image of the sky with an absence of precipitation. Hence we can say that human decision making is a mind, body, and context problem.

Brains are Embodied and Bodies are Embedded

As Figure 2.2 illustrates, our brain is embodied and it communicates with and depends upon other biological processes and systems to function effectively. However, at any given time, our brains and bodies are embedded in physical, social, and institutional environments of varying degrees of richness. Any particular set of biological decision making process is situated in a physical

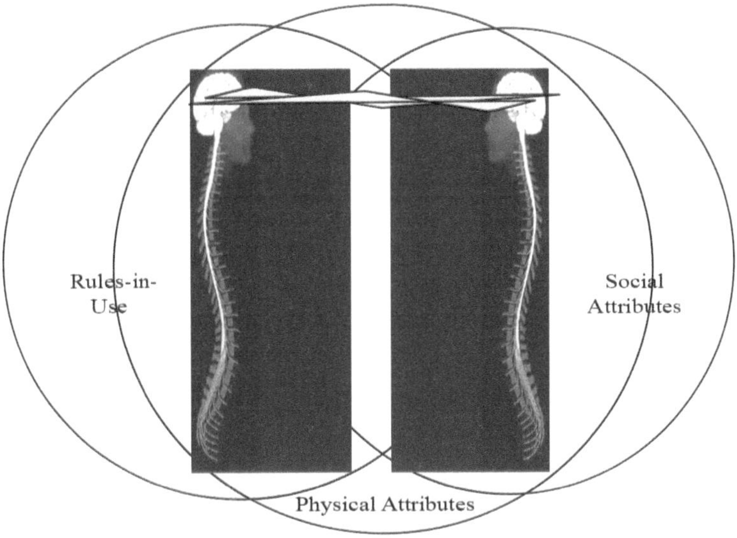

Figure 2.3 The Human Decision Making Ecosystem. *Source*: Created by author.

context (where we are located in space and time) and a social context (with whom we are located). As Figure 2.3 illustrates, this means that human decision making is shaped by our innate capacity—how we are wired at birth, our current functionality, and the extent of our previous experience—and the physical and social decision ecosystem within which we are embedded.

While we can often observe and estimate the effects of physical aspects of a decision environment on biological processing such as temperature, altitude, and so on, the effects of the social aspects of our environment are seemingly invisible. Yet the ability to understand social signals, represent the values and the experience of others in our own minds, and to perceive and transmit mental desires and beliefs is a cornerstone of our intelligence and functionality. What is sometimes called social or emotional intelligence is rooted in biological mechanisms that allow us to read others' minds and to integrate this information with our previous experience and training (Polski 2008).

One line of research on the transmission of social information focuses on a system of "mirror neurons" that allows us to simulate and mimic the states of others—to "get inside their head"—and thereby estimate their intentions and respond accordingly. When we simulate the actions or feelings of others, functional Magnetic Resonance Imaging (fMRI) evidence suggests that it triggers the same neurobiological activity that we would experience if we were directly engaged in the identical action or emotional state.

Another line of research is related to micro expressions. This research is based on evidence that suggests that a good deal of what we learn and experience becomes embodied in facial expressions, postures, gestures, and so on. These expressions then become associated with specific sensations, emotions, memories, and thoughts. In social interaction we take cues from the expressions and gestures of others: what we used to call "body language" and now call "biometrics." Wittingly or unwittingly, we convey our personal values, beliefs, and experience to others through our expressions and gestures. These often very subtle cues from others trigger biological signaling that affects how we feel and what we think, which in turn, affects our motivation, decision making, and performance.

Homeodynamics

Policy making involves creating incentives for behavior, and it often aims to change behavior. Change would be a relatively simple exercise in individual decision making except for the fact that we live in social groups in particular contexts, which may or may not be conducive to the changes we wish to or ought to make. Although changing ourselves when we want to change is difficult in the best circumstances, changing an entire social order when not everyone wishes to do so is an even greater challenge. Well-intended, large-scale social change efforts fail more often than they succeed because to change outcomes, one must change patterns of behavior.

A biological perspective on change implies that to change patterns of behavior, one must change minds *and* bodies, which involves restructuring the rules that govern biological signaling. The ability to change our biological rules of the game also varies across individuals based on genetic wiring, injury, illness, or environmental factors such as being too hot or too cold to "think straight." For example, in addition to psychometric evidence of differences in cognitive processing capacities or intelligence, neuroscience studies have consistently identified distinctive, inheritable differences in the biological structures associated with certain decision making disorders such as schizophrenia, autism, and attention deficit and hyperactivity.

Sensing and pattern recognition processes that are hardwired cannot be changed until or unless we experience injury, disease, or some sort of environmental or technological intervention. However, sensing and pattern recognition processes that are based on experience and training can be changed, but change requires creating new biological maps, which literally requires embodying new experiences.

Implications of the Biological Perspective for the IAD

Lin used to argue that if we want to change behavior, our options include changing people, changing technology, or changing institutions. In her view, it was potentially easier to change institutions than it was to change people *or* to change technology. However, if we take the biological perspective on institutional analysis and design seriously, it seems to me that the evidence suggests that the only way that we can change institutions or technology is to change *people*, and specifically, to change the biological maps and processes that govern their behavior in a particular context.

But how on earth can a policy analyst investigate biological preconditions for policy change or advise policy makers on creating incentives for biological change? It seems to me that a biological perspective on institutional analysis provides additional support for the necessity for institutional analysis and it also demonstrates the need for a tool like the IAD framework in policy work. For if we are to properly understand and affect the dynamics of a policy action arena at a biological level, we absolutely must do the kind of far-reaching specification of the decision making ecosystem that the IAD framework demands.

A biological perspective on institutional analysis also provides even more rigorous empirical support for assumptions that are critical for policy analysis and design, namely that institutions are locally shared concepts, and that humans are fallible. However, it seems to me that the biological perspective requires that we further extend our assumptions about institutions and institutional analysis by demonstrating that:

1. Institutions exist in ways that can be only partially discerned by language and by investigating formal "rules of the game," a point I discuss in more detail in the third section of this chapter, Emerging Challenges for Institutional Analysis and Design;
2. Humans are not just fallible in the sense that we make mistakes, but our decision making processes are fundamentally and irreducibly biased by our innate capacities and experience;
3. Pattern recognition is a better approximation of human decision making processes than logical or computational processes;
4. While many humans have the ability to discern patterns from very different types of data, we must account for the fact that we have processing limits as well as innate biases.

Finally, it seems to me that a biological perspective demonstrates that institutional analysis and design are exceedingly complex endeavors. The Ostroms never shied away from complexity: as Vincent argued, ". . .both biological and cultural evolution is accompanied by the development of increasingly complex patterns in human institutional arrangements" (V. Ostrom 1988). And Lin was often the leader of the pack in both expanding the complexity of a policy analysis, and in seeking new approaches and methods to handle increasingly complex sets of observations.[9]

A Complex Systems Perspective on Institutional Analysis and Design

Few policy action arenas are simple or even merely complicated: many are situated in complex adaptive physical and social systems such as forests, fisheries, local economies, or national security systems. Behaviors in many complex adaptive policy arenas are emergent and cannot be attributed to an aggregation of existing properties. Behaviors are often robust and resilient and survive because actors or organisms adapt to changes in their environment. Adaptive behaviors are typically associated with dynamic networks of interactions, and self-organizing micro-level structures.

Complexity has a number of implications for decision making. In operations research, many decision making problems associated with complexity are sometimes called "wicked problems." Wicked problems cannot be formulated definitively. They do not have a well-defined set of right or wrong solutions, or a well described set of permissible operations. Discrepancies can be explained in many different ways, and there is no immediate or ultimate test of a solution to a wicked problem.

Whereas complicated policy arenas have hard parameters and a fixed number of alternative courses of action, complex systems have fuzzy boundaries and a potentially unlimited set of alternative courses of action. We may be able to observe patterns in the behaviors that emerge from complex arenas, but we cannot eliminate the possibility that these patterns are transitory. Similarly, we may find correlations in the behavior of components of complex arena, but it may not be possible to rigorously demonstrate causal relations.

For example, reflecting on game-theoretic analyses of conflict and strategy that were increasingly popular in the early years of the Cold War, Schelling (1980 [1960]) observed that formal models could not handle unbounded strategic behavior. In complex policy arenas participants can and do change the rules while playing by manipulating their operating space, the types of participants in this space, the positions of participants, information, resources including technologies, the scope of permissible action, the enforcement of rules, the imposition of costs and benefits, and the allocation of payoffs.

The Characteristics of Complex Adaptive Policy Arenas

Complex adaptive policy arenas have a number of characteristics that differentiate them from other types of dynamic systems, or systems that are merely complicated.[10] Perhaps most importantly, they are self-organizing and exhibit both deliberate and spontaneous order. Self-organizing behavior occurs without explicit command or control, and it is associated with locally operating social and technical processes, which may be quite difficult to observe.

Complex adaptive policy arenas are also polycentric and multi-scale. They have many centers of inter-dependent decision making and control, and the arena cannot be described as governed by a single, hierarchical form of command and control, even though some sub-systems may be centralized or decentralized hierarchies. Multi-scale behavior cannot be described by a single rule or analyzed at a single level: the structure of behavior exists on multiple scales and multiple levels.

While complex adaptive policy arenas are sensitive to initial conditions, they often exhibit path dependencies, and stable equilibrium; they are dynamic, subject to punctuated equilibrium and "black swans," and they are rife with interdependencies and non-linearity. Comprehending complex adaptive policy arenas is difficult but not impossible and the IAD framework is a useful tool.

The Implications of a Complex Systems Perspective for the IAD

Complex adaptive policy arenas can be studied over time, and emergent properties and behavior can be rigorously explored. However, in addition to using the IAD framework as a guide in specification, it seems to me that policy analysts must learn to use tools and methods from the computational sciences, such as artificially intelligent analytics that can crawl through "big data," network analyses, visualization tools, and simulation methods such as agent-based modeling. For example, analysts may find data mining and social network analysis tools to be useful for analyzing complexity problems; Monte Carlo and graph theory may be useful for diagnostic problems; cellular automata and agent-based models may be useful for modeling; and genetic algorithms and particle swarm optimization may be useful for synthesis.

In addition to embracing new tools, policy analysts who are interested in complex adaptive policy arenas may also find it useful to reconsider their analytical objectives. It may be futile to search for causal relations or deterministic "drivers" in these arenas. Instead, it may make more sense to focus on identifying associations and correlations, valuing tangible and intangible assets, estimating stocks and flows, monitoring emerging behavior, tracking "outliers," mapping interactions, and identifying patterns and trends. Realistic analytical questions include:

- What is the structure of the arena and what are its boundaries? How permeable are these boundaries?
- What are the properties of the arena and how does it behave, for example, what emerges from the arena?
- How could the arena evolve and what are the implications for emergent properties and behaviors?

- What is the logic of adaptation? Which aspects of the arena are critical for resiliency? Which groups are most likely to survive? Prevail? Which groups are vulnerable?

Comprehending complex adaptive policy arenas involves many different types of knowledge from a variety of perspectives; activities are organized at multiple levels, and any given policy situation overlaps with other policy situations so that activities in one situation affect activities in others. No single discipline covers all of the issues that humans address when they interact in these types of arenas. In order to understand what is actually going on in a policy arena as well as how things might proceed differently, it is important to incorporate input from multiple disciplines and to use multiple methods of analysis. One of the reasons for developing the IAD framework was to provide a common basis for specifying and integrating the work of these types of diverse policy analysis activities. So let us now reconsider the IAD framework in light of the biological and complex systems perspectives on policy analysis and decision making.

The IAD Framework Reconsidered

I continue to find the IAD framework enormously helpful in my work as a policy analyst and researcher. However, as Figure 2.4 shows, I have made some modifications to the framework for analyzing particularly wicked, complex adaptive policy arenas. Apart from some slight changes in terminology, I have preserved the essential elements of the original IAD framework as well as the extensions that Lin and I made in 1999. However, I make subtle but I

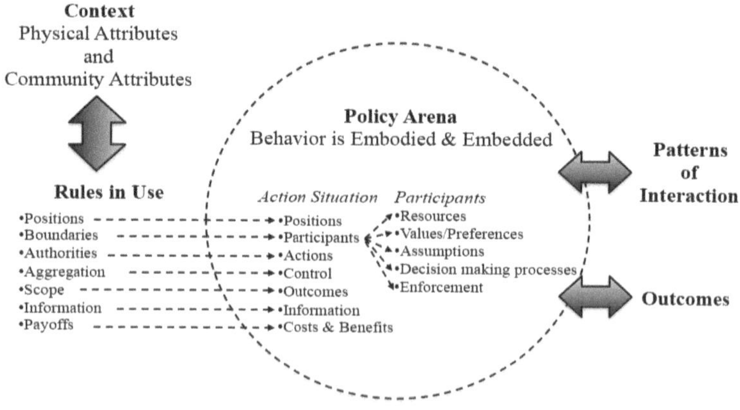

Figure 2.4 The IAD Framework Reconsidered. *Source*: Created by author.

think important distinctions based on my understanding of developments in the cognitive neurosciences and the complexity sciences.

First, I conceptualize the policy arena as a complex adaptive system with permeable boundaries, which is reflected in the depiction of the policy arena as a circle bounded with dashed lines rather than a box with solid lines. I label the behavior that emerges in the action arena as "embodied and embedded," which reminds me to consider the biological rules that govern behavior in the action situation under consideration, as well as the impacts associated with the social and physical context of the action situation. I replace the term "Actors" with the term "Participants" to explicitly indicate that the focus of interest is those who are directly engaged in the action situation rather than those who are merely playing a role.

Second, I have combined the boxes "Physical World" and "Community" into a concept depicted as an unbounded "Context." I include the labels "Physical Attributes" and "Community Attributes" to remind me to consider the geophysical, demographic, and cultural aspects of the context that are relevant to the action situation that I am considering.

Third, I have retained the "Rules in Use" category and the specification of different types of rules. However, I have removed the box and hence the boundaries, and inserted a two-way arrow between "Context" and "Rules in Use," which reminds me to consider that there may be interdependencies. For example, as population demographics change, rules-in-use may also change or if they do not, if we are alert to them, we may find perverse effects. Similarly, if attributes of the physical situation change, rules-in-use are subject to change.

Fourth, I have also removed the one way arrow that connects the set of contextual attributes and "Rules in Use" to the "Action Arena." It seems to me that the arrow in earlier versions of the IAD framework could be understood to imply that there is a linear or causal relationship between contextual attributes, rules, and the behavior that emerges in the action arena. In my view, understanding and specifying these elements is crucial. However, attempting to find causal relations or linearity between contextual attributes, rules, and emergent behavior in a policy action arena is potentially futile or at the very least, beyond the scope of a given policy analysis project.

Finally, I have retained the "Patterns of Interaction" and the "Outcomes" categories but I have removed the boundaries and the one way arrow that connected them. Instead, I have inserted two-way arrows that permeate the action arena, which reminds me to consider the interdependencies between emergent behavior in the policy action arena and the potential feedback associated with patterns of interaction and outcomes. Moreover, the previous construction of the framework could be understood to imply that the action arena is a kind of production function that "produces" patterns and outcomes in the same way that an enterprise produces products or services. I find it more useful to think of patterns and outcomes as a way of describing and categorizing emergent behavior, rather than as distinct analytical constructs.

EMERGING CHALLENGES FOR INSTITUTIONAL ANALYSIS AND DESIGN

When Lin and I applied the IAD framework to policy analysis in our 1999 paper, we focused exclusively on issues related to governing human behavior. However, increasingly we operate in policy arenas that involve complex operations, and include human *and* artificially intelligent participants. These complex, "heterogeneous systems" will continue to proliferate as advances in the computational sciences are applied to a wide range of action situations that go far beyond shopping, navigating, or selecting films, to encompass driving, healthcare, and warfare, among many other action arenas. In the near future, some societies will include humans *and* machines, which will be capable of operating autonomously, semiautonomously, and in symbiotic groups. With advances in artificial intelligence, the machines we create and deploy are potentially capable of self-governance and self-replication. These developments will generate entirely new patterns of order and governing dilemmas.

For example, today, many of the traders in modern financial systems are algorithms or artificial agents. Humans create the algorithms and the trading platforms. Human traders start and stop trading in a particular market or on a particular platform, develop investment strategies, and issue "buy" and "sell" orders. However, as the mysterious "flash crashes" in recent years demonstrate, we cannot completely account for the behavior that emerges from the interaction between human and artificial decision making in financial markets. Being "in the loop" and in control are two entirely different propositions and, in my view, present novel analytical challenges.

Reconsidering the Role of Language in Institutional Analysis and Development

The Ostroms and many other institutional analysts have defined institutions primarily as linguistic concepts, which presupposes the use of human language(s) as the primary mode of interpretation, transmission, design, and implementation in establishing and maintaining social order.[11] For example, Vincent (1988) specifically defined an institution as a linguistic structure, and his discussion of achieving "shared communities of understanding" contemplates language-based dialogue, contestation, and negotiation over the meaning of specific words, concepts, requirements, permissions and prohibitions. In this 1988 essay, a 1985 essay, and a great deal of his other work, he dwells at length on the key role of the rule of law and jurisprudence in creating and maintaining social order.[12]

The institutional definitions and concepts that Lin and I used in our 1999 paper potentially provide for a very broad conceptualization of institutions, and institutional analysis and design that goes beyond linguistic structures and concepts. However, we did not explicitly contemplate an extension beyond language centric concepts at the time we wrote this paper. In fact, Lin, like Vincent, steadfastly defined institutions and institutional concepts consistent with linguistic structures. For example, in her most comprehensive and refined effort to articulate her perspective on institutions and institutional analysis, she defines institutions as rules, which she asserts "are formulated in human language," and her conceptualization of the source of rules is related to a general legal framework (Elinor Ostrom 2005).[13]

More generally, as Collins (1998) argues, language is an established and unavoidable tool in intellectual endeavors. Consistent with Collins' notion of how knowledge is created and transmitted across people and time, we may wish to see the IAD framework as a helpmate in using language to better connect more abstract ideas about institutional design with observable instances and actions. It is natural for those of us for whom language is our primary tool to see the world through this lens and to wish to persist in creating intellectual scaffolding in this way. However, as the old adage warns, if our only tool is a hammer, everything looks like a nail. It seems to me that if we fall into the trap of limiting our definition of institutions to human linguistic structures, we foreclose the opportunity for creativity and innovation in institutional analysis, design, and development. While I do not dispute a role for language in institutional analysis and design or intellectual life—indeed, I am using language to make this argument—it seems to me that both the biological and the complexity perspectives on institutional analysis, as well as the prospect of symbiotic human-machine societies, challenge us to explicitly search for additional ways to understand and create concepts of institutions and institutional orders that go beyond linguistic constructs even while we continue to use language to communicate about these ideas.

For example, the biological perspective on the IAD framework leads us to assume that the first-order rules of the game are in fact observable biochemical interactions. Moreover, in many situations, humans communicate order to each other through observable images, nonverbal expressions, and sensations. The use of emoticons to convey meaning without words is rapidly becoming ubiquitous in everyday text communications among family and friends who stay in nearly constant communication with mobile phones. Videotaping is routinely used to monitor, analyze, and report actions and reactions in many policy arenas. Expert negotiators and diplomats are able to "read" what their interlocutors are saying "between the lines." The primary way that musicians convey their understanding of a musical composition to an audience is with sound, not with words. In improvisational music, musicians make decisions about what, when, and how to play based on an exchange of glances, gestures, and rhythms. They aim to "find the groove" and "get into the groove" without the benefit of a script or a score. Ensembles of musicians who play together regularly have a shared community of understanding that cannot be captured by language or formal rules. Every parent and some teachers understand the value of a single look, a gesture, or a tone in establishing order. Less benignly, the use of physical violence and various psychological operations triggers human action and generates patterns of order that words alone often cannot achieve.

The complex systems perspective on the IAD framework also challenges us to search for additional ways to understand and craft institutions and institutional orders. This perspective leads us to assume that in complex operations, behaviors can emerge that are not based on linguistically facilitated deliberation, debate, shared understanding, or intentional action. Emergent behaviors may or may not be directly associated with micro-level behaviors in a causal sense, but they can influence the behavior of individuals, things, and organisms in ways that lead to new forms of order in particular systems.

Similarly, the prospect of human-machine symbiosis challenges us to think about how we interact with and establish order with machines in particular contexts. For example, expert sailors and pilots are able to navigate based as much on "reading" cues in the sky, the sea, and the wind and then interacting with these speechless flows as they do based on their language-based decision support systems and their training. Expert fleets of sailors and squadrons of pilots can assemble and disassemble human-machine formations (patterns of order) without language, without direct communication, and in response to unanticipated events for which they have no previous experience or training.

Toward a Broader Definition of Institution and Institutional Analysis and Design

Policy analysis focuses on function and functionality: analysts want to understand how social coordination process work, why they work the way they do, and how they might work in a specific application. The functional essence of the idea of an institution is that it is something that helps us to coordinate our behavior with the behavior of others. And our concept of order embraces micro, meso, and macro level patterns of coordination.

In thinking about a broader definition of institution to meet the emerging challenges of institutional analysis and design, it seems to me that we can look to Thomas Schelling's extensive work on strategy and conflict for inspiration.[14] In the course of his career, Schelling has considered a wide range of coordination problems that have involved behavior in global social orders such as limiting the risk of a nuclear attack; behavior in domestic social orders such as segregation; bilateral and multilateral bargaining behavior; and individual self regulating behaviors such as smoking cessation. In each of these endeavors he has considered a wide range of cues that he has argued enable coordination by communicating meaning about motives, intentions, expectations, limits, and constraints. His willingness to take a wide angle view of communication with respect to coordination problems has provided us with a remarkable set of useful policy concepts and principles such as deterrence, compellence, and focal points.

My understanding of coordination behavior suggests to me the following refinement in our definition of an institution: *an institution is a signaling mechanism that facilitates coordination by conveying information about motive, intent, expectations, permissions, limits, and constraints.* Mechanisms may include but are not limited to language-based constructions such as policy statements, laws, regulations, norms, and standard operating procedures; other symbolic representations such as numbers, signs, and computer code; images; sounds; gestures; odors; touch; flavor; and other mechanisms associated with sensation.

CONCLUSION

In 1999, Lin and I wrote a paper that extended the IAD framework to address policy analysis tasks. In this extension, we added a typology of rules-in-use, and we included typologies of the institutional characteristics of the environment and the actors in the action arena. We also drew a distinction between the terms "institutions" and "organization." While we drew on theory and practice in a number of areas in the decision and management sciences, we did not explicitly articulate how these influences affected the way that we thought about applying the IAD framework to policy analysis and design.

Since 1999, I have further extended the way that I think about the IAD framework based on research in the decision sciences, the cognitive neurosciences, and the complexity sciences. These extensions challenge institutional analysts to consider the biological rules that govern decision making, the implications of complexity for formulating analytical objectives, and the tools and methods we use for analysis. In particular, it seems to me that we need to work with colleagues in the neurosciences and the computational sciences, and learn to integrate new sources of data and new analytic methods such as biometric analyses, data mining techniques, network analyses, visualization tools, and simulation tools such as cellular automata and agent-based modeling with institutional analyses.

As we build and extend our partnerships with machines, we will need to learn to do institutional analyses of heterogeneous policy arenas and action situations. This means that the art and science of institutional analysis and design must evolve to address emerging policy concerns. Analysts will have to develop skills and methods to rigorously analyze and compare autonomous human decision making, autonomous machine decision making, human-machine social orders, and the processes of integrating and governing human-machine teams.

I propose that as a first step in addressing emerging challenges in institutional analysis and design that we broaden our definition of institutions to include ways of achieving understanding and order, which do not require language such biochemical signaling, gestures, micro expressions, symbolic representations, and so on. Specifically, I propose the following general definition: an institution is a signaling mechanism that facilitates coordination by conveying information about motive, intent, expectations, permissions, limits, and constraints. Developing a broader definition of institution, a wider scope for institutional analyses and intellectual collaborations, and new methods of data collection and analysis will present new challenges for the IAD framework but ones that I predict it will easily accommodate.

NOTES

1. In her professional and personal life, Elinor Ostrom preferred to be called "Lin": I honor this preference in all subsequent references.
2. See for example, Poteete et al. (2010) and Anderies et al. (2004).
3. Lin and Vincent Ostrom not only shared a name, they were tightly integrated work partners. While they had independent research agendas and both were extraordinarily productive scholars, they shared a core set of intellectual ideas and assumptions. Vincent Ostrom preferred to be called "Vincent" and so to avoid confusing the two Ostrom and to honor their preferences, hereinafter I will refer to him as Vincent.
4. Examples of physical attributes include geographic features; geological or atmospheric conditions; natural resource stocks and flows; physical assets such as infrastructure, equipment, stocks of goods, and facilities; and technologies. Examples of community attributes include demographic characteristics; historical experience; social networks; and know-how. The action arena is the set of activities and behaviors that may be associated with policy making. Patterns of interaction are observable patterns of physical and social behaviors that may be associated with policymaking activities. Outcomes are effects that may be associated with policy and policymaking activities.
5. In fact, Lin and I both started our careers in the field that was known as Personnel Administration in Lin's era, and Human Resource Management in my era. While we

had the shared experience of thinking about organizations from the perspective of recruiting, selecting, and developing people to achieve an organizational purpose, I do not recall that we consciously incorporated this experience in writing the 1999 paper.

6. For an accessible discussion of the implications of findings in cognitive neuroscience research for the role of intentionality in human decision making, see Gazzaniga (2005).

7. Cognitive activities are information and integration intensive. Raicle et al. (2001) estimate that the brain consumes over 20 percent of the body's total energy allowance. They further speculate that 60–80 percent of the brain's energy consumption is associated with glutamate cycling, which they associate with neurons talking to each other to sustain system balance. This "spontaneous intrinsic activity" limits the capacity of the brain to handle external inputs and to engage in integrative processing. With limited processing capacity, it makes sense for human systems to default to pattern recognition as a primary decision analysis strategy.

8. Cognition (thinking and deciding) and action are a function of the interaction of genes/DNA (instructions for making proteins), RNA (regulates cellular activity), and physiological systems, for example, the nervous system, the motor system, the autonomic system, the endocrine system, the immune system, and so on. Until fairly recently, it has been assumed that communication between the brain and the body is principally mediated by the somatosensory system. However, emerging evidence suggests that RNA may play a greater role in system control than previously thought. For a primer on what we are learning from the neurosciences about the biological basis of decision-making, see Polski (2008).

9. For a detailed discussion of Lin's approach to institutional analysis as it evolved over time, see Elinor Ostrom (2005).

10. For a primer on complex adaptive systems, see Miler and Page (2007).

11. See for example, Douglass North (2005, 48), who defines the term "institution" as "formal rules, informal norms, and their enforcement characteristics"; or Williamson (1985, 4) who differentiates between the "rules of the game," which he characterizes as the "institutional environment," and "institutions of governance," which he characterizes as mechanisms for ordering relations such as markets, hybrids, hierarchies, and bureaus.

12. Vincent Ostrom (1985). For a comprehensive overview of Vincent's work, see Allen (2011; 2012) and Sabetti et al. (2009).

13. After some discussion of different types of rules based on her understanding of Max Black's work, Lin, with reference to others, defines rules as: "shared understandings by participants about enforced prescriptions concerning what actions (or outcomes) are *required*, *prohibited*, or *permitted* (Ganz 1971; V. Ostrom 1980; Commons 1968). All rules are the result of implicit or explicit efforts to achieve order and predictability among humans by creating classes of persons (positions) who are then required, permitted, or forbidden to take classes of actions in relation to required, permitted, or forbidden outcomes or face the likelihood of being monitored and sanctioned in a predictable fashion (V. Ostrom 1991)" (El. Ostrom 2005, 18). Similarly, she defines working rules that individuals use in making decisions as ". . . the set of rules to which participants would make reference if asked to explain and justify their actions to fellow participants" (El. Ostrom 2005, 19.).

14. See for example, Schelling (1980 [1960]; 1987; 2005; 2006 [1978]; 2008 [1977].

REFERENCES

Allen, Barbara, ed. 2012. *The Quest to Understand Human Affairs: Natural Resources Policy and Essays on Community and Collective Choice. Volume I.* Lanham, MD: Lexington Books.

Allen, Barbara, ed. 2011. *The Quest to Understand Human Affairs: Essays on Collective, Constitutional, and Epistemic Choice. Volume II.* Lanham, MD: Lexington Books.

Anderies, John M., Marco A. Janssen, and Elinor Ostrom. 2004. "A Framework to Analyze the Robustness of Social-Ecological Systems from an Institutional Perspective." *Ecology and Society* 9(1): 18, [online] URL: http: www.ecologyandsociety.org/vol9/iss1/art18.

Axelrod, Robert. 1984. *The Evolution of Cooperation.* New York, NY: Basic Books.

Collins, Randall. 1998. *The Sociology of Philosophies: A Global Theory of Intellectual Change.* Cambridge, MA: The Presidents and Fellows of Harvard College.

Crawford, Sue E. S., and Elinor Ostrom. 1995. "A Grammar of Institutions." *American Political Science Review* 89(3): 582–600.

Gazzaniga, Michael. S. 2005. *The Ethical Brain.* New York, NY: The Dana Foundation.

Miller, John H. and Scott E. Page. 2007. *Complex Adaptive Systems: An Introduction to Computational Models of Social Life.* Princeton, NJ: Princeton University Press.

North, Douglass C. 2005. *Understanding the Processes of Economic Change.* Princeton, NJ: Princeton University Press.

Ostrom, Elinor. 2005. *Understanding Institutional Diversity.* Princeton, NY: Princeton University Press.

Ostrom, Elinor, Roy Gardner, and James Walker. 1994. *Rules, Games, and Common-Pool Resources.* Ann Arbor, MI: University of Michigan Press.

Ostrom, Vincent. 1988. "The Foundations of Institutional Analysis and Development," in *The Quest to Understand Human Affairs: Natural Resources Policy and Essays on Community and Collective Choice. Volume I*, edited by Barbara Allen, 2011, pp. 451–75. Lanham, MD: Lexington Books.

Ostrom, Vincent. 1985. "Conceptualizing the Nature and Magnitude of the Task of Institutional Analysis and Development," in *The Quest to Understand Human Affairs: Essays on Collective, Constitutional, and Epistemic Choice. Volume II*, edited by Barbara Allen, 2012, pp. 181–217. Lanham, MD: Lexington Books.

Polski, Margaret M. and Elinor Ostrom, Forthcoming [1999]. "An Institutional Framework for Policy Analysis and Design," in *Elinor Ostrom and the Bloomington School of Political Economy: Volume 3, Frameworks and Methods of Institutional Analysis*, edited by Daniel Cole and Michael McGinnis. Lanham MD: Lexington Books.

Polski, Margaret M. 2009. "Essays on *Wired for Survival*: Integrating Neuroscience and IAD." Presentation for the Workshop on the Workshop at Indiana University, Bloomington, IN. June 5.

Polski, Margaret M. 2008. *Wired for Survival: The Rational and Irrational Choices We Make From the Gas Pump to Terrorism*. Upper Saddle River, NJ: FT Press.

Poteete, Amy R., Marco A. Janssen, and Elinor Ostrom. 2010. *Working Together: Collective Action, the Commons, and Multiple Methods in Practice*. Princeton, NJ: Princeton University Press.

Raicle, Marcus E., Ann Mary Macleod, Abraham Z. Snyder, William J. Powers, Debra A. Gasnard, and Gordon L. Shulman, 2001. "A Default Mode of Brain Function." *Proceedings of the National Academy of Sciences*. Inaugural Article Neurobiology: 98(2): 676–82. January 16.

Raiffa, Howard. [1968] 1970. *Decision Analysis: Introductory Lectures on Choices Under Uncertainty*. Reading, MA: Addison Wesley Publishing Company.

Sabetti, Filippo, Barbara Allen, and Mark Sproule-Jones. 2009. *The Practice of Constitutional Development: Vincent Ostrom's Quest to Understand Human Affairs*. Lanham, MD: Lexington Books.

Schelling, Thomas C. [1977] 2008. *Arms and Influence*. New Haven, CT: Yale University Press.

Schelling, Thomas C. [1978] 2006. *Micromotives and Macrobehavior*. New York, NY: W.W. Norton and Company.

Schelling, Thomas C. 2005. "An Astonishing Sixty Years: The Legacy of Hiroshima." Nobel Prize Lecture. December 8.

Schelling, Thomas C. 1987. "The Role of War Games and Exercises," in *Managing Nuclear Operations*, edited by Carter, Ashton, John Steinbruner, and Charles Zraket. Washington, DC: Brookings, 426–44.

Schelling, Thomas C. [1960] 1980. *The Strategy of Conflict*. Cambridge, MA: Harvard University Press.

Simon, Herbert A. 1957. *Models of Man: Social and Rational—Mathematical Essays on Rational Human Behavior in a Social Setting*. New York, NY: John Wiley and Sons.

Williamson, Oliver E. 1996. *The Mechanisms of Governance*. New York, NY: Oxford University Press.

Chapter 3

Framing the State of Nature through Institutionalist Lenses

Paul Dragos Aligica and Ion Sterpan

The work of Elinor Ostrom, a co-recipient of the 2009 Nobel Prize in Economics, defines the core of an important school of thought in contemporary institutionalist political economy, but at the same time has a dimension that goes beyond the strict boundaries of political science and economics, crossing into the domain of political philosophy. This fact becomes obvious when we consider the relationship between her efforts and Vincent Ostrom's work, the other founding figure of the Bloomington School of institutionalism (Mitchell 1988; Aligica and Boettke 2009, 2011). One of the most consequential contributions of the group of scholars associated with the Ostroms' research program was the creation of the IAD framework, a heuristic and analytical framework to be used in specifying and examining the relationships between the environmental, social and individual elements (Bloomquist and DeLeon 2011). The objective was not so much the discovery of general laws or grand theory building but to capture the dynamics of different action arenas under different constellations of

The IAD framework was born from the empirical examination of a diversity of institutional settings and human interactions. It was further applied to explore how social actors respond to various sets of rules in real-life situations as well as in an abstract configurations of variables or "theoretical scenarios." The framework enabled the construction of scenarios where participants in a social arena arrive at new rules starting from a "default condition," a condition where participants have not yet come to either know or follow the rules pertaining to a resource (Ostrom 2005; 2007; 2010). Together with the distinction between phenotype and genotype (a situation's observed final, compound, properties as opposed to the initial properties of its separate elements), the IAD framework's idea of a baseline value of rules defined as values yet unspecified to participants, proved useful in constructing rigorously disciplined scenarios about real-world arenas. By these two ideas, the IAD framework revealed knowledge about the dynamics of individual, physical and social variables. It answered questions about which variables are pushed to acquire a value by existing configuration of variables which have a specification.

Before IAD, this domain of concern used to be addressed with a classical device in social and political philosophy: "the state of nature thought experiment." This paper argues that the IAD framework should extend its analytical and assessment role from real-life policies and concrete institutional arrangements, to the deceptively simple state of nature theoretical scenarios. Our argument is that the IAD framework advances a broader and more precise perspective on action situations that helps us conceptualize, chart and critically evaluate the diversity of thought experiments evoking the notion of state of nature.

We warn our readers that we are moving on abstract ground. The reasoning from state of nature makes two movements. First it abstracts from unessential aspects of reality so as to arrive at a stylized, cleaner slate, and then from there proceeds to logically reconstruct reality or develop some alternative scenario. Both movements are if-clauses. For instance, someone argues that the absence of such and such political aspects would be or would not be enough to erase such and such social or moral aspect. Then, the argument continues that some social aspect which would still be present in the reduced state would, or would not be enough to generate such and such political aspect. Because grand scale state of nature reasoning does not expose itself to crucial observation, if we wish to probe this device at all, then we must probe its steps. And because intuitive reasoning is made implicitly, its steps and their assumptions must first be detected. In other words, we are in a realm where the test must be more complicated than the device tested.

Our motivation in revisiting the state of nature instruments of abstraction and reconstruction of the world and compare them with Ostrom's newer and more empirically informed device is that many people use the more rudimentary devices to wrongly support institutional prescriptions of great consequence. The old state of nature instruments are simpler to use and for that reason more appealing than Elinor Ostrom's state of nature. But their simplicity is double edged: when their results are incorrect, their simplicity attracts more supporters on the wrong side.

Reasoning from simple states of nature offers a simplified insight precisely because it glosses over nuances and distinctions. The Hobbesian device for instance, does not clearly distinguish between a pre-social and a pre-political state of affairs. Such conflations lead to overstate the risks to social order brought by civic and political contestation even when such actions would serve order. The failure of the old state of nature device to help the user separate between an arena's physical and institutional attributes also corrupts institutional claims made by one of the most careful political philosophers of the twentieth century. On the other hand, the IAD framework helps us distinguish between several aspects in imagined social arenas and reduces the chance of wrongful institutional claims and civic and political prescriptions.

Our scrutiny of the state of nature will also bring something back from political philosophy to social science and serve Elinor Ostrom's initial motivation. E. Ostrom built the IAD framework to tax the employment of metaphors in supporting policy prescriptions (Ostrom 1990, 23). Her favorite example, Garrett Hardin's model for evaluating institutional settings, shares the metaphorical quality with state of nature reasoning. Like state of nature reasoning, it serves as an intuition pump to evaluate situations not yet governed by markets or states as tragic, when in fact the Bloomington School, armed with the IAD, showed ways in which that may not be the case.

THE IAD FRAMEWORK: STRUCTURE AND APPLICATION

The IAD framework (Figure 3.1) as described by the Ostroms, is an analytical and heuristic instrument which consists of "nested sets of components within components." This method aimed at mapping diverse institutional arrangements "overtly analyzes the deeper structures that constitute any particular action situation" (Ostrom 2005, 7). The framework grew around a set of "basic units," atomic "building blocks" of human interaction which Ostrom identified in all cases of collective action and social coordination from a commodity market to a university, a religious order, a transportation system, or an urban public economy (Ostrom 2007).

The framework is intended to contain the most general set of variables useful to examine a diversity of institutional settings including human interactions within markets, private firms, families, community organizations, legislatures, and government agencies (Ostrom 2007). The framework is neither the product of speculative thought on the categories of understanding, nor committed to essentialism. It is the product of empirical studies of common pool resources and of an effort to create a uniform database for appropriation and collective choice arenas involving fisheries, irrigation systems, forestry, social choice situations, development processes, constitutional dynamics, social-ecologic systems. Its set of variables have been arrived at by detecting the common elements in the answers to the various questions asked so far from different perspectives. And if questions within social science about reforms and transitions are fair candidates to the IAD framework, so might the philosophical question about generic transitions from states of nature to government.

The challenge institutional theorists face, explains Ostrom, is to use just enough variables in the structure of a situation to explain, understand, and predict outcomes in relevant settings (Ostrom 2005, 7). The IAD framework's contribution is to enable them to pre-identify the basic structures embedding and defining all key variables of interest.

The IAD framework pivots around individual actions each taking place in their own "action situation." The individuals and their action situations taken together make up the "action arena." Social actors use information, make decisions, engage in interaction, and evaluate consequences of actions in a specific social-cultural, institutional, and biophysical context. The framework is not itself a map or a theory but a meta-theoretical mapping principle of the "action arena" in its context (Aligica 2006).

The underlying theme is obviously that the social and institutional outcomes of individuals' interactions occurring in action arenas are composites of different variables. This means we should not fixate only on actors' attributes ("human nature") and their endowments when explaining social outcomes. One should also consider the attributes of the community (including the heterogeneity and homogeneity of preferences, the levels of trust and norms of reciprocity), the rules-in-use (to be distinguished from the rules-on-paper) and the attributes of the "resource" (the underlying nature of the "goods" in play even if we are talking about an abstract object such as social coordination). The kind of goods social actors may want to generate in their collective action coordination (private, public, toll/club or a common pool) makes a huge difference because each type induces different dynamics and patterns of interaction (Ostrom and Ostrom 1971; 1977).

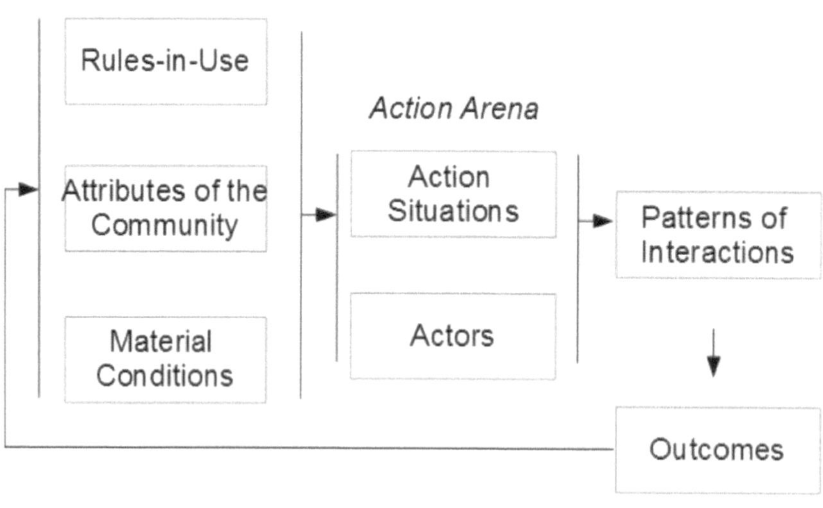

Figure 3.1 IAD Framework. *Source*: Adapted from Ostrom (2007, 27).

The IAD mapping process proceeds in three steps: the first is to map the action arena by identifying the action situation and the actors. The second is to identify the determinants of the action arena: the rules-in-use, the nature of the community, and the physical attributes and aspects of the world some of which might be targeted for change. The third is to elaborate scenarios on how the arena and its determinants generate specific patterns of interactions and specific outcomes (which in turn feedback the determinant variables).

The framework and its application have an extensive and robust track record in the domain of empirical analysis from commons, natural resources, fisheries, forests and water management to public services delivery systems, the economy of foreign aid and constitutional analysis (Polski 2005; Oakerson 1999; McGinnis and Ostrom 1996; Gibson et al. 2005; Agrawal 1999; Sproule-Jones 2002; Hess and Ostrom 2006; Shivakumar 2005).

As already suggested, methodologically speaking, the framework should not be read as a social theory in the standard, mainstream sense. Its epistemological nature requires a discussion in itself (Aligica 2006), but briefly and somewhat imprecisely put, frameworks specify the structural variables relevant to a pretheoretical question while theories (such as microeconomic theory, game theory, transaction cost theory, public choice theory) make assumptions necessary for explanation and prediction of phenomena. Models make further assumptions on the values of the parameters involved: markets or states count as models of arenas while the economic man, or the informed unbiased agent, are models of the individual actor (Ostrom 2005, 2007, 2008).

For the purposes of the current paper it is sufficient to note that the key elements of the framework are abstract, formal in the broad sense of the term, being better seen as just placeholders. For instance, the "actor" may be defined in various ways, according to the case, circumstances and the analytical or theoretical interests of the researcher. Different models of the agent may be used. One may start with a model of homo economicus (maximization-driven, fully informed and fully rational) in an action arena with minimal rules and incentives and with patterns of interaction driven by the maximizing logic. Starting with this austere model of man and action arena, new features may be added step by step. But one may decide to make a theoretical jump and use instead, for instance, behavioral models of agents and action in more complex environments. In brief, as Ostrom (2005, 7) explains, one has a wide range available, from neoclassical economics to "broader theories that assume individuals are fallible learners trying to do the best they can in the long term by using norms and heuristics in making their immediate decisions."

As we shall see later, the physical or material attributes of the world of production and consumption also have an essential role to play. They are as important for analytical and prediction purposes as the attributes of the community, the rules-in-use, the action situation, and the attributes of the individual. Indeed one can think of many sorts of variations in material conditions and many combinations between classes of attributes. In brief, while the IAD framework remains a framing constant, one could use a variety of theories and models and accommodate a wide range of perspectives. It is now understandable why Ostrom presents the framework as providing a "metatheoretical language" that can be used to analyze a diversity of problems to compare theories and results (Ostrom 2007, 24).

From the perspective of the current discussion, note that the IAD framework is well positioned to specify the structural variables relevant to an entire array of pre-theoretical questions about what we casually call "the" state of nature. Rather than naming a particular model, a state of nature is a specification of rules about a largely indeterminate set of combinations of attributes. The absence of a body politic whose representatives are set up as, pose as, or spontaneously arise to be ultimate third parties for others is compatible with very different physical attributes of the worlds, attributes of communities, of individuals and rules-in-use. The same argument holds about "the" transition from a state to a different state. There are many possible transitions. The IAD institutionalist device should be a neutral frame able to encompass different perspectives on the origins of the state, contractarian or evolutionary such as Hume's (Hume 1896, Book III.). Similarly, parameters like rules-in-use and attributes of the community should, only by taking different values, be able to frame abrupt changes from the state of nature, such as Hobbes' transition to the Leviathan as well as nonradical changes such as Locke's transition from an ordered state of nature to an ordered commonwealth (Hobbes 1651, Chapters 13, 15; Kavka 1986, 88; Locke 2015, Chapter 2. Section 15).

The relevance of the IAD framework is also evident when considering the classic theme of "human nature." The so-called state of nature is obviously a situation in which outcomes of the patterns of interaction are determined by social actors in action situations. The logic of the IAD approach flows naturally from here. Specifying actors means indeed (as the typical state of nature narrative does) specifying the resources that an individual brings to a situation, the valuations actors assign to states of the world, the way actors process information and the processes they use to select a particular course of action (Ostrom 2007, 28). However, as we have already seen, the framework has an additional strong message to deliver: the rules-in-use, the physical conditions, and the attributes of the community, are together determining the actors and their action situation in ways that make them crucial for any relevant analysis or thought experiment. The immediate insight that emerges even at a superficial reading is that examining the traditional state of nature thought experiments requires not just specifying several action arena attributes and examining the kind of rules that are set to default, but also revealing implicit assumptions in the attributes of the community and the material/physical conditions that are determining conditions for the entire exercise.

Last but not least, when the assessment of the parameters describing state of nature is being done, it is imperative to try to determine the likely configurations between the entire set of parameters, as opposed to a selective reading. These are far from straightforward but they may be decisive: Ostrom's achievement stands as evidence that it takes intense fieldwork to understand the relationships between the elements involved. Ostrom found that fieldwork was necessary because the impact of one rule was not independent of the configuration of other rules (Ostrom 2007). The lesson for thought experiments is clear: before assessing a rule's impact (for instance the rule of non-ultimacy of any authority), the whole configuration of that imagined state of affairs must be determined or made explicit. The reason why we need to circumscribe the famous scenarios as particular configurations in a space of possibilities is simple: we can prevent the overreach or "metaphorical employment" of any specific model in explaining or prescribing institutions only after we uncover all hidden assumptions about initial conditions and processes. The IAD framework is a guide to detecting these assumptions.

The capacity of the approach is thus rather evident. Using it, one may be able to systematically compare classical accounts such as those of Hobbes, Locke and Nozick or may be able to test in each case the carrying capacity of such classical models, while exploring the limits of different interpretations. The analytic potential of the IAD approach is bolstered by its flexibility. The strengths come from the fact that, in using the framework, one may focus on only one component or building block and go in-depth in specifying it. Done under *ceteris paribus* conditions, such exercises amount to a rather sophisticated form of analytical and heuristic theoretical scenario-building, as Ostrom would put it. Needless to say, the exercise of looking at different sub-elements of a building block and their impact on other components of the framework similarly specified as well as at the general dynamics of the system resulting from various configurations of variables, opens the door for insights that were not available to the classics.

STATES' OF NATURE GENOTYPIC ASPECT

The rise of evolutionary conceptions of law called into question the dichotomy between nature and convention (Hayek 1992), and with it, the conceptual baggage around the state of nature. Nevertheless, the core aspect of a state of nature as the "absence of a common power to keep all parties in awe" (Hobbes 1651, Chapter XIII) is still coherent and legitimate. This aspect pertains to the rules-in-use. The IAD framework is able to capture this notion in various state of nature scenarios, where the three variables—rules-in-use, attributes of the community, physical/material conditions—can take different values. Since the rule aspect has been the main research motivation behind authors' appeals to the concept of state of nature, we shall next see how Ostrom developed this aspect.

Ostrom uses the concepts of phenotype and genotype to separate the rules or instructions initially put into place, from an institutional system's observable characteristics, codetermined by the environment.

> A rule configuration is parallel in function to a genotype in that rules, like genotypes, are mechanisms that transmit information about how to produce something (a protein of a particular organ or an action situation in a particular environment). In other words, rules are a set of instructions of how to produce the expressed situation or the structure of relationships among individuals that is also affected by the biophysical world and the kind of community or culture in which an action situation is located. (Ostrom 2010, 325)

The genotypic structure of a governing system is the rule configuration or the set of instructions on how to produce or "express" a functional system in the biophysical world. A quaker may approach his interactions with a fixed inherited internal instruction of honest dealing. Someone else may be flexible, open and willing to try out several behaviors. The phenotypic structures characterize the "expressed" system, the way it functions in a particular environment. Ostrom explains that the genotypic institutional structures are changed through blind variation and to some extent by design. The genotypic structures' distribution in the world depends on the survival rate of the phenotypes they produce.

Even more interesting, Ostrom provides a seven rule matrix describing the genotypic source of structure for an action situation (Ostrom 2010, 322–23). The rules are classified according to their impact on the seven elements, variables or "working parts" of an action situation: *Participants* in *Positions* who must decide among diverse *Actions* in the light of the *Information* they possess about how actions are *Linked* to potential *Outcomes* and their *Payoffs* (Ostrom 2007, 38; Ostrom, Gardner, Walker 2003, 29–31). Each of the rules or categories of the genotypic structure can feature different specifications or "values" that take the form of deontic operators. When one of the categories is left unspecified, it is said to be in a "default" condition. When all of them are, the whole genotypic structure is being set to default. That condition may be seen as the genotypic recipe for a "complete" state of nature. When individuals have no deontic instructions all social behavior is being left to trial and error starting only from individuals' internal biological instructions.

The rules or categories of the genotypic matrix are the following: rules that create *Positions* (1); rules that specify *Entry and exit* in and from these positions (2); rules that attach deontic operators to particular types of *Choices* that can be physically made from those positions (3); *Aggregation* rules determining who decides for whom (4); rules affecting the flow of *Information* available (5); rules determining the *Payoffs* attached to certain actions, positions or outcomes (6); and rules establishing the *Scope* of outcomes that may, must or must not be affected (7).

Lists like this of separate elements and variables may look intimidating. But the list's manifest testimony is quite accessible: no two variables in this list are equivalent. Empirical work showed each of the elements makes a separate difference. This testimony already provides a filter and a guard against theories models, questions, which presuppose that the value of one variable entails a certain value of another variable across all settings. Thus, one easy use of such lists is to pre-articulate criticism of theories and models. The IAD because it suggests the main possible warps, conflations they can make and the main traps in which they may fall. Thus, before reaching the stage of building new theories using this apparatus, there is a separate, immediate payoff in simply understanding its concepts.

Ostrom stipulates the default condition for position rules to be (1) "No formal positions exist." The default entry condition is formulated as (2) "Anyone can enter." The default choice condition as (3) "Each player can take any physically possible action." The default aggregation condition as (4) "Players act independently. Physical relationships present in the situation determine the aggregation of individual moves into outcomes." The default information condition is (5) "Each player can communicate any information via any channel available to the player." The default payoff condition is (6) "Any player can retain any outcome that the player can physically obtain and defend." And finally the default scope condition is (7) "Each player can affect any state of the world that is physically possible (Ostrom and Basurto 2011, 324)."

Ostrom's stipulation of the default conditions needs qualification. Some of the stipulations have a clear meaning. For example "no formal positions exist" simply means there is no formal position to be filled. But other conditions have unclear or equivocal formulations. The modal "can" in "Anyone can enter any position" should not be interpreted as a deontic operator since all deontic forms of permissions, prohibitions or requirements describe rules-in-use (Ostrom and Basurto 2011, 324). This means they would describe generally *enforced* permissions, prohibitions, or prescriptions and that would not be a default. But by definition, in a default condition, whether anyone can enter anywhere is something yet unspecified to actors, something that actors seek to learn once the experiment or model is run. A default situation should be that in which, initially, from each actor's perspective, expected enforcements of alternative deontic operators are equiprobable. This can hardly be described as "anyone can enter."

Elinor Ostrom started to develop the concept of default condition for rules only at the end of 2000s. At an early stage of developing the IAD framework, she did not have a complete grasp of that concept. In *Governing the Commons*, Ostrom wrote that "the absence of a rule forbidding or requiring an action is logically equivalent to the presence of a rule that permits an action. The Hobbesian state of nature is logically equivalent to a situation in which rules exist permitting anyone to take any and all desired actions, regardless of the effects on others (Ostrom 1990, 140)." However, if the rules of interest are the rules-in-use, then the Hobbesian state of nature is not logically equivalent to such permissions. We need to bear in mind that we are not describing a functional situation in a given setting, but merely specifying the genotypic structure, that is, a set of instructions that are yet to produce a setting. The formulations "anyone can physically enter," and "each player can take any physically possible action" may wrongly suggest an information on some positive state of affairs regarding rules-in-use. When we formulate a state of nature's genotype, we formulate "unspecifications" of rules. We "uninstruct" each actor of any institutional guidance. Thus, the following formulations would be correct: (2) "no prescription regarding entry and exit at a very first stage of a dynamic setting are being observed," (3) "no prescription regarding what choices can be made from any position exist at a very first stage of a dynamic setting," and so on. In state of nature dynamic settings actors start experimenting on their own with these rules as well as with respect to others, including the aggregation rule. Players do not necessarily "act independently" even in the first stage of the dynamic setting. As long as there is equiprobability of rule enforcement, they simply act according to their non-deontic impulses, their internal biological instructions, which may include several dependencies. At subsequent stages of the dynamic setting, we may observe that some actors act even less independently toward various actors. In a state of nature dynamic setting, and successive changes in phenotype are occurring, the rules-in-use are respecified at each round as a result of polycentric trial-and-error learning occurred in previous rounds.

Setting all rules to default across the board means unspecifying all rules of interaction and, for the first stage of a dynamic setting, unspecifying interaction itself. We may then speak of an "absence-of-society state of nature." This is implicitly the case with Hobbes's state of nature initial condition, and explicitly the case in Hume's discussion of a hypothetical state of nature lacking any rules regarding property at all, which for Hume is the essential societal feature (Hume 1896, Book III). But not all seven rules are set to default in all state of nature thought experiments. Locke's state of nature is only an "absence-of-government state of nature." The most significant rule set to default in the first stage of the dynamic setting would be the aggregation rule (who decides for whom).

How this alone plays out in the long run and affect other rules is less obvious. In empirical settings this would simply require an observation of expressed (phenotypic) aspects. We would observe how with each successive period, the phenotype acquires positive specifications through feedback from jointly caused, or emergent outcomes. In thought experiments, we need to examine the arguments and the conclusions of various state of nature thought experiment to detect the presuppositions at work.

To identify which of the seven rules are set to default condition, that is, to identify state of nature genotypic structures in classical state of nature scenarios, we must look for what traditional philosophers called, in the normative sense "laws of nature." The Lockean law of nature is a set of prohibitions on infringing on others' lives, health, liberty or possessions (Locke 2015, Chapter 2, Section 6). We can interpret these as specified, non-default, scope rules (7). In the Lockean state of nature—the dynamic setting where patterns of behavior are observable, where, in other words, there is a phenotype, the scope rules are left to develop without an actor being in a formal position of monopoly on coercive third-party enforcement. The relevant modifications are to rules (1) and (4). In a dynamic setting these rules acquire values in successive stages. Any such dynamic setting which would manifest some degree of stability, would qualify as a functional Lockean state of nature (Locke 2015, Chapter 2, Section 13).

Similarly, the Hobbesian "right of nature" exercised in an initial stage of the dynamic setting, is itself a set of internal individual instructions according to which every individual, acts under an initial internal impulse equating might with right. This is the meaning of individuals having a "right to everything" (Hobbes 1651, 98). A Hobbesian state of nature is a dynamic setting in which everyone's war against everyone is taking place and so, at least temporarily reiterating, stable, self-enforcing. Hobbes claims that starting from a Hobbesian genotype, only a comprehensive monopolistic position rule and aggregation rule can end the dreadful predicament of disorder where no rules can crystalize.

We established that it is the default character of some rules that lets us call a variety of initial conditions "states of nature." Our main point was that state of nature arenas can differ from one another on many accounts. This means that if we want a precise evaluation of state of nature thought experiments and of state of nature arguments, the building blocks and traits of these arenas will also require careful specification. For any given setting, when explaining institutional change starting from a genotypic default position, one also needs to specify the values of other elements being given in that setting. These are the non-rule parameters involved in the dynamics, the other building blocks" or "working parts," of an action situation (Ostrom and Basurto 2011, 323). We cannot ignore the quality of non-rule elements of the IAD framework when assessing the impact of a rule change because the impact of a rule's value (permission, prohibition, requirement) is not linear, but dependent on the configuration of all other variables.

STATES' OF NATURE MATERIAL CONDITIONS

Using the IAD framework, we have reviewed the idea that genotypes are expressed in particular arenas which are a joint outcome of rules, attributes of community, and material attributes of the world. Clearly the material attributes of world are a non-rule element. In this section we discuss the importance of the non-rule aspect in state of nature thought experiments.

Ostrom (2007, 41; 43) notes that social reality is composed of multiple arenas linked sequentially or simultaneously. In empirical settings we distinguish between market and nonmarket arenas, between an operational level arena and collective level arenas. But even when the genotype is set to default as in a state of nature thought experiment, what is not warped down to default is physical space. Classical state of nature theorists provided scenarios with homogenous and large-scale settings comprising large sets of actors presumably spread across large geographical distances (e.g., Hobbes 1651, 129). Hobbes misses the relevance of a simple physical attribute of the environment: geographical distance. Since geographical distances between various actors are different across these settings, it is only reasonable to break the single initial arena in many arenas. A plausible thought experiment on a large number of individuals must take into account that each arena is sufficiently isolated from the others to gain some separate dynamics and analytical identity. One may not simply assume that the costs of conflict, negotiation and communication faced by actors are homogenous over the domain of large settings or the thought experiment loses all plausibility.

The differences in proximity are of course just one of the possibly heterogeneous factors at work. Ostrom's eight design principles of robust institutions (and at the same time conditions for successful collective action) provide a broad and telling picture (Ostrom 1990, 90; 178–79). According to the differences in the attributes of the physical world that can surround each participant in a large size arena, subsets of actors in each scenario may present different distributions on these eight dimensions relative to other subsets. Some subsets of actors will be objectively more likely than others to successfully gestate collective action, since the difference in distributions represents the difference in obtaining the ingredients required for successfully enforced aggregation rules.

But if genotypes are only expressed in many arenas, then the initial state of nature predicament too should be partitioned and the resulting predicaments recalibrated. The overwhelming variety of conditions documented by Ostrom in empirical settings creeps in the realm of thought experiments. And that has implications on what the thought experiment shows. The simple fact that we are dealing with multiple arenas across a large geographical surface, each counting a smaller numbers of actors than we initially thought, makes coordination and interdependent action in each of these arenas more plausible than a symmetrical war of all against all. Cooperators in smaller settings must benefit from their relative isolation from geographically distant defectors. One can thus see how merely noting that sometimes arenas are sufficiently autonomous from one another to gain independent identity, raises important questions about which of these arenas is likely to engender a social contract first and with what consequences for the others, and thus opens the way to a nuanced criticism of many arguments that operate in the shadow of the state of nature classical approaches.

To further illustrate the importance of the non-rule aspect we shall revisit Robert Nozick's state of nature thought experiment in the first part of *Anarchy, State and Utopia* purporting to show that a Lockean state of nature would lead us back into a state (Nozick 1999, 10–17; Gaus 2011). We shall see that Nozick overgeneralizes the result of his thought experiment and makes an insufficiently founded claim about the „inevitability of the state" precisely because he does not critically examine the physical/material attributes of his imagined world.

Nozick starts from the Lockean state of nature, which he defines as a state governed by a Lockean law of nature (Locke 2015, Chapter 2, Section 4; Nozick 1999, 10). This is a state where individuals' negative rights to life, liberty, property, health are generally respected and enforced informally by all individuals (Locke 2015, Chapter 2, Section 8). Locke's state of nature is particular version of a state of the world without a common power to keep all parties in awe. In Ostrom's terms, this definition of Lockean state of nature is telling us something very clear about the rule aspect of a world state, but nothing clear about the material attributes of that world.

Suppose we proceed to imagine a Lockean-inspired state of nature starting from the status quo as working material for our imagination. Taking the IAD framework as a guide we must set to default a number of features in the "control panel." What is the minimum number of aspects we need to set to default, to unspecify, or about which we should uninstruct actors? To eliminate the ultimacy of authority we go to the genotype and unspecify the formal positions rules and decision aggregation rule. Other aspects of the genotype might also require change. But how are we supposed to deal with the non-rule aspect of the state of nature for example, with the physical attributes/material conditions?

The difference between the genotypic aspect and the material aspects that the material aspect cannot possibly be reduced to default. A state with a rule reduced to default is a state where actors do not have any instruction in that respect. A setting where fishing rules are set to default is not under open access, it is a setting where, by trial and error, initially uninstructed participants learn what the regime is, specify and build a regime, or reach an equilibrium through gameplay. Actors have equiprobable expectations and no initial grasp on a regime because no regime is there to have a grasp of. But unspecifying the material attributes of a world leaves that world in metaphysical indeterminacy which means it would not yet possibly unattainable. To uninstruct actors in regard to certain conditions is part of the concept of state of nature, but to "unspecify" the material characteristics of a world of which actors can have any grasp cannot be part of the concept, since such non-instruction is impossible. The material aspect needs to be positively specified exogenously by the thought experimenter.

While an infinite array of specifications is possible, if the practical research interest behind a thought experiment is the institutional improvement of the status quo then our working material should be the status quo. We have no reason to imagine away the already accumulated, human capital, social capital, and physical capital which are present in the status quo. These material factors, together with their consequences for the attributes of the individuals, are a part of the world. If we imagine away or ignore this partly reusable capital, then our thought experiment would lose its relevance for today's world. To imagine a Lockean-inspired state of nature we only need to imagine that incumbents of an organization claiming ultimate authority repudiate their positions within such an organization, but not that they give up all their social, human, and physical capital accumulated in the historical process.

Yet Nozick, even though his stakes are to show the inevitability in a world like ours today, uncritically adopts a model of the state of nature where attributes of the individual, of the community, and of the material are those of a primitive and atomized society more resembling to Locke's century than to his. Nozick's uncritical move is a rolling back of material conditions to a primitive state but this positive specification is very different from setting anything to default condition. That the non-rule aspects of his scenario are those of a civilizational primitive world is implicit in his argument throughout. Like Locke and Hobbes, he envisions atomic solitary individuals who, first "naturally" become enforcers of their own rights (Nozick 1999, 11). But if we start our thought experiment from here and now, personal enforcement is not likely even in the initial stage of the experiment, because even after dismantling all formal agencies, the fruits of police, courts, insurance companies, already make up for a heterogeneous social and human capital and an unequal distribution of comparative advantages in protection or violence.

Let us pursue Nozick's argument to demonstrate the consequences of confusing setting an attribute to default with positively specifying it in a way resembling a primitive atomized state. We shall see why Nozick's thought experiment material attributes make it irrelevant for a contemporary institutional debate on the inevitability of government.

Nozick's scenario treats arbitration and protection agencies as extensionally identical: "for obvious reasons, he says, there will be strong tendencies for the functions of [detection, apprehension, judicial determination of guilt. . .] to converge in the same agent or agency" (Nozick 1999, 14). But this again ignores the already existing fruits of division of labor in terms of human and social capital. These fruits are here to use, regardless of how much of their existence is due to government.

Then he asks: "What happens if [two agencies] reach different decisions as to the merits of the case and one agency attempts to protect its client while the other is attempting to punish him or make him pay compensation?" (Nozick 1999, 16). The question is charged with the false assumption that it falls on protection agencies to sit in judgment. When answering it anyway, he builds a constructive dilemma*:* legal disputes can be solved either through conflict or through arbitration. In both cases, Nozick says, the unintended result of individual acts will be a de facto legal territorial monopoly. In case of conflict, goes the argument, violence separates territorial influence. Consequently, the clients whose agency has been weakened in their geographical area will find it to their advantage either to change the supplier or move to the new area of operation of their original supplier. In case of arbitration, if a dispute between two codes governing a geographical territory appeal to a third protection-arbitration agency, the new resolution, even though administered by two agencies, starts to uniformly apply over that territory (Nozick 1999, 17).

It is not our intention here to prove this argument wrong, but irrelevant. None of the two options, conflict or arbitration, work toward de facto territorial legal monopoly in a scenario where material conditions and the attributes of the community are those of the twentieth or the twenty-first century. Both horns assume material conditions where geographical proximity defines interactions. The first horn of the dilemma unnecessarily assumes conflict would be constrained to be territorial. But in a world with our physical attributes, the network of interaction is not dictated by geographical proximity (there is air traffic, Internet traffic, and different social distances). The already existing physical and social infrastructure enables individuals to avoid territorial collateral damage and risking retaliation from bystanders to a larger extent than in the seventeenth century. Similarly, the second horn of the dilemma unnecessarily constrains legal codes to apply geographically. Nozick knows that in a Lockean-inspired state of nature, arbitration codes apply according to legal insurance contracts. But Nozick presumes that customers' networks are dictated by geographical proximity because in his thought experiment arbitration agencies' operative scope overlaps with that of protection agencies, which are themselves imagined to operate territorially. This need not be the case in a Lockean state of nature where the attributes of the individual, of the community, and the material or technological conditions were those of today. In a Lockean state of nature like ours today, the scope of initial arbitration codes would not overlap with territorial enforcement agencies because previous period's division of labor between enforcement and arbitration, would have already determined different initial distributions of human and social capital.

The undue importance Nozick gives to the geographical element rests with his tacit assumption about initial material conditions: in a primitive civilization, interaction is more likely to be confined to geographical proximity. But, as we showed above, a thought experimenter has no reason to imagine away today's material conditions, attributes of community and the consequent attributes of the individual. Such a choice is unmotivated and also responsible for making the whole experiment irrelevant. Our point is then that even if Nozick's argument were correct, it would merely prove that a Lockean state of nature with material characteristics of a primitive civilization would lead back to a state. A consistent application of the IAD framework showed that even if Nozick's thought experiment perfectly ran through, it would not prove that if we adopted a Lockean state of nature rules, we would inevitably be driven back to a state.

General Lessons of the IAD Framework for State of Nature Thought Experimenters

The fact that the IAD logic can be usefully applied to the entire family of the state of nature arguments and models needs not further explanations. The IAD framework gives us an insight about the complexity of the theme, of the intricacies of the conceptual space in play, of the diversity of the possible interpretations as well as of the sources of that diversity and complexity. While granting added expert insight in the ways in which a setting might develop, it mostly gives reasons against the idea of grand reform. If anything, the IAD framework warns against grand prediction as well as against what Hayek called constructionism. In multicentered, multivariable social arenas where nonlinear relationships abound, there is no locus of policy design any more than there is for grand prediction.

As we mentioned earlier, in Ostrom's vocabulary, theories make general assumptions necessary for explanation and prediction of phenomena while models make further assumptions about the values of the parameters involved (Ostrom 2007, 26). Simply put, theories have higher generality claims. The IAD framework warns us against the metaphorical use of state of nature thought experiment. For instance, it helps us see more clearly why traditional state of nature thought experiments are models of change, even though they are sometimes disguised as theories. State of nature thought experiments are in no way standard theories. In this respect, the Ostromian framework to be used in the study of state of nature thought experiments, allows us to discover a set of hidden assumptions that are induced unawaringly in the thought experiments but may be nevertheless responsible for the result.

A key corollary of this entire discussion is that, assuming the description of the processes involved in unfolding the initial conditions is accurate, the extended validity of a state of nature thought experiment depends on whether the conclusion of the experiment is predicated over the same set of parameter values as those describing the initial conditions—including not just rules-in-use but also attributes of the community and of the physical world. If the conclusion is predicated on a wider set of parameters, then the argument is invalid and the model is masquerading as theory. We studied a problem of overgeneralization in a state of nature scenario where the material conditions were presumed to have certain specifications and values, but the conclusion of that thought experiment was predicated over a wider interval of material conditions. If an argument predicates that *the* Lockean state of nature is unstable (e.g., Nozick 1999, 10–17), then, what is being claimed is a universal proposition about all worlds qualifying, from a genotypic point of view, as Lockean states of nature. For such an argument to be legitimate, not just the default genotypic aspect, but also the initial physical conditions had better hold true for all worlds that qualify as Lockean states of nature. If the conclusion is a universal proposition, the state of nature and the empirical laws described in that thought experiment should be as universal.

We discussed earlier the genotypic aspect of the state of nature as a cluster of rules set to a default condition. Hence the key question about the possible expressions of that genotype: can any state of nature thought experiment, say, a state of nature thought experiment testing for the self-enforcing potential of a state of nature, be correctly performed such that its conclusion be universal? Could the conclusion of that state of nature thought experiment be predicated for all possible specifications of material conditions and for all attributes of the community? Ostrom's work is very clear evidence that such overgeneralizations would not be justified. Models are used inappropriately when applied to the study of problematic situations that do not closely fit the assumptions of the model (Ostrom 2005, 29).

We must emphasize that state of nature thought experiments go beyond mere conceptual analysis. They should be seen as experiments using imagined empirical elements. Any state of nature usable in thought experiments needs some empirical determinations, and since empirical elements are contingent, no universal theory denying the self-enforcing potential of the "Lockean state of nature" is justified. That is to say, conclusions of state of nature thought experiments cannot be universal statements, holding true about all possible worlds possibly supporting Lockean relationships. The argument is simple. On the one hand, claiming to control for all secondary variables is impossible, as there are too many things that could significantly change the landscape. On the other hand, dropping that claim would weaken the justification of the theory (Socaciu 2001, 245). The project of formulating a universal theory of the self-enforcing character of state of nature cannot escape this dilemma.

CONCLUSION

To conclude, Elinor Ostrom's work draws our attention to the measure in which traditional analyses of states of nature were "too sparse" in the sense that key internal and external variables needed to explain self-organization were missing from consideration (Ostrom 1990, 189). The development of a framework to specify the elements and relationships between elements that one needs to consider for institutional analysis covers naturally the idea of theoretical scenarios in which participants in an arena craft rules starting from a default condition (Ostrom 2005, 2007; Ostrom and Basurto 2011). So far scholars have applied the framework to the analysis of real-life situations. But as we tried to show above, state of nature thought experiments are easily amenable to the same treatment. Our paper has identified in an exploratory manner the potential of this approach. Based on that, one could thus outline a very interesting agenda: a systematic comparative IAD framework analysis of specific themes underlying several well-known classical state of nature arguments from Hobbes to Nozick and beyond. What would this entire discussion look like, once systematically framed using Ostrom's institutional analysis instruments? This seems to be indeed the next important test of the relevance of the IAD framework for political theory and political philosophy and of its potential to extend the field of institutional economics.

REFERENCES

Agrawal, Arun. 1999. *Greener Pastures: Politics, Markets, and Community among a Migrant Pastoral People*. Durham, NC: Duke University Press.

Aligica, Paul D. 2006. "Institutional and Stakeholder Mapping: Frameworks for Policy Analysis and Institutional Change." *Public Organization Review* 6 June: 79–90.

Aligica, Paul D. and P. Boettke. 2011. "The Two Social Philosophies of Ostroms' Institutionalism." *Policy Studies Journal* 39(1): 29–49.

Blomquist, William and P. deLeon. 2011. "The Design and Promise of the Institutional Analysis and Development Framework." *Policy Studies Journal* 39: 1, 1–7.

Gaus, Gerald. 2011. "Explanation, Justification, and Emergent Properties: An Essay on Nozickian Metatheory," in *The Cambridge Companion to Nozick's Anarchy, State, and Utopia*, edited by R. M. Bader and J. Meadowcroft. Cambridge: Cambridge University Press, 116–42.

Gibson, Clark C., K. Andersson, E. Ostrom and S. Shivakumar. 2005. *The Samaritan's Dilemma: The Political Economy of Development Aid.* Oxford: Oxford University Press.

Hess, Charlotte and E. Ostrom. 2006. "A Framework for Analysing the Microbiological Commons." *International Social Science Journal* 188: 335–49.

Hayek, Friedrich. 1992. *The Fatal Conceit.* London: Routledge.

Hobbes, Thomas. 1651. *Leviathan; or, The Matter, Forme, & Power of A Common-Wealth, Ecclesiasticall And Civil.* London: Printed for Andrew Crooke, at the Green Dragon in St. Paul's Church-yard. Printed by Viviane Ridler. Oxford: Oxford University Press.

Hume, David. 1896. *A Treatise of Human Nature.* Reprinted from the Original Edition in Three Volumes and Edited, with an Analytical Index, by L. A. Selby-Bigge, M.A. Oxford: Clarendon Press, 1896. http://oll.libertyfund.org/titles/342.

Kavka, Gregory. 1986. *Hobbesian Moral and Political Theory.* New Jersey: Princeton University Press.

Locke, John. 2015. *The Second Treatise of Civil Government.* The Constitution Society. http://www.constitution.org/jl/2ndtreat.htm.

McGinnis, Michael and E. Ostrom. 1996. "Design Principles for Local and Global Commons," in *The International Political Economy and International Institutions. Vol. II.*, edited by O. R. Young, 465–93. Cheltenham, UK: Edward Elgar.

McGinnis, Michael, ed. 1999. *Polycentric Governance and Development: Readings from the Workshop in Political Theory and Policy Analysis.* Ann Arbor: University of Michigan Press.

McGinnis, Michael, ed. 2000. *Polycentric Games and Institutions: Readings from the Workshop in Political Theory and Policy Analysis.* Ann Arbor: University of Michigan Press.

Mitchell, William C. 1988. "Virginia, Rochester, and Bloomington: Twenty-five Years of Public Choice and Political Science." *Public Choice* 56(2): 101–19.

Nozick, Robert. 1999. *Anarchy, State and Utopia.* Oxford and Cambridge: Blackwell Publishers.

Ostrom, Elinor and Xavier Basurto. 2011. "Crafting Analytical Tools to Study Institutional Change." *Journal of Institutional Economics* 7(3): 317–43.

Ostrom, Elinor, Roy Gardner and James Walker. 2003. *Rules, Games and Common Pool Resources.* Ann Arbor: The University of Michigan Press.

Ostrom, Elinor. 1990. *Governing the Commons: The Evolution of Institutions for Collective Action.* New York: Cambridge University Press.

Ostrom, Elinor. 2005. *Understanding Institutional Diversity.* Princeton: Princeton University Press.

Ostrom, Elinor. 2007. "Institutional Rational Choice: An Assessment of the Institutional Analysis and Development Framework," in *Theories of the Policy Process, edited by* P. Sabatier. Boulder, CO: Westview Press, 21–64.
Ostrom, Elinor. 2008. "Developing a Method for Analyzing Institutional Change," in *Assessing The Evolution and Impact of Alternative Institutional Structures*, edited by Sandra Batie and Nicholas Mercuro. London: Routledge Press, 89–98.
Ostrom, Vincent and Elinor Ostrom. 1971. "Public Choice: A Different Approach to the Study of Public Administration." *Public Administration Review* 31 (March/April): 203–16.
Ostrom, Vincent and Elinor Ostrom. 1977. "Public Goods and Public Choices," in *Alternatives for Delivering Public Services. Toward Improved Performance*, edited by E. S. Savas, Boulder, CO: Westview Press, 7–42.
Shivakumar, Sujai. 2005. *The Constitution of Development: Crafting Capabilities for Self-Governance*. New York: Palgrave Macmillan.
Socaciu, Emanuel. 2001. "Starea Naturala ca Experiment Mental," in *Filosofia Politica a lui Thomas Hobbes*, edited by Emanuel Socaciu. Iasi: Polirom, 56–72.
Sproule-Jones, Mark. 2002. *The Restoration of the Great Lakes*. Vancouver: University of British Columbia Press.

Part II

INSTITUTIONAL CREATIVITY AND GOVERNANCE

Chapter 4

Representation

A Slender Thread?

Ronald J. Oakerson

Mainstream democratic theory views representation—and the electoral process on which it depends—as the institutional core of modern democracy.[1] Vincent Ostrom demurred:

> The term democracy implies that people govern. "The government," however, is plainly not the people. People vote and elect representatives who participate in the government. Voting is a *very slender thread*, hardly strong enough to let us presume that people, by electing representatives, govern (Ostrom 1991, 5 emphasis added).

Others have made similar or complementary observations. If democracy is understood as rule by the people, Henry S. Richardson writes that claims of democratic governance are without credibility anywhere in the world (Richardson 2002, 3). Bernard Manin (1997) sought to explain why this might be so—building a persuasive case that no political system based on representation is capable of democratic governance. Conclusion: because it cannot be scaled up, democracy is impossible to practice in the modern world of nation-states. If the alternative is governance by elites, the conclusion is not one that Ostrom was prepared to accept.

In his careful study of the intellectual origins of representative government Manin drew on conceptions advanced by James Madison in *Federalist* 10, where he distinguished a "democracy," in which the people assemble to rule directly, from a "republic," in which the people elect representatives to rule on their behalf. Republics do not enable the people to rule but, rather, subject rule by representative elites to the "verdict of the people" through popular election (Manin 1997, 161–92). Retrospective accountability, administered *ex post*, does not require (or allow) the represented to instruct their representatives *ex ante*.[2] Although elections have a democratic element in the equal right of citizens to vote, representation has an elitist element in the ability of representatives to act independently. What the represented retain is not the power to govern but rather the right to replace those who govern at the next election.

Ostrom, in contrast, viewed the "slender thread" of representation as insufficient, not only from a democratic standpoint, but also from a republican standpoint. Dissenting from Madison's identification of "republican form" with representation, Ostrom insisted that a republic requires more than a system of representation as ordinarily understood (1991, 199); republics need strong democratic elements, including more than one-person, one-vote. Madison too, in *Federalist* 51, suggested the need for "auxiliary precautions" in addition to the "primary" instrument of popular control over government. Madison's auxiliaries included constitutionalism, the separation of powers, and federalism—institutions widely regarded as anti-majoritarian and, therefore, nondemocratic (see, e.g., Zakaria 2007, 22; Levinson 2008). In Ostrom's hands, these same institutions would become instruments of democracy.

Ostrom and Manin shared the same premise—that representation by elected officials is unable to support democracy—but reached opposite conclusions.[3] Unlike Manin, Ostrom did not abandon the concept of democracy as unrealistic. Instead, he pressed the underlying question: can the people govern? Is democracy possible? Ostrom's entire body of work can be construed as an effort to demonstrate that democracy is possible in the modern age—*possible* even though "improbable" (Ostrom 1987, 34, 165).

Ostrom viewed the design of the American political system as both republican and democratic. His approach sheds new light on the arguments posed by would-be reformers of the system in twenty-first-century America: Fareed Zakaria (2007) sees an increasingly "illiberal" democracy suffering from democratic excess; Steven Teles (2013) finds a "kludgeocracy," an ill-designed collection of assorted parts that has become too cumbersome to operate with even tolerable efficiency; Francis Fukuyama (2014) assails the design of the American political system as a "vetocracy" that yields only stalemate; and Martin Gilens and Benjamin Page (2014) find a system of national representation distorted by elite and special interest influences, more oligarchic than democratic. Set against this assemblage of critics, Ostrom offers a radically different perspective on American political experience—one that enables us to reframe democratic theory and reimagine democracy for the modern world.

In what follows I first reconstruct Ostrom's argument for democracy as possible under modern conditions.[4] If democracy is possible, it must also be sustainable, meaning that serious institutional weaknesses in a democratic system must be open to democratic solution. Accordingly, I apply Ostrom's argument to two current problems with the performance of the American political system: legislative deadlock in the Congress and the use of deadly force by police in urban areas.

THE LIMITS OF REPRESENTATION

Ostrom concurred with Madison's sense that electoral representation has limits—that it is necessary but not sufficient for republican governance. The limits derive from several sources:

- *Voters must consider a number of issues simultaneously and are limited to binary choices regarding those issues* (Bish and Ostrom 1973, 23). Unless a voter happens to agree with a candidate's position on all issues, the vote cast both represents and misrepresents the voter. Moreover, a voter cannot negotiate conditional support for a candidate; voter choice is binary, confined to yes or no, severely limiting the *ex ante* accountability of candidates to voters.
- *Voters have highly imperfect information due to the costs of disseminating and collecting information* (Downs 1957). Unlike consumers in the marketplace, voters have only weak incentives to invest in political information given the negligible influence of a single vote on the election outcome. This implies that the quality of representation is a collective good limited by free-rider incentives among voters. In the aggregate, the purchase of major appliances in the marketplace may be better informed than the choice of representatives in Congress.
- *The selection of nominees to be considered by voters in the election of representatives is potentially subject to manipulation by party leaders.* Ostrom considered the period of "boss rule" in late nineteenth-century America a serious challenge to democracy (Ostrom 1987, 182–90). The accountability of elected representatives to the electorate was distorted by accountability to the party machine, which selected the candidates to be placed on the general election ballot. The introduction of direct primaries for choosing nominees, one of a series of progressive reforms intended to combat political corruption, significantly reduced the power of the machine—though support or opposition from party organizations often continues to matter a good deal.
- *Representative assemblies exhibit oligarchical tendencies, which limit and distort the process of representation.* Legislative oligarchy derives from the need to rely on leaders to govern the deliberative process. Drawing on Madison's analysis in *Federalist* 58, Ostrom expected oligarchical tendencies to increase with the size of the assembly (1987, 92–97). Representation

depends on the liberty of legislators to give voice to their constituent's interests. Legislative oligarchy is destructive of the liberty of legislators and therefore destructive of representation, as illustrated by the dominance of the U.S. House of Representatives by the Speaker of the House at various points in its history. New York is notorious for the dominance of its budgetary process by "three men in a room"—the governor, speaker of the assembly, and majority leader of the senate (Creelan and Moulton 2004, 1, 47).[5]

Subject only to retrospective accountability, representatives must anticipate how voters will respond to their legislative decisions rather than carry out voter intentions (Manin 1997, 178–79). Nonetheless, accountability rendered *ex post* can tie representatives closely to public opinion if competitive nomination and election contests draw public attention to a legislator's voting record. Today, what is called "opposition research" nearly guarantees that an incumbent's record will be selectively exposed to voters.[6] Retrospective accountability applies mainly, however, to actions taken—bills introduced and votes recorded—but less so to inaction, including the failure to address issues of concern to constituents. Inaction reflects power over agenda setting, the selection of issues to receive attention on a limited legislative calendar. G. K. Chesterton saw the deficiency in what is called "representative democracy," which he stated with characteristic terseness:

> We have not got real Democracy when the *decision* depends upon the people. We shall have real democracy when the *problem* depends upon the people. The ordinary man will decide not only how he will vote, but what he is going to vote about. (Chesterton 1912, emphasis added)[7]

GOVERNANCE, REPRESENTATION, AND ACCOUNTABILITY

The weakness of representation by elected officials does not, of course, establish the feasibility of rule by the people. A key to Ostrom's argument is his insistence that democracy must embrace the whole process of governance,[8] not only law making. He emphasized that rules of law are "not self-formulating, self-applying, and self-enforcing" (Ostrom 2011, 463). We can add that neither are rules self-invoking; rather, someone must claim injury from the violation of a rule and seek its application and enforcement.

The process of governance has four distinct dimensions: *prescribing, invoking, applying,* and *enforcing* law.[9] Once a rule is *prescribed* as law, it can be *invoked*—this is the process of laying claim to legal rights and authority. Once invoked, the general language of law must be *applied* to the particulars of a specific case—the essence of the judicial process. Having been applied, the resulting judgment must be *enforced*, if necessary, by means of coercive sanctions—an executive function. Considerations of representative government are usually focused on the process of *prescribing* law—the work of legislatures. The governance process is incomplete, however, until legislation is also invoked, applied, and enforced. In addition to who makes law, we need to ask: who invokes law, who applies it, and who enforces it?

Governance cannot occur in any of these four dimensions without some mode of representation. Though frequently contested, representation is a central concept in many fields of inquiry, including art,[10] linguistics,[11] and Christian theology.[12] In politics, representation refers to the process by which some persons make decisions on behalf of others. The right to act for others is authority. In a guardianship, for example, one individual is authorized to act for another in his or her interest. What distinguishes *political* authority is the right of officials to act on behalf of a collectivity in relation to the individuals who compose it. Those who represent the group have coercive power over individuals within the group.

Political authority introduces a strong element of inequality between officials and the citizens they represent, as Ostrom emphasized (1987, 139–41). It is also possible, however, for *citizens* to exercise authority that is equally distributed among them—in effect, to *represent one another*. The official-to-citizen relationship might be characterized as *vertical* representation and the citizen-to-citizen relationship, as *horizontal* representation. Vertical representation leads to inequality, whereas horizontal representation is based on equality. The use of selection by lot and rotation in office in premodern democracies was intended to provide equal and direct citizen participation in governance, avoiding the creation of vertical elites (Manin 1997, 132–60). As instruments of horizontal representation, lot and rotation provide a key to understanding how democratic features can be integrated into a republican system of government.

Alexis de Tocqueville argued in *Democracy in America* that officials—vertical representatives—can fail to perform as expected in three ways: (1) doing "what the law forbids"; (2) neglecting "what the law requires"; and (3) executing the law "without energy or zeal" (1945, I, 79). His distinctions provide the basis for a framework that distinguishes among modes of accountability. Doing "what the law forbids" is to exceed the limits of one's authority, and neglecting "what the law requires" is to fail the public trust: both can be addressed legally, as Tocqueville observed, through the courts. Executing the law without energy or zeal is not to violate the law, however, but to misuse lawful discretion. As Madison remarked in *Federalist* 41, all authority involves a discretion that can be misapplied and abused (Ostrom 1987, 84); Tocqueville, however, makes us aware of the other side of the coin—without discretion there is no energy or zeal, only rule following.[13] Accountability for the use of discretion is either hierarchical—to administrative superiors—or political—to an electorate—but not judicial. Tocqueville noted that Americans preferred political accountability to administrative, producing a large of number of elected officials in a variety of jurisdictions.

Each stage in the governance process—prescribing, invoking, applying and enforcing law—is dependent on the "energy or zeal" of which Tocqueville wrote. Legislation involves much more than voting up or down on proposed legislation; laws need to be crafted in a process that requires considerable energy and zeal. Likewise, invoking and enforcing law require initiative, and applying law requires faithfulness to the law as prescribed—all dependent on discretion. Moreover, evaluating the energy and zeal of official performance is highly information-dependent, requiring knowledge of inaction as well as action.

THE REPUBLICAN TRADITION IN AMERICA

Ostrom drew much of his argument from Madison's work in *The Federalist*, reconstructing the argument that Madison advanced in concert with Alexander Hamilton for ratification of the US Constitution (Ostrom 1971; 1987). Madison was immersed in the republican thought of his generation, an inheritance from the Glorious Revolution of a century earlier in England. Within the republican tradition Madison was an innovator who sought to accommodate its precepts to the requirements of governing a republic of potentially continental proportions. He nonetheless remained a republican who sought to design a new—untried—republican experiment. Although *The Federalist* was written in response to arguments being made in the press by Madison's republican colleagues, Ostrom did not address this body of writing, known as Antifederalist. Nevertheless, the full body of republican thought, embracing both Madison and his critics, has relevance to Ostrom's basic question—is democracy possible?

The purpose of representation in republican thought was to obtain the "consent of the governed," as Thomas Jefferson put it in the Declaration of Independence. Britain, so the Declaration argued, had failed to seek the consent of colonial legislatures on a number of key issues—taxes, trade, immigration, and a standing army. Republican consent was understood as given through elected representatives; though not given individually, the required consent was no mere formality. Substantively, consent required that representatives be held strongly to account by the represented, both *ex ante* and *ex post*. Accepting no "slender thread," traditional republicans demanded *strong representation*, including these core features:

1. Short terms of office. The prevailing standard was annual election—reflected in the popular republican slogan, "Where annual election ends, tyranny begins" (Wood 1969, 166–67; Rakove 1996, 304). Among the first state legislatures, South Carolina's two-year term was the single exception.
2. Small, community-based constituencies. The average ratio of constituent to representative among the 13 state legislatures formed prior to the US Constitution was 1,700 to 1; in 1830, the ratio in Massachusetts was 1,000 to 1 (Storing 1985, 7; Shain 1994, 93).
3. A right of instruction. Explicitly protected in three state constitutions, instruction was feasible because small local constituencies were able to assemble and deliberate and thereby instruct their representatives on particular issues (Adams 1980, 248). Instruction provided *ex ante* accountability and therefore gave the represented a role in agenda setting, otherwise lacking in vertical representation.

In republican thinking representatives could provide consent on behalf of the represented only because of natural sympathy (Rakove 1996, 204–5), referring to the ability of an individual to identify with the problems and interests of others—identified by Adam Smith in 1759 as the basis for moral sentiment (Smith 1966). Although it was unnecessary, therefore, for people to give consent individually,[14] small communal constituencies were a necessary element of representation, needed to nurture sympathetic understanding and sustain a strong social bond between a representative and the represented.

Republican insistence on strong representation was problematic when circumstances seemed to require that Americans somehow scale up the republican project. Because the mode of representation prized by republicans was possible only in a small republic, scale became the major source of disagreement between Federalists and Anti-federalists in the debate over ratification of the Constitution. In *Federalist* 10, Madison defended the increased size of constituencies in the House of Representatives beyond ordinary republican standards—to 30,000 inhabitants or more. Although this modification made larger republics feasible, it abandoned the accepted theory of representation. Madison sought to make a virtue of the necessity: larger constituencies would result in the selection of representatives of wider reputation, who would be better able to discern the common good of the greater community. Representation would rely more on discernment, less on sympathy, in order to "refine and enlarge" the raw material of public opinion.

Madison built his theory of institutional design around the need to counteract an inherent weakness of republican form—the problem of faction, a group of citizens who combine to seek their own interest at the expense of the greater community. Minority factions, though problematic, were less troublesome than majority factions, which could claim legitimacy based on the majority principle on which republics operated. Democracies had no means to restrain majority faction; only republics could do so—by accommodating a larger scale of organization than a democracy. The larger the republic, the greater is the variety of interests within it and the less likely that a single factional interest would constitute a majority.

Traditional republicans responded to *Federalist* 10 with trenchant criticism: democratic and republican principles were not inherently in conflict, and democracy did not require direct rule by the whole people in assembly, if representation were "substantial."[15] Madison spoke of "republican form" as no more than a requirement of representation by means of election. Such formalism, in the eyes of his critics, was no substitute for substantive representation, which depended on small constituencies.[16] At stake was an outcome of great importance to republicans: the confidence of people in their government.[17] Without confidence, republicans saw the core republican value of liberty at risk: liberty could be sustained only if people tended to comply with governmental authority willingly, requiring only marginal resort to governmental coercion. Lacking the confidence that government represented their interests, people would evade and resist authority, and government would necessarily use coercive force to obtain compliance. No doubt, traditional republicans would view with alarm the collapse of public confidence in the federal government that has occurred since the mid-twentieth century.[18]

Also at issue in the ratification debate was the meaning of representativeness—the qualities that make an assembly representative. John Adams argued for a representative assembly that closely resembled the represented on key characteristics, such as social and economic class (Wood 1969, 165; see also Rakove 1996, 203). Today, the same argument is inclined to focus on characteristics such as race and gender. For Adams, the perfectly representative assembly was a society in miniature. Hamilton challenged this vision in *Federalist* 35, arguing that it contradicted the free choice of representatives by constituents; moreover, he thought, it was not sympathy but inquiry that was the mark of a good representative.[19] Frequent election would create strong incentives for representatives to inquire into the interests of constituents, and constituents would tend to choose representatives who would be able students of the common good, not simply people who share their social position. Unless Adams' view is pushed to the extreme, however, it is not inconsistent with the elective principle: a legislative body elected from local districts can in fact reflect much of the diversity of society, in particular geographically based diversity in an extended republic.[20]

Madison's theory of representation left no place for the republican right of instruction, nor did the design of the US Constitution. Enshrined in the Massachusetts Constitution alongside freedoms of speech and assembly and the right of petition, instruction was omitted from the First Amendment. Without constituencies small enough to assemble for discussion, *ex ante* accountability would be infeasible.

Republican thought, however, did not confine the requirement of consent to law making. Representation was relevant also to the application of law in individual cases. This is the political significance of trial by jury—an institution equal in importance, for republicans, to representation in the legislative process. Tocqueville (1945, I, 293) argued that the jury "places the real direction of society in the hands of the governed, or of a portion of the governed, and not in that of the government. . . . He who punishes the criminal is therefore the real master of society." Applied to civil penalties as well, trial by jury seeks to ensure that the coercive powers of government are not employed without the consent of citizens, who as peers of the defendant are members of the same community, not unlike their elected representatives.

The means of representation in juries is quite different from legislatures, jurors being chosen randomly within the relevant community. Selection of representatives by lot dates to ancient Athens (Manin 1997, 31–41). Although it disappeared as a means of selecting legislative representatives, random selection has remained in use for jurors. If Adams' concept of a representative assembly as society in miniature were the prevailing model, the selection of representatives by lot would come much closer than election to meeting the standard. Manin argues that the introduction of the principle of consent led to the abandonment of random selection (1997, 42–93). Whereas the use of lot served well the democratic principle of equal opportunity to participate, the use of consent as a test of legitimacy required that officials have a means to obtain the consent of those they represent; election provided that means. In the case of trial by jury, however, the driving consideration is not equal opportunity to serve but impartiality and the lack of a pro-government bias. Jurors are unaccountable for their decisions, deliberately so; their status as citizens and disinterested third parties is what qualifies them to decide. The use of citizens as jurors, selected from a pool chosen by lot, is a democratic element in an otherwise republican system. In short, as Tocqueville contended, it is an element of rule by the people.

Republican thinking also addressed the *enforcement* of law. The possibility that the authority to enforce law might be abused was much on the mind of republicans. Because coercion can require recourse to armed force, republicans sought to tame the use of coercion by limiting and conditioning the availability of force. "No standing army," a principle associated with the contribution of Niccolò Machiavelli to republican theory, was as important to many republicans as "no taxation without representation." Republicans instead established a military force composed of citizens: the local militia. Alongside the jury, it was one of two local institutions deemed essential to republican form. Reflected in the Second Amendment by the right of citizens to bear arms, the militia required direct citizen participation in the use of coercion.

Before the law can be applied and enforced, however, it must be invoked: how might citizens invoke the law? The answer depended in part on whether the law is criminal or civil. Citizens were understood as the invokers of criminal law in the institution of the grand jury, and individual citizens could invoke civil law against other citizens in court. The remaining gap was a process for invoking civil law against officials of government. The traditional republican answer was contained in the right of citizens to petition for the redress of grievances—another democratic element of republicanism. Petition was closely connected in republican thought to a bill of rights, which specified legitimate grounds for grievance (Rakove 1996, 336). Formal petition was the accepted republican means for bringing grievances to the attention of officials, whether elected or unelected. The purpose of a bill of rights was primarily civic, not legal, providing citizens with a common set of principles, publicly shared, for coordinating the expression of grievance. The First Amendment, as drafted by Madison in the first Congress, retained the right of petition even as it omitted the right of instruction.

Traditional republicanism addressed the entire process of governance, not just law making, and did so drawing on principles of democracy. Though Madison identified republican form with the election of a representative assembly to make law, the republican tradition was concerned with much more: not only representation but *strong* representation, both *ex ante* and *ex post*, in the process of prescribing law; the right of petition, enabling citizens to invoke civil law against officials; the application of law by citizen-jurors chosen randomly; and the right of citizens to bear arms, so as to participate in the enforcement of law through the citizen militia.

In contrast to Madison, but arguably consistent with traditional republicanism, Ostrom identified the core of a republic as the *public* itself—the realm of public activity. Its critical attribute is its *openness* to citizens (1989, 146; 1991, 210).[21] Though not private, he wrote, the open public realm lies "outside the jurisdiction of governments as such," and is the source of "many features pertaining to a democratic society: public opinion, civic knowledge, and a culture of inquiry" (Ostrom 1991, 200). Sustained by the liberties of citizens, including the freedoms of speech, press, and assembly, as well as the freedom to enter into enforceable contracts, the productivity of the public realm is the primary aim of a republic, enabling citizens to act in association with one another. An autonomous public realm also provides "a necessary complement to representative institutions" (Ostrom 1991, 211),[22] an independent platform for scrutinizing government.

By providing institutional space for organizing a variety of common endeavors, the public realm nurtures a "community of understanding," derived from joint problem-solving (Ostrom 1991, 217–18). Without mutual understanding, similar to the mutual sympathy prized by traditional republicans, Ostrom implied that democracy is not sustainable (Ostrom 2012, 20). The community of understanding depends on individuals who engage in "normative inquiry" based on the Golden Rule (Ostrom 1991, 213). Ostrom thus extended Smith's concept of sympathy from the problem of how to secure the consent of the governed to the larger problem of how to sustain the mutually productive character of the public realm.[23]

Ostrom's conception of a republic, much like the traditional republican view, requires that democratic and republican principles fit together as close complements in contrast to the stark alternatives of *Federalist* 10. The scaling-up of the republican project, however, raises new questions of representation in the process of governance:

- In the process of prescribing law: Given the weakness of representation by means of elections in a scaled-up republic, how can public voices be strengthened, particularly in agenda setting?
- In the process of invoking law: Is petitioning for the redress of grievances the only feasible means by which citizens can invoke civil law against officials? When officials neglect "what the law requires" or do "what the law forbids," judicial remedies are appropriate—but who represents a wronged public in court?

MULTIPLE-AGENCY FOR PRESCRIBING LAW

From the standpoint of principal-agent theory the "slender thread" of representation is rooted in information asymmetry: agents are better informed than their principals. The remedy in American politics is redundant representation, achieved by means of "multiple agency relationships" (Ostrom 1991, 210), providing both redundant sources of information and redundant means of legislation in federal, state, and local legislatures. The basis for multiple-agency is found in what Ostrom termed "constitutional choice" (1987, 60–62), which supplies the fundamental law used to organize and govern the process of governance. If the distinction between (1) the fundamental law of a constitution and (2) ordinary law made by legislators is to be more than a nominal distinction, there must be separate procedures for making and altering fundamental law distinct from those used for making and altering ordinary law. Although the United States has never convened a second constitutional convention, relying instead on the proposal of amendments by two-thirds of both houses of Congress followed by ratification in three-fourths of the states, the states have repeatedly used separately elected conventions to rewrite state constitutions—averaging almost three conventions per state. Constitutional conventions provide a separate path of representation for making fundamental law. During the progressive era, constitutional conventions provided citizens with the alternate means of representation needed to secure reforms resisted by legislative oligarchies (Ostrom et al. 1988, 33).

In the making of ordinary law, federalism creates alternate paths of representation (Ostrom 1987, 134). Madison redesigned federalism: originally conceived as a union that governed domestically only through the agency of its member states, federalism took the form of a "compound republic," smaller republics nested inside a larger, more inclusive republic (*Federalist* 51). In *Federalist* 46, Madison grounded the concept of multiple-agency in a representational division of labor: "The federal and state governments are in fact but different agents and trustees of the people, constituted with different powers, and designed for different purposes." In *Federalist* 28, however, Hamilton stressed the redundancy of concurrent powers held at federal and state levels, arguing that multiple-agency would greatly amplify the voice of citizens:

> Power being almost always the rival of power, the general government will at all times stand ready to check the usurpations of the state governments, and these will have the same disposition towards the general government. The people, by throwing themselves into either scale, will infallibly make it preponderate. If their rights are invaded by either, they can make use of the other as the instrument of redress.

Hamilton's redundancy is readily apparent throughout the structure of federal and state governments. Both are involved in the governance of forests and parks, schools and roads, air and water, the control of crime and the facilitation of commerce, among other policy domains.

Governance is inherently complex because it requires trade-offs among competing values that cannot be measured on a single utilitarian scale—the recent preoccupation of Americans with trade-offs between security and liberty being a case in point. The diversity of competing values increases with the growth and development of societies. A republic depends on representation to bring diverse values onto the legislative agenda for consideration: multiple-agency facilitates this process by multiplying the paths of representation. Ostrom devoted much of his career to a defense of multiple-agency against the charge of "fragmentation," arguing that a complex environment requires complex means of representation (Ostrom 1989). In addition to elected representatives, non-elected officials also function as representatives of diverse publics.[24] Different administrative agencies with partially redundant responsibilities make somewhat different trade-offs, allowing for a broader range of values to be represented. Reformers who seek to sort functions neatly between federal and state levels of government fail to understand the complexity of broadly defined policy domains, such as education or the environment.[25]

The greatest threat to multiple-agency, however, comes from what Ostrom called the "central government trap" (1991, 112–26), a consequence of treating all major public problems as national problems requiring a uniform national response (Ostrom 1987, 205–7). Overloading the Congress with non-national concerns creates opportunities for minority factions to clog the legislative arena, as Madison anticipated in *Federalist* 10. Factions can then play what Ostrom derisively termed "the game of raiding the national treasury," the use of national revenues for non-national purposes, including private rather than public interests (Ostrom 1987, 206). For this reason he emphasized the *limited* nature of the authority constitutionally assigned to the federal government and advocated the consistent application of those limits in court (Ostrom 1991, 107–12).

Drawing on the work of Mancur Olson (1969), Ostrom argued for observing a principle of fiscal equivalence in the federal system—diverse state and local communities benefiting from public services ought to pay for those services, requiring the national community to pay only for services of national benefit (Ostrom 1989, 61). However, fiscal equivalence cannot always be strictly observed. General benefits, those available to everyone in a community without exclusion, can be distinguished from selective benefits, available only to particular recipients (Olson 1965). The problem is this: *the provision of public goods, which supply general benefits to a community, always generates selective benefits as well.* National defense is a pure public good in terms of its general benefits, but its production generates selective benefits for particular firms and localities, sure to find supporting voices in Congress. If legislators are free to represent the interests of their particular voting constituency, there will always be vote trading—in the political vernacular, logrolling. To paraphrase Madison, liberty is to logrolling as air is to fire! If representation depends on the liberty of legislators to represent their constituents, the appropriate fix is not to destroy liberty but—following the logic of *Federalist* 10—to limit its ill effects.

Vote trading is more likely to produce a fair distribution of selective benefits that emerge as a by-product of public good provision than a process dominated by a single majority coalition.[26] Without fiscal constraint, however, logrolling can drive up aggregate spending and distort policy in the process.[27] Dwight D. Eisenhower, the five-star general who as President repeatedly vetoed defense appropriation bills as too generous, warned against the influence of a military-industrial complex in his Farewell Address. The military-industrial complex is what Madison feared most—a majority faction.

His primary remedy—the variety of interests inherent in the extent of the Union—proved to be insufficient in the face of a national public good as gigantic as national defense in terms of budget share. The republic is forced instead to rely on Madison's secondary remedy—the "proper structure" of the Union—to which Madison referred at the conclusion of *Federalist* 10 and Ostrom emphasized (1987, 104–5). When the extent of the Union fails, the remaining guard against majority faction is the openness of the legislative process to public scrutiny (Ostrom 1987, 161), an openness nourished by multiple-agency and sustained by the Union's proper structure.

Ostrom understood federalism as "*constitutional choice reiterated*" (1987, 25, Ostrom's emphasis), carried out as states write constitutions and communities write municipal charters, extending the principles of federalism and constitutionalism to the most local levels. Home-rule provisions, added to state constitutions by progressive reformers to enhance local autonomy, effectively broadened the intersection of constitutionalism and federalism (Ostrom et al. 1988, 34–35). Small municipalities, townships, homeowners associations, and organized urban neighborhoods are the "primary units" of democratic governance (Oakerson 1988), enabling citizens to address a multitude of small-scale collective problems on the basis of fiscal equivalence (Ostrom 2011, 339–48). Given the number of relatively autonomous local governments in the United States—some 89,000—the strong representation sought by traditional republicans is alive and well in many parts of local America (Oakerson 1999), though tragically missing in others.

Multiple-agency is sustained by constitutionalism, federalism, the separation of powers, and bicameralism—the "auxiliary precautions" recommended by Madison in *Federalist* 51. When viewed as anti-majoritarian, Madison's auxiliaries appear to create opportunities for elite manipulation and special interest influence and, moreover, engender a pronounced status quo bias (Gilens and Page 2014, 573). *Ostrom's argument is the reverse:* misrepresentation is *inherent* in the "slender thread" of vertical representation; the remedy is to multiply representational channels, equipping citizens with multiple agents and providing the (mis)represented with multiple opportunities to challenge the status quo.[28]

Multiple-agency mitigates, but it cannot eliminate, the weakness of the principal-agent relationship between voters and their elected representatives. The only way to avoid the slender thread of legislative representation entirely is to enable the electorate to legislate directly. Initiative and referendum procedures, found in 26 states plus the District of Columbia and in thousands of local jurisdictions, do exactly that: citizens petition to place a legislative proposal on the ballot and then accept or reject it in a popular vote.[29] Referenda are unavailable at the national level because Congress may not constitutionally delegate its legislative authority. National initiative and referendum proposals nonetheless have broad public support.

If one adheres to Madison's conception of a republic as representative government, initiative and referendum appears to be un-republican, bypassing the refining quality of representation that Madison lauds in *Federalist* 10. The signers of an initiative petition, however, can be viewed as horizontal representatives of the citizenry, enabling citizens to legislate directly rather than indirectly through vertical representatives. Initiative and referendum can have a democratizing effect on the whole process of prescribing law: if the legislature fails to act, the people can do so, affording voters the opportunity to participate directly in agenda formation. Progressive reformers introduced initiative and referendum in response to the dominance of state and local legislatures by party machines. Any legislative body can develop vested interests that prompt representatives to ignore popular interests and preferences. The process of initiative and referendum can therefore be viewed as an important complement to electoral representation rather than its antinomy.[30]

The major weakness of popular referenda is the binary choice offered to voters—the absence of popular deliberation in shaping the content of the proposal. Used too frequently, referenda can convert the legislative process into the same low-information affair found in elections, all too easily manipulated by well-funded promotional campaigns.[31] In this sense there is no substitute for the representation-cum-deliberation that characterizes a good legislature. If limited, popular referenda can create incentives for legislators to address issues they prefer to avoid, so as to craft legislation themselves instead of its being written by others. At the same time, if referenda are to be reserved for exceptional cases, access to the referendum ballot needs to be restricted to a relatively few issues of serious public concern.[32]

Multiple-agency and popular referenda bring the process of prescribing law into the open public realm—the core of the republic—but there is more: with the process of prescribing law comes the whole governance process. Laws prescribed must also be invoked, applied, and enforced. As Ostrom put it, "The process of governance occurs in the public space afforded by the concurrent operation of these multiorganizational arrangements" (2009, 37). While the separation of powers sorts the processes of prescribing, applying, and enforcing law into separate decision structures that interact publicly, multiple-agency reiterates the entire process at constitutional and operational levels in every unit of government throughout the compound republic.

THE ANYONE RULE FOR INVOKING LAW

Ostrom understood the provisions of the Bill of Rights as an assignment of authority to persons—including authority to invoke the protection of fundamental law (Ostrom 1987, 152–64). Madison initially resisted inclusion of a bill of rights in the US Constitution, despite its centrality in republican thought and ubiquity in state constitutions. Traditional republicans reacted in astonishment, but Hamilton insisted in *Federalist* 84 that a bill of rights was unnecessary given the limited assignment of authority to the federal Congress. Jefferson wrote Madison from Paris to suggest that a written constitution—an American innovation—could greatly strengthen the provisions of a bill of rights.[33] If rights were to be understood as part of the fundamental law, individuals could invoke those rights in court against officials of government. No longer would citizens be limited to making humble petition to those who govern them—with their only further recourse the right of revolution.[34]

The authority of persons extends potentially to the rule of law in general, including ordinary law. A law can be construed as an n-person contract among the people, agreed to by the people's representatives in Congress assembled. Just as a contract is potentially enforceable on the petition of any party, so a law might be viewed as enforceable when invoked by any citizen. Ostrom understood the authority of persons as an example of the "anyone rule" (1987, 34, 154–59), a rule that has broad application in the process of governance. The anyone rule enables any person to obtain collective action in his or her own behalf as well as on behalf of others, such as invoking service delivery (Ostrom 1989, 60). In effect, the anyone rule allows citizens to exercise executive authority by commanding the delivery of a public service or performance of a public obligation (Ostrom 1987, 158). The simple act of calling 911 allows anyone to cause emergency responders to respond.

The anyone rule is an element in the framework of constitutional choice developed by James Buchanan and Gordon Tullock in *The Calculus of Consent* (1962), a work upon which Ostrom drew extensively. In this framework the range of possible collective-choice rules extends from anyone to everyone—unanimity. Buchanan and Tullock clearly distinguished the anyone rule from a one-person rule that identifies a unique individual, for example, the President or a governor (1962, 67). Shown in Figure 4.1, simple majority rule occupies a position just to the right of mid-point on the range; to the left of the mid-point are various less-than-majority-rules (such as used in initiative petitions) and to the right are various super-majorities (such as used to amend constitutions).

Although democracy is frequently identified with simple majority rule, the entire range of Buchanan and Tullock's decision-rule continuum can be viewed as democratic.[35] Each point on the continuum specifies a decision rule by which a democracy can act collectively. The choice of decision rule depends in part on the circumstances surrounding various types of decisions and in part on how the collective-choice rule fits with other rules in an institutional configuration. Buchanan and Tullock used two cost functions to determine the optimal decision rule: external costs and decision making costs (1962, 63–84). External costs are the costs that some members of a

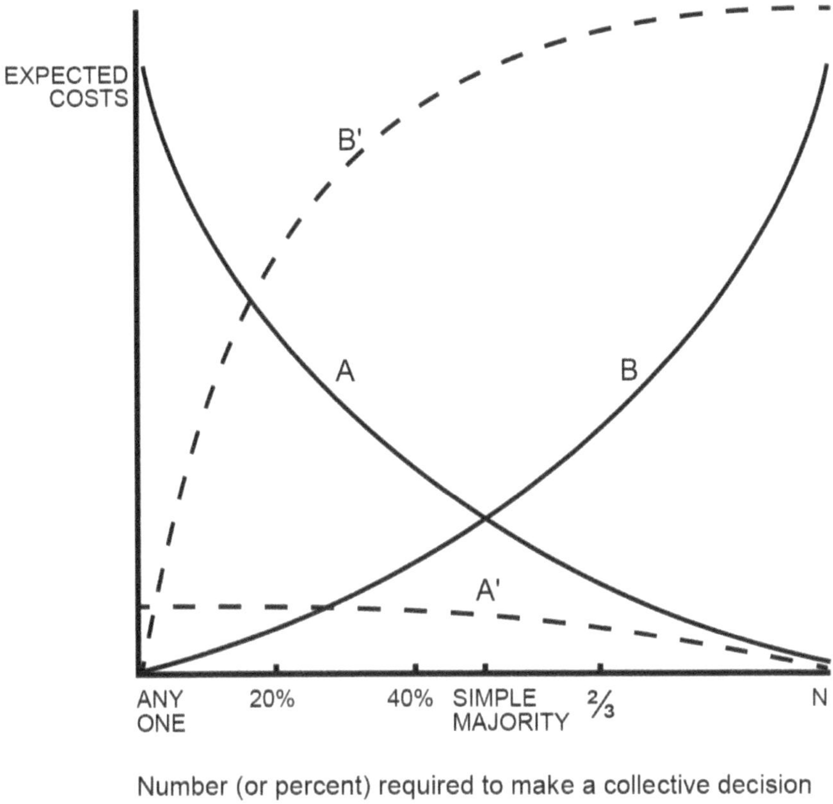

Figure 4.1 Cost Functions for Collective Choices. *Source*: Created by author.

collectivity can potentially impose on other members by means of a collective decision. Decision making costs are the costs of time and effort devoted to the process of coming to a collective decision. External costs (the curve marked A in Figure 4.1) are 0 under a rule of unanimity, while decision making costs (curve B in Figure 4.1) are at their peak; decision making costs are 0 under the anyone rule, while external costs are at their peak. Although the cost functions are drawn in Figure 4.1 to indicate simple majority rule as optimal, the functions can vary so as to produce other optimal rules.

Buchanan and Tullock erred, I believe, in conceptualizing the decision-making cost function entirely in terms of time and effort, that is, the costs of procedure. The costs of collective inaction (or delay) are not simply costs of time and effort. Some members of society may be able to continue privately to externalize their costs to others if collective action does not occur; indeed, the control of external costs among private individuals is a principal rationale for collective action. I have recast the cost functions as liability costs and disability costs, using language drawn from the institutional economist, John R. Commons: "liability" costs are the costs that some can impose on others through collective action, and "disability" costs are the costs that some can impose on others by collective inaction (Commons 1959, 106).[36] Disability costs are the opportunity costs of time and effort in decision making—the value forgone by not acting. Whereas liability costs are borne by those who would oppose collective action, disability costs are borne by those who seek collective action, including its beneficiaries.

Buchanan and Tullock saw little or no practical utility for the anyone rule (1962, 67). By associating collective choice exclusively with the process of prescribing law, they missed its importance. For prescribing law (or for applying and enforcing law), an anyone rule would amount to anarchy: when anyone can make his or her own "rule," liability costs skyrocket. When invoking law or commanding service delivery, there are still potential liability costs—whether it is the cost of a false alarm or frivolous lawsuits. The liability costs of invoking law are sharply constrained, however, by the terms of the law being invoked: this makes the anyone rule a potentially optimal rule (shown in Figure 4.1 as the liability cost function A′). The disability costs for invoking law (B′ in Figure 4.1) rise steeply as the rule moves to the right on the continuum—in part because the use of the anyone rule can create external benefits. Reporting a crime or a fire in process benefits a community; so does invoking a law of general benefit. More inclusive rules are preferred when liability costs are somewhat higher (e.g., when a person is asked to demonstrate some level of support from fellow citizens before invoking a procedure that, in the end, requires agreement from a wider group). Rules of petition fall into this category, used in initiative procedures that lead to a referendum as well as in nomination processes.

As a rule for invoking law, the anyone rule is qualified by judicial doctrines that pertain to "standing" in court—the authority to bring a lawsuit. Rules of standing further limit the potential liability from use of the anyone rule. In general terms, standing requires legal injury. Due process would seem to require standing when there is private injury caused by an act of government; otherwise, officials of government are generally considered the proper parties to invoke the law on behalf of the public. Many state jurisdictions, however, allow taxpayer standing: any taxpayer may challenge the legality of an act of the tax-receiving jurisdiction.

What constitutes injury is the threshold question. When the injury is a pure public bad (citizens are jointly affected and no one can be excluded, like a pure public good), citizens have ordinarily lacked standing unless statutorily granted. If government agencies fail to enforce environmental regulations, allowing the degradation of shared resources, the result is often close to a pure public bad. Joseph Sax (1970) advocated citizen standing to invoke environmental protection laws, giving rise to a host of federal and state statutes authorizing citizen suits.

How far legislation may go in authorizing citizen standing is a constitutional question of considerable importance to democracy: can members of the public represent public interests in court, or are citizens reliant exclusively on elected officials and their subordinates? The *Endangered Species Act* (16 U.S.C. ξ 1540, 1973) declares that "any person may commence a civil suit on his own behalf . . . to enjoin . . . the United States and any other governmental instrumentality or agency . . . who is alleged to be in violation" of the relevant law. The US Supreme Court disallowed a citizen suit based on this act in *Lujan v. Defenders of Wildlife* (504 U.S. 555, 1992). Associate Justice Antonin Scalia wrote for the Court:

> Vindicating the *public* interest (including the public interest in governmental observance of the Constitution and laws) is the function of the Congress and the Chief Executive. [A] statute . . . that permits all citizens . . . to sue . . . is to permit Congress to transfer from the President to the courts the Chief Executive's most important constitutional duty, to "take Care that the Laws be faithfully executed" (emphasis in the original text)

Scalia's opinion denied horizontal representation in favor of vertical: only officials, not citizens, are entitled to represent *public* interests in the courtroom. Tocqueville's accountability framework would produce a different result: when the President or any executive officer, acting on the basis of statutory authority, proceeds to do what the law forbids or fail to do what the law requires, the appropriate remedy is judicial. The anyone rule as established in the statute required that citizens allege a violation of the law to gain standing. If citizen suits are disallowed, *no one* outside the government is authorized to invoke the law unless privately injured. Scalia's point applies to the "energy or zeal" with which law is executed—accountability that is necessarily political or administrative in nature—but not to actions or inactions contrary to statutory requirements.[37]

Ostrom's reworking of democratic theory allowed him to revive Max Weber's rejected category of administration: *democratic* administration in contrast to bureaucratic administration (Ostrom 1989, 68).[38] The ability of citizens to make legal claims on behalf of a public brings democracy squarely into the administrative process. Conventional democratic theory would channel citizen influence on administration exclusively through vertical representatives who supervise a bureaucratic hierarchy, but with the leverage supplied by anyone rules, citizens can participate directly in shaping administrative decisions.

The courts are conventionally viewed as a non-democratic element in an otherwise democratic system of governance. If, however, we consider the courts to be an institutional facility specialized to the unbiased application of law, the important question in a democracy is one of access: who has access to this institutional facility and on what terms and conditions? The anyone rule, Ostrom wrote, was the only basis on which he could conceive of the "possibility of *equality* in a democratic republic" (Ostrom 1971, 102, Ostrom's emphasis). Rather than simple majority rule, which creates inequality between citizens in the majority and those in the minority, anyone rules are foundational for democracy. The logic of horizontal representation allows anyone to represent everyone when invoking law: "If an 'any-one' rule can be sustained, then the authority of everyone is assured" (Ostrom 1987, 34). Surprisingly, the same collective-choice rule supports both democracy and the rule of law—often thought to be in tension with one another.

While multiple-agency brings law making into the public realm, anyone rules allow any member of the public to invoke those laws—representing the public and laying claim to public interests. This is democracy resting on a broad foundation, not hanging by a slender thread.

INSTITUTIONAL FAILURE AND REFORM

Methodologically, Ostrom was an institutionalist who understood institutions as configurations of rules that define decision making arrangements. Within the opportunities afforded by *rules*, as commonly understood by members of a community, individuals choose *strategies* that guide their choices in some *material and social context*, producing a set of *consequences*.[39] Given a material and social context, if the consequences fail to satisfy evaluative criteria, a modification of the rules may induce individuals to choose different strategies. Shifts in the context—whether environmental, technological, or cultural—can cause institutions to malfunction. Designing reforms that yield the desired results requires an institutional analysis: first to identify the sources of institutional failure, then to anticipate how decision makers are likely to respond to rule changes. Below, I analyze two cases of institutional failure that have recently dominated public discussion in America.

Prescribing Law: Overcoming Deadlock

A growing ideological polarization in American politics has produced ongoing deadlock in the Congress, with consequent inattention to long-standing national problems. The material and social context in a legislative body includes both the size of the assembly[40] and the distribution of prior opinion among legislators—measuring opinion on a liberal to conservative scale—relative to the division of the legislative body between political parties. If this is the "ground," so to speak, on which the legislative process must be built, it has shifted dramatically over roughly the last twenty years. While the distribution of opinion in Congress has always been bi-modal, reflecting the two-party system, the two modes have moved farther and farther apart, away from the median of the distribution. The ideological overlap between the two parties in the middle portion of the distribution has shrunk, almost to zero: the most liberal Republicans now seem more conservative than the most conservative Democrats. Usefully, ideologies supply legislators with criteria for choice; competing ideologies can share some criteria and not others. When legislators are firmly committed to mutually exclusive criteria, however, they are unable to resolve their differences. Ostrom commented that no political system is able to cope adequately with such deep disagreement (Ostrom 1997, 286).

Drawing on the work of John Dewey (1938, 508–9), Ostrom argued that policies should be viewed as hypotheses, subject to inquiry (Ostrom 1971, 9). He sought a political system structured so that conflict—even stalemate—occasions inquiry and deliberation, leading to an informed resolution; the mutual veto positions inherent in the American separation-of-powers/checks-and-balances arrangement then become a prelude to negotiation and settlement, not deadlock (Ostrom 1987, 163). Inquiry-based deliberation, however, requires a substantial set of shared criteria among legislators. Ongoing deadlock indicates institutional failure.

Persistent disagreement without resolution has diminished the culture of inquiry long characteristic of Congress. Committee work—historically the bulwark of congressional power and influence—has declined in importance. Traditional norms of specialization and reciprocity, including a large element of bipartisanship (especially in the Senate), have eroded. The "energy and zeal" of which Tocqueville wrote applies to the work of legislators. Retrospective accountability in elections, however, is ineffective as a means of holding legislators accountable for their work as legislative artisans. Although legislators must do much more than simply show up and vote, it is their voting record that is the focus of retrospective accountability. Without a shared set of norms that enables legislators to hold one another accountable for their work ethic, a representative assembly becomes increasingly unproductive, provoking efforts in the executive to bypass the legislature when possible. The retrospective accountability characteristic of electoral politics—the slender thread of representation—is unlikely to reverse the decline of Congress.

Most analyses of congressional dysfunction focus on the Senate and its rules of debate, which permit any 41 senators to prevent legislation from being brought to a vote. Nonetheless, the Senate retains some capacity for bipartisan action: in the current configuration, if enough Democrats join with Republicans, a filibuster can be overcome. The situation in the House is more problematic. The larger size of the House makes a tradition of open debate impossible; the House Rules Committee, dominated by the majority party leadership, schedules bills for floor debate. If the Rules Committee declines to schedule a bill, the only recourse is a discharge petition signed by a majority of the House—218 members. This rarely occurs because the petition rule requires some members of the majority party to oppose a decision taken by their leadership, exposing them to informal sanctions (Sinclair 2007, 17–18; Jackman 2013).[41]

Former House Speaker Dennis Hastert established the principle that no bill should be brought to the floor without the support of a majority of the Republican Conference—a majority of the majority party. The so-called Hastert Rule, though informal, is simply the latest manifestation in the House of the oligarchical tendencies Madison predicted in large representative assemblies. It provides an interesting variant of Madison's concept of majority faction. Although a bare majority of the majority party is a minority of the full House, it is able to mask its minority character by its dominance of the majority party. The majority appears to rule even as it prevents a majority of the House from acting.[42]

When a majority of the majority party is ideologically committed to a set of principles that make inquiry and deliberation superfluous, the stage is set for deadlock. On numerous important issues, Republicans in the House have adopted a blocking strategy that prevents the enactment of legislation by not bringing it to the floor. When the Senate passed a comprehensive immigration reform bill with bipartisan support in 2013, acting to resolve a long-standing national problem, the House declined to consider the bill; even though knowledgeable observers believed that it had majority support from House members, it was opposed by a majority of the majority party (Jackman 2013). Unlike the Senate, where any 60 senators can act on the floor to approve legislation, an equivalent percentage of the House may be unable to act without a discharge petition. This result is clearly a failure of the republican form Madison sought to build into the design of the House. The republicans who designed the Constitution intended the House of Representatives to be the people's house, the one place where a majority of the people's representatives could prevail. If the House is unable to act, the popular majority *has no voice* in the making of law, an outcome that is neither democratic nor republican.[43]

The institutional source of the difficulty is the petition rule that requires a simple majority of House members to discharge the Rules Committee (or any other committee blocking legislation).[44] The disability costs associated with the petition rule are extremely high, while liability costs are low. A discharge petition does not enact legislation nor even require floor debate; it simply allows the full House to decide whether to debate the bill in question. Although control of the agenda prevents the floor from being clogged with legislation, justifying a more inclusive petition rule, to require a majority to get a bill to the floor seems extreme.[45]

Suppose that 40 or 45 percent of members could discharge legislation.[46] Such a rule would not flood the floor with bills, but it would undermine the ability of a minority to block full consideration of legislation that enjoys significant support in the House—substantially reducing disability costs without unduly increasing liability costs. Relaxing the discharge rule might lead members of the majority caucus to choose a much different legislative strategy—to help shape legislation so that it conforms more closely to their legislative criteria instead of blocking it. Ideological purists would be constrained to join the deliberative process in order to be effective. They might even learn to adopt less restrictive criteria of choice.

The main objection to relaxing the discharge rule is a belief that the majority party ought to control the legislative agenda (Jackman 2013).[47] Advocates of "responsible party government" hold that majority party control of the House agenda makes the majority party fully responsible for House action and therefore more easily held accountable by voters. However, efforts to establish party government in the House potentially make the House dysfunctional when the power to legislate is shared with the Senate and the President. The House is not the government; but a majority of the House is intended to speak for the people in the process of prescribing law.

Enforcing Law: Constraining Police

Traditional republicans viewed the local militia as a means of citizen participation in law enforcement, long since displaced by police. Philip Pettit notes that professionalized police may today pose a threat to republican values similar to the dangers once associated with a standing army (1997, 155). As I write, public attention has been focused for more than a year on a series of highly publicized police abuses that often resulted in the death or serious injury of citizens. Preventing police abuse has become a nation-wide concern, spurred in great part by the widespread availability of video on the street, enabling citizens to record the interaction between police and citizens visually. The relevant material and social context is the problem of keeping order on city streets—the urban commons. Safe use of the streets requires that individuals be restrained from actions that threaten the safety of others. The use of force by police, however, puts an officer in the triple role of law invoker, applier, and enforcer. No jury stands between police and citizen when police use deadly force.

The concern with police accountability has focused largely on legal accountability in the criminal courts—in Tocqueville's words, accountability for "doing what the law forbids." Keeping order on the street, however, requires discretion and judgment—in particular, when and when not to use physical force. Accountability for the use of discretion has to do with "energy and zeal," extended in this case to include an equal concern for judgment and restraint. The remedies identified by Tocqueville apply: administrative and political accountability. Administrative accountability operates through the chain of command of a police department. Political accountability in large cities works through administrative accountability as mayor and council attempt to control police work by means of the police hierarchy. Paul Chevigny (1969, 1997) has described the many ways that officers on the street can evade effective supervision by bureaucratic superiors. The larger the police department, the more problematic administrative and political accountability becomes (see Ostrom 1989, 51–56).[48]

Some police departments have begun to require that officers wear body cameras, institutionalizing the informal monitoring of citizens with smart phones. Others fear, however, that the use of body cameras will cause officers to avoid situations that hold the potential for violent interaction, failing to keep order on the street. Cameras alone are not an adequate constraint when the intended result is a proper use of discretion. Although cameras can capture an officer "doing what the law forbids," cameras cannot record a lack of "energy and zeal."

The question is how to create a mode of accountability that fits the material and social context—the use of police discretion on the street. Control of discretion demands both prospective and retrospective accountability. Local elections are mostly retrospective and do not directly affect police, who are insulated from political accountability by layers of bureaucracy and, often, by police unions. A police officer with discretion is a representative of the relevant public as much as any other public officer, elected or unelected. William K. Muir (1979) rightly characterized police officers as "streetcorner politicians." Representation depends on the tie between representative and represented, a linkage that needs to be as direct as possible.

From a republican standpoint, the most effective way to control police discretion is to embed officers in the neighborhoods they patrol. Officers should not only resemble the community they serve but also function as members of that community. Because residents possess place-based information that bureaucratic superiors lack, they have an essential role as monitors of the urban commons. Throughout urban America neighborhood associations enable urban residents to monitor their neighborhoods and interact with respect to neighborhood issues. In traditional republican fashion, police should become participating members of a neighborhood association that organizes the public they in effect represent. If neighborhood associations are authorized to monitor police behavior and officers were instructed to function as association members, the relationship between police and community can become mutual: each can monitor the other, learn from the other, and be accountable to the other. To constrain police to give serious attention to neighborhood advice and counsel, citizens also need access to police superiors through elected representatives at city hall. Political and administrative accountability is nonetheless secondary: the primary source of accountability is in the public realm, where police and citizens can interact as equals, fostering mutual respect and empathy.[49]

CONCLUSION

Ostrom understood the American political system as a democratic republic—an institutional configuration that combined democratic and republican features as complements.[50] By expanding the scope of democracy to include the whole process of governance—prescribing, invoking, applying, and enforcing law—he was able to demonstrate, contra Madison, how a republic can, and ought to, provide rule by the people. The "slender thread" of representation is strengthened by adding horizontal representation to vertical, including the anyone rule to invoke law—thus allowing citizens to participate directly in all four stages of the governance process. Multiple-agency yields not only multiple paths of representation for prescribing law but also multiple arenas of governance, each of which embraces the whole governance process, multiplying the opportunities for public participation. The core of a compound republic is a set of publics where citizens relate as equals—a complex public realm with smaller arenas (such as urban neighborhoods) geographically nested in larger ones (state and nation). The meaning is clear: *a republic is democratic at its core.*

In Tocqueville's terms, a democratic republic yields "a society that governs itself for itself" (1945, I, 59), a self-governing society that allows the people to rule without recourse to a Hobbesian or Weberian state possessed of a monopoly of legitimate coercive power (Ostrom 1989, 152; 1991, 15). The polycentric distribution of authority inherent in multiple-agency avoids the monopoly condition and creates a multiplicity of opportunities for citizens to participate *directly* in governance, giving substantive meaning to democracy.

Ostrom concluded that democracy, though improbable, is possible in the modern world. In contrast to realists who see only the facts of history, Ostrom was a "possibilist" (Aligica 2014a) who dared to dream *possible* dreams, imagining alternate possibilities to those that dominated the past (Ostrom 1997, 288–89). He also recognized that *impossibility* theorems are powerful because they are falsifiable. The American case, while imperfect, falsified the proposition that democracy is impossible, or for that matter unsustainable;

after all, the American political system is the oldest in the world. This does not mean it can last indefinitely.

Democracy is improbable in part because it is necessarily complex, and complexity makes strong epistemic demands upon its designers and users. Sustaining the knowledge base needed to design, use, and maintain a democratic system of government is an ongoing challenge. Ostrom saw American democracy, approaching the end of the twentieth century, as seriously at risk—in need of reform (see Ostrom 1989, Chapters 6 and 7). Unfortunately, reformers can make matters worse rather than better. Reforms that grease the wheels of a parliamentary system may throw sand in the gears of the separation of powers. If reforms are system repairs, then reform surely requires an understanding of the system being repaired.

Sustaining a polycentric system and its democratic-republican character in the midst of accelerating technological and social change depends on an institutional capacity to alter the configuration of rules by which the system operates. Francis Fukuyama, who sees American democracy as a "vetocracy" increasingly incapable of action, despairs of reform as untenable given American devotion to the Constitution and the polycentric structure it established (2014, 467–505). His despair suggests the absence of institutional resources for reform in American democracy. Ostrom presents the counterargument (1991, 257–58): reformability requires institutions open to change: openness is facilitated by multiple-agency, which is sustained by multiple veto capabilities. In a democratic republic the process of reform emerges from within the open public realm rather than government. This has consistently been the path of basic political reform in the United States—reform that defeated the political bosses of the late nineteenth century and ended de jure discrimination against African-Americans in the mid-twentieth century.

There is, however, a further question: if confidence in government has fallen so low, why has a viable reform movement not emerged? Institutional resources are not lacking, but institutions are not all that is needed: the "moral and intellectual" qualities of democratic citizens are also essential resources (Ostrom 1997, 114). The intellectual dimension of the problem turns upon epistemic choice, the choice of paradigm for understanding relationships of governance: Americans may have misplaced the repair manual needed to maintain the American political system. The root cause of the deep ideological divide that characterizes American politics in 2016 is epistemic, not institutional. But there is also a moral dimension: a principal vulnerability of democracies is "neglect" on the part of their citizens (Ostrom 1997, 283). If the core of a republic is its public, the keepers of the republic are its citizens. The decline in civic engagement and social capital among Americans, traced by Robert Putnam (2000), is the loss of a critical resource for reform. Traditional republicans understood that the viability of democratic republics depends on civic virtue. Just as the passion for equality—the democratic impulse—can be joined to republicanism, it can also be joined to despotism (Tocqueville 1945, II, 334–39). If there is cause for despair, it is not from devotion to the Constitution—as Fukuyama claims.

Many astute observers have concluded that America has become "too democratic," that less democracy is needed to clear the way for action by vertical representatives (e.g., Zakaria 2007). This is a recipe for reform based on a profound misunderstanding of democracy and its connection to republicanism. Ostrom joined Madison to urge that we "rest *all* our political experiments on the capacity of mankind for self-government" (*Federalist* 39, emphasis added; Ostrom 1987, 103–4). The present moral and intellectual condition of American society may make this exhortation difficult to follow, but as Ostrom well understood, neither the creation nor the destruction of a democracy is short work (Ostrom 1997, 114). Tocqueville (1945, I, 97) saw each new generation as a potential source of renewal, for "nations do not grow old as men do." It is never too late to begin the work of reform.

NOTES

1. I owe a considerable debt of gratitude to my life-long colleagues Roger Parks, Fil Sabetti, and Jamie Thomson, each of whom provided helpful comments on earlier drafts of this chapter.

2. William H. Riker (1982, 9) was emphatic on this point: it is "fear of the next election" alone that controls the conduct of officials.

3. Riker (1982) shared the same premise, and like Ostrom, he considered constitutionalism and the separation of powers necessary to sustain republican government; but akin to Manin, he rejected rule by the people, arguing that it is a "populist" fallacy.

4. When a work appeared in more than one edition, I reference the latest work when possible.

5. The most recent incumbents of the two legislative leadership positions are, at this writing, under federal indictment.

6. R. Douglas Arnold used the analogy of an audit to explain the role of opposition research in holding representatives accountable to the represented (1990, 272–73).

7. In the same essay, Chesterton continued: "The democracy has a right to answer questions, but it has no right to ask them. It is still the political aristocracy that asks the questions." I am indebted to Graham Badger, a former student, for directing me to Chesterton.

8. Paul Dragos Aligica (2014b, 181) recognized this same point: "The Ostromian perspective on democracy is broad, flexible, and sometimes made to look coextensive with a broader governance process that includes the standard institutional arrangements typically associated with democracy but goes beyond them. Hence, democracy

in relation to governance is a source of ambiguity and an area in which further work in clarification and elaboration is needed."

9. This formulation combines Ostrom's categories with a model of the decision process proposed by Harold Lasswell, a mid-twentieth-century American political scientist from whom Ostrom drew many key concepts. See Lasswell (1971, 28–29).

10. See for example, John Dewey (1934, 82–105).

11. See Chomsky (1980).

12. "For Christ's love compels us, because we are convinced that one died for all, and therefore all died." 2 *Corinthians* 5: 14 (*The New Testament*, New International Version).

13. Ostrom (1997, 275) wrote that detailed regulation of human relationships "makes everyone a slave of legalities." The need of institutional space for discretion implies the correlative need of political and administrative accountability. Freedom implies politics.

14. There was no need in traditional republicanism for a qualified doctrine of tacit consent, though see Pettit (1997, 63) for a different point of view.

15. This critique was well articulated by the Federal Farmer, whose published letters paralleled the publication of the *Federalist* essays. See Storing (1985, 76–77).

16. Hanna Pitkin used this same distinction to frame her central argument in *The Concept of Representation* (1967), distinguishing between "formalistic" concepts of representation (which she found wanting) in contrast to "substantive" views—without drawing, however, on the arguments advanced by Anti-federalist writers.

17. The Federal Farmer vigorously argued the point, concluding that a legislature "must possess the confidence, and have the voluntary support of the people" (Storing 1985, 74).

18. In 1958, the University of Michigan National Election Study measured public confidence in the federal government at 76 percent; in 2010, using the same question, Gallup measured public confidence at 19 percent. Although there are peaks and valleys in between, the long-term trend has been downward. See Gallup: http://www.gallup.com/poll/5392/trust-government.aspx.

19. Pettit makes a case for an "inclusive legislature," one that includes voices that can credibly represent all of the important groups in society, however defined (Pettit 1997, 190–91). Neither sympathy nor inquiry on the part of elected representatives is sufficient in this perspective to provide for representation. Committees, Pettit points out, are more likely to use the standard of inclusion rather than the principle of consent as the means of securing representation (Pettit 1997, 239). Richardson (2002, 199–200) uses a variant of the inclusion standard to argue that representation is strengthened when the process of election allows various political views or ideologies to be represented, presumably in proportion to their relative strength within the electorate. He suggests that proportional representation (PR), in contrast to single member districts, is more likely to secure this sort of representation. To my knowledge, Ostrom nowhere directly addressed the issue. I offer this conjecture: representatives ought to represent real people in discrete circumstances, not abstract political views. In PR, voters choose among political parties, which select representatives by means of slating; elected representatives represent their party, representing voters only through the party apparatus. Indirect representation is a likely source of distortion, obscuring accountability to voters.

20. A leading student of representation in the House of Representatives, Richard Fenno, Jr., has noted that Congress does mirror much of the great diversity of America (Fenno 2003, 244).

21. Ostrom (1991) identified the core of the "republic" with its Latin root: *res publica*, literally, the public thing. Most commentators on republicanism render *res publica* as the "public good." I construe Ostrom's "open public realm" as the public together with its common wealth—the sum of all values or goods shared by the public, both tangible (e.g., roads and schools) and intangible (e.g., liberty and security).

22. Manin (1997, 169–70) made a similar point about the freedom of public opinion and argues that it can be understood as a substitute for the right of instruction, allowing the governed to communicate among themselves as well as with their representatives and thus informing the process of legislation from outside the legislature.

23. Richardson (2002) advances a highly congruent concept of the public and elaborates upon its nature in *Democratic Autonomy*, Chapter 13.

24. John Dewey viewed all officials as "public agents . . . doing the business of others in securing and obviating consequences that concern them" (Dewey 1927, 19). Ostrom relied on Dewey for his conception of a "public" as a group affected by the indirect consequences of private transactions (Ostrom 1997, 40–43).

25. Teles (2014) takes issue with the complexity defended by Ostrom, arguing that the compound republic would be well served by a clear sorting of broadly defined functions, such as education or economic regulation, between federal and state levels. His approach would not only erase Hamilton's redundancy and thereby reduce the efficacy of multiple-agency for citizens but also reduce the efficiency he seeks to increase. See my discussion of public economies (Oakerson 1999) and multiple-agency in an administrative context (Oakerson 2008, 174–76).

26. Writing before rent-seeking behavior became a concern among political economists, Buchanan and Tullock provided an economic defense of vote trading (1962, 131–45).

27. Robert L. Bish (2014) notes that when the treasury becomes an unregulated commons, the result is a fiscal tragedy.

28. Richardson (2002, 70) makes a congruent point: democratic governance, rather than being concentrated in a single center of decision making, is dispersed among an array of institutions that operate in the context of a public realm.

29. See Cronin (1989) for a useful description and evaluation.

30. One source of frustration with vertical representation is the disproportionate influence of highly intense minorities who focus on a single issue. Legislators may ignore the opinion of a large majority of voters on an issue if it has low salience for them while a small minority holds the opposite opinion but regards the issue as highly salient. The regulation of handguns illustrates the point: large majorities support modest gun-control measures well within the scope of the Second Amendment, but fail to pass muster in Congress because the issue is much more salient to minority opponents, who can spell the difference between victory and defeat at the polls. Popular referenda avoid this scenario: intensity adds no influence to a small minority when voting in a referendum.

31. Zakaria (2007, 187–98) has rightly criticized states, most notably California, that rely heavily on referenda. However, the problem is not that referenda are too democratic but rather that deliberation is severely limited.

32. Initiative petition rules typically require the signatures of some 8 percent of the number of voters who cast votes in a previous election (Cronin 1989, 62). If an 8-percent rule crowds the ballot and threatens to subvert the legislative process, it can be increased substantially. Use of the Internet can perhaps reduce the costs of securing signatures and at the same time allow the requirement of a much larger percentage of the electorate to sign an initiative petition.

33. Thomas Jefferson, Letter to James Madison, March 15, 1789. See Veit et al. (1991, 218).

34. The use of the anyone rule to invoke constitutional and statutory limits on official discretion seems to me consistent with Pettit's (1997) view of republican governance as the non-arbitrary use of governmental power. Pettit sees the capacity of citizens to contest and resist the arbitrary exercise of governmental power as crucial to republican governance (Pettit 1997, 202).

35. See also Richardson (2002, 11), who views the identity of democracy with simple majority rule as mistaken.

36. Ostrom drew extensively on Commons' work (see, e.g., Ostrom 2012, 194–96).

37. The *New York Times*, in an editorial of May 10, 2016, commented on a law suit filed against President Barack Obama by an army captain serving in Kuwait, who alleges that the conduct of war against ISIS violates the *War Powers Act*—a point on which many commentators would agree. It will be interesting to see whether the federal district court grants standing.

38. Richardson (2002) highlights bureaucratic autonomy as a principal threat to democratic governance.

39. This is my shorthand summary of Ostrom's formulation (1989, 48–49; 1997, 103.) I first drew upon these ideas in my doctoral dissertation (Oakerson 1978) and developed them further in a paper prepared for the Panel on Common Property Resource Management of the National Academy of Sciences in 1985, later published (Oakerson 1992). Elinor Ostrom (1990) elaborated upon her husband's original formulation to build the IAD framework, which became the signature contribution of the Ostroms to the methodology of institutionalism.

40. Ostrom (1987, 95) emphasized the physical constraint that only one person in an assembly can speak and be heard at a time.

41. See Sinclair (2007, 17–18). As I was writing this chapter, a discharge petition succeeded in bringing to the floor a bill to reauthorize the Export-Import Bank, opposed by the conservative wing of the Republican Conference. It passed the House 313–118 and was sent to the Senate.

42. Teles (2014) argues, for example, that the Senate needs to become as majoritarian as the House. Manifestly, the House is not a majoritarian body. If it were, institutional deadlock would be greatly relieved.

43. Ostrom (1991, 43): "A democracy survives only so long as the rule of assembly is maintained with effective limits upon those who exercise leadership prerogatives and serve as agents of the assembly." By "democracy" in this passage Ostrom meant what he called a "simple, direct democracy." The same proposition would apply, nonetheless, to a representative assembly.

44. Molly C. Jackman (2013) provides a very useful history and analysis of the discharge rule in the House.

45. Ostrom (1987, 223) wrote as follows: "There may be counterintuitive circumstances, such as the oligarchical tendencies that arise in all deliberative assemblies, which require special safeguards. In such circumstances, people may find themselves trapped by preemptive moves where a few players learn how to set the agenda and dominate the play of the game. All of these contingencies require cautious regard for rules that establish appropriate restrictions."

46. Historically, the rule has varied from a low of one-third of the House (in 1931) to the simple majority now required (Jackman 2013).

47. In 2015, The *New York Times* published a discussion of the "Hastert Rule" that includes responses from former Republican House Speaker Newt Gingrich (in support of the rule) and former Republican member Mickey Edwards (opposed). See "Paul Ryan, the 'Hastert Rule' and Democracy on the Hill," October 23. http://www.nytimes.com/roomfordebate/2015/10/23/paul-ryan-the-hastert-rule-and-democracy-on-the-hill.

48. Elinor Ostrom conducted a series of highly influential studies of police services focused on the effects of department size. She concluded that small to medium-size departments consistently outperform large departments on a number of indicators. For summaries of the research program see Ostrom, Bish, and Ostrom (1988, Chapter 7) and Parks (2009).

49. Community monitoring is no easy fix. Efforts to introduce and sustain something called "community policing" have been active for decades—with federal grant support (Reisig 2010). Police professionalism and autonomy pose serious obstacles to substantive community involvement, as do collective action problems within neighborhoods (Kahan 2002; Herbert 2005). There are no shortcuts to representation on either side of the relationship, but I see no other workable means of accountability.

50. Although others might call the same combination a "liberal democracy," Ostrom did not employ this commonly used terminology, nor did he, to my knowledge, explain why. I suspect that he saw no purpose to be served—and much confusion to be sowed—by a qualification of "democracy" with the adjective "liberal," as if an "illiberal democracy" is possible. Only if democracy is identified solely with the unlimited power of popular majorities (or their elected representatives) to prescribe law is "illiberal democracy" a coherent use of language. The equal authority of persons to invoke rights protected by constitutional processes is not undemocratic; rather than limiting democracy, it enhances rule by the people.

REFERENCES

Adams, Willi Paul. 1980. *The First American Constitutions: Republican Ideology and the Making of the State Constitutions in the Revolutionary Era.* Chapel Hill: University of North Carolina Press.

Aligica, Paul Dragos. 2014a. "Citizenship, Political Competence, and Civic Studies: The Ostromian Perspective," in *Civic Studies: Approaches to the Emerging Field*, edited by Peter Levine and Karol Edward Sołtan, 33–44. Washington, DC: Bringing Theory to Practice.

Aligica, Paul Dragos. 2014b. *Institutional Diversity and Political Economy: The Ostroms and Beyond.* New York: Oxford University Press.

Arnold, R. Douglas. 1990. *The Logic of Congressional Action*. New Haven: Yale University Press.

Bish, Robert L. 2013. "Vincent Ostrom's Contributions to Political Economy." *Publius: The Journal of Federalism* 44: 227–48.

Bish, Robert L. and Vincent Ostrom. 1973. *Understanding Urban Government: Metropolitan Reform Reconsidered*. Washington, DC: American Enterprise Institute.

Buchanan, James M. and Gordon Tullock. 1962. *The Calculus of Consent: Logical Foundations of Constitutional Democracy*. Ann Arbor: The University of Michigan Press.

Chesterton, G. K. 1912. "The Voter and Two Voices." In *A Miscellany of Men*. Norfolk, VA: HIS Press. www.cse.dmu.ac.uk/~mward/gkc/books/misc.html.

Chivigny, Paul. 1969. *Police Power: Police Abuses in New York City*. New York: Vintage Books.

Chivigny, Paul. 1997. *Edge of the Knife: Police Violence in the Americas*. New York: The New Press.

Chomsky, Noam. 1980. *Rules and Representations*. New York: Columbia University Press.

Commons, John R. 1959. *Legal Foundations of Capitalism*. Madison: The University of Wisconsin Press. First published in 1924.

Creelan, Jeremy M. and Laura M. Moulton. 2004. *The New York State Legislative Process: An Evaluation and Blueprint for Reform*. New York: Brennan Center for Justice, NYU School of Law. http://www.brennancenter.org/publication/new-york-state-legislative-process-evaluation-and-blueprint-reform.

Cronin, Thomas E. 1989. *Direct Democracy: The Politics of Initiative, Referendum, and Recall*. Cambridge: Harvard University Press.

Dewey, John. 1927. *The Public and Its Problems*. New York: Holt.

Dewey, John. 1934. *Art as Experience*. New York: Capricorn Books.

Dewey, John. 1938. *Logic: The Theory of Inquiry*. New York: Holt.

Downs, Anthony. 1957. *An Economic Theory of Democracy*. New York: Harper and Row.

Fenno, Richard F., Jr. 2003. *Home Style: House Members in Their Districts*. New York: Longman.

Fukuyama, Francis. 2014. *Political Order and Political Decay: From the Industrial Revolution to the Globalization of Democracy*. New York: Farrar, Straus, and Giroux.

Gilens, Martin, and Benjamin I. Page. 2014. "Testing Theories of American Politics: Elites, Interest Groups, and Average Citizens." *Perspectives on Politics* 12: 564–81.

Hamilton, Alexander, John Jay, and James Madison. n.d. *The Federalist*. New York: Modern Library.

Herbert, Steve. 2005. "The Trapdoor of Community." *Annals of the Association of American Geographers* 95: 850–65. http://www.jstor.org.stable/3694016.

Jackman, Molly C. 2013. "Letting Majorities Rule: The Potential Impact of the Discharge Rule on the Fate of Immigration Reform," in *Governance Studies at Brookings* (August). Washington, DC: The Brookings Institution.

Kahan, Dan M. 2002. "Reciprocity, Collective Action, and Community Policing." *California Law Review* 90, 1513–39. http://www.jstor.org/stable/3481363.
Lasswell, Harold D. 1971. *A Pre-View of Policy Sciences*. Elsevier Publishing. www.policysciences.org/classics/preview.pdf.
Levinson, Sanford 2008. *Our Undemocratic Constitution*. Oxford: Oxford University Press.
Manin, Bernard. 1997. *The Principles of Representative Government*. Cambridge: Cambridge University Press.
Muir, William K. 1979. *Police: Streetcorner Politicians*. Chicago: The University of Chicago Press.
Oakerson, Ronald J. 1978. *The Erosion of Public Highways: A Policy Analysis of the Eastern Kentucky Coal-haul Road Problem*. PhD diss., Indiana University, Bloomington.
Oakerson, Ronald J. 1988. "Reciprocity: A Bottom-Up View of Political Development," in *Rethinking Institutional Analysis and Development: Issues, Alternatives, and Choices,* edited by Vincent Ostrom, David Feeny, and Hartmut Picht, 141–58. San Francisco: International Center for Economic Growth.
Oakerson, Ronald J. 1992. "Analyzing the Commons: A Framework," in *Making the Commons Work: Theory, Practice, and Policy*, edited by Daniel W. Bromley, et al., 41–59. San Francisco: ICS Press.
Oakerson, Ronald J. 1999. *Governing Local Public Economies: Creating the Civic Metropolis*. Oakland: ICS Press.
Oakerson, Ronald J. 2008. "The Politics of Place: Linking Rural and Environmental Governance," in *Frontiers in Resource and Rural Economics: Human-Nature, Rural-Urban Interdependencies,* edited by JunJie Wu, Paul W. Barkley, and Bruce A. Weber, 169–91. Washington, DC: Resources for the Future.
Olson, Mancur, Jr. 1965. *The Logic of Collective Action: Public Goods and the Theory of Groups*. Cambridge: Harvard University Press.
Olson, Mancur. 1969. "The Principle of 'Fiscal Equivalence': The Division of Responsibility among Different Levels of Government." *American Economic Review* 59: 479–87.
Ostrom, Elinor. 1990. *Governing the Commons: The Evolution of Institutions for Collective Acton*. New York: Cambridge University Press.
Ostrom, Vincent. 1971. *The Political Theory of a Compound Republic*. Blacksburg, VA: Public Choice.
Ostrom, Vincent. 1987. *The Political Theory of a Compound Republic: Designing the American Experiment*, 2nd ed. Lincoln and London: University of Nebraska Press.
Ostrom, Vincent. 1989. *The Intellectual Crisis in American Public Administration*, 2nd ed. Tuscaloosa and London: The University of Alabama Press.
Ostrom, Vincent. 1991. *The Meaning of American Federalism: Constituting a Self-Governing Society*. San Francisco: ICS Press.
Ostrom, Vincent. 1997. *The Meaning of Democracy and the Vulnerability of Democracies: A Response to Tocqueville's Challenge*. Ann Arbor: The University of Michigan Press.

Ostrom, Vincent. 2009. "Federalism, Polycentricity, and *Res Publica*: Some Reflections on the American Experiments in Republican Government," in *The Practice of Constitutional Development: Vincent Ostrom's Quest to Understand Human Affairs,* edited by Filippo Sabetti, Barbara Allen, and Mark Sproule-Jones, 31–57. Lanham, MD: Lexington Books. Originally presented to "*Res Publica*: East and West," Dubrovnik, Yugoslavia, October 10–14, 1988.

Ostrom, Vincent. 2011. *The Quest to Understand Human Affairs*, Vol. I., edited by Barbara Allen. Lanham, MD: Lexington Books.

Ostrom, Vincent. 2012. *The Quest to Understand Human Affairs*, Vol. 2, edited by Barbara Allen. Lanham, MD: Lexington Books.

Ostrom, Vincent, Robert Bish, and Elinor Ostrom. 1988. *Local Government in the United States*. San Francisco: ICS Press.

Parks, Roger B. 2009. "Metropolitan Organization and Police," in *The Practice of Constitutional Development: Vincent Ostrom's Quest to Understand Human Affairs*, edited by Filippo Sabetti, Barbara Allen, and Mark Sproule-Jones, 183–201. Lanham, MD: Lexington Books.

Pettit, Philip. 1997. *Republicanism: A Theory of Freedom and Government*. Oxford: Oxford University Press.

Pitkin, Hanna Fenichel. 1967. *The Concept of Representation*. Berkeley and Los Angeles: University of California Press.

Putnam, Robert D. 2000. *Bowling Alone: The Collapse and Revival of American Community*. New York: Simon & Schuster.

Rakove, Jack N. 1996. *Original Meanings: Politics and Ideas in the Making of the Constitution*. New York: Vintage Books.

Reisig, Michael D. 2010. "Community and Problem-Oriented Policing." *Crime and Justice* 39: 1–53, University of Chicago Press. http://www.jstor.org.stable/10.1086/652384.

Riker, William H. 1982. *Liberalism Against Populism: A Confrontation between the Theory of Democracy and the Theory of Social Choice*. Prospect Heights, IL: Waveland Press.

Sax, Joseph L. 1970. *Defending the Environment: A Handbook for Citizen Action*. New York: Vintage Books.

Shain, Barry Alan. 1994. *The Myth of American Individualism: The Protestant Origins of American Political Thought*. Princeton: Princeton University Press.

Sinclair, Barbara. 2007. *Unorthodox Lawmaking: New Legislative Processes in the U.S. Congress*, 3rd ed. Washington, DC: CQ Press.

Smith, Adam. 1966. *The Theory of Moral Sentiments*. New York: Augustus M. Kelley. Originally published in 1759.

Storing, Herbert J., ed. 1985. *The Anti-Federalist: Writing by Opponents of the Constitution*. Chicago and London: The University of Chicago Press.

Teles, Steven M. 2013. "Kludgeocracy in America." *National Affairs* 17. http://www.national affairs.com/publications/detail/kludgeocracy-in-america.

Tocqueville, Alexis de. 1945. *Democracy in America*, Vols. I and II. Translated by Phillips Bradley. New York: Vintage Books. Originally published in 1835.

Veit, Helen E., Kenneth R. Bowling and Charles Bangs Bickford, eds. 1991. *Creating the Bill of Rights: The Documentary Record from the First Federal Congress*. Baltimore and London: the Johns Hopkins University Press.
Wood, Gordon S. 1969. *The Creation of the American Republic 1776–1787*. New York and London: W. W. Norton.
Zakaria, Fareed. 2007. *The Future of Freedom: Illiberal Democracy at Home and Abroad*. New York and London: W. W. Norton.

Chapter 5

Polycentricity, Culture, and Covenant

Anas Malik

Does polycentricity have a particular, historically specific, cultural lineage, particularly in its covenantal origins? Are there particular intersubjective understandings and metaphysical foundational assumptions that lend themselves well to polycentric orders? Would a truly alien metaphysics render a polycentric order irreconcilable to the point of producing severe dysfunction or a split? This chapter explores the suggestion that covenanting implies a moral dimension that spurs deep trust and reciprocity, which precedes and cements the covenant underlying a polycentric order. I consider the Golden Rule basis of such a dimension, and suggest that this dimension can be apprehended by a style of research that integrates humanities and social sciences.

An apparent stream of thought that goes from Ibn Khaldun to Tocqueville to Vincent Ostrom's assessment (V. Ostrom 1997) seems to cross epistemological and ontological lines, and better explaining these helps map the potential for the legitimacy, success, and constitutional understandings on which polycentric arrangements are based. This provides motivation for my own research on inter-religious covenants, which I see as part of a broader effort to more thoroughly integrate or at least engage marginalized or underexplored political literatures from different cultural contexts into the literature on governance.

I note that my own training is in social science, rather than philosophy, and this exploration is an open-ended way to build dialogue around these questions. This chapter builds on my interactions with the Vincent and Elinor Ostrom and others in the Workshop in Political Theory and Policy Analysis when I was a graduate student in the 1990s. Covenant can be understood as a cultural feature, and I begin the chapter with a general description of culture and cultural variation as it relates to polycentricity. Next, the chapter introduces some ways of thinking about covenant in light of the Vincent Ostrom's engagement with the concept, and considers the significance of the concept for scholars in the present time. The chapter then describes some definitions of the term covenant, considers some of Vincent Ostrom's reflections on the challenges of building and maintaining covenant. Finally, the chapter considers some aspects of the legacy of the Enlightenment for our approaches to inquiry, particularly the split between sciences and humanities, and ends with some suggestions for continuing exploration of covenant in an integrative way.

CULTURE, SELF-GOVERNANCE, AND POLYCENTRICITY

Culture-based explanations of politics persist, even though "culture" is a much-contested concept. The presumption that covenant is a cultural feature necessitates a discussion of cultural variation. Samuel Huntington's widely cited "clash of civilizations" thesis asserts the essential primacy of several distinct major cultural groupings, such as "Islam" or "West" (Huntington 1993). From the perspective associated with Edward Said's influential *Orientalism*, large-label civilizations are characterized by profound hybridity, cross-fertilization, and coexistent internal contradictions. Any attempt to positively define a cultural essence is suspect, as it marginalizes other views (Said 1979, 2001).

In surveys of comparative politics, cultural variation or diversity is often understood as diversity in identities, attitudes, and ideas, and institutions (although institutions are sometimes conceived narrowly as only formal organizations of official government, rather than the fuller range of formal and informal rules that structure social interactions). A common assumption, usually implicit and unquestioned, is that institutions flow automatically or monotonically from identities, attitudes, and ideas. Many "cultural" practices can be readily mapped onto an institutional grammar. Mapping rules-in-use in different cultures and within shared cultures as shared expectations and "institutional facts" helps illuminate the complexity of cultural diversity. Much of the content of what is termed "culture" has to do with logics of appropriateness—tied to world-views, religious injunctions, customs and mores.

"Culture" can be understood as a community attribute that shapes the structure of action arenas (E. Ostrom 2005, 26).

> The term "culture" is frequently applied to the values shared within a community. Culture affects the mental models that participants in a situation may share. Cultures evolve over time faster than our underlying genetic endowment can evolve. Cultures have in turn affected how the human brain itself has evolved. . . . The history of experience with governance institutions at multiple

> levels affects the way local participants understand, implement, modify, or ignore rules written by external officials. . . .
>
> For example, when all participants share a common set of values and interact with one another in a multiplex set of arrangements within a small community, the probabilities of their developing adequate rules and norms to govern repetitive relationship are much greater. . . . The importance of building a reputation for keeping one's word is important in such a community, and the cost of developing monitoring and sanctioning mechanisms is relatively low. If the participants in a situation come from many different cultures, speak different languages, and are distrustful of one another, the costs of devising and sustaining effective rules are substantially increased. (E. Ostrom 2005, 27)

The above quote seems to suggest that cultural diversity is potentially a problem for governance in a small community. Shared cultural understandings can promote self-governance, and thus the autonomous capacities of local units. Diversity means fewer coordination solutions and more mistrust, which makes governance more costly at the local level.

This takes on a different level of meaning when there are multiple local decision units that must interact with and resolve collective action problems with each other. The situation where there are many local units with their own unique and distinct cultures (in Elinor Ostrom's sense) and that then have to deal with an "institutional collective action problem" (Fieock and Scholz 2009)—creating the collective arrangements for mutual well-being and productivity between collective choice units. The prospects for this would be greatly enhanced, and the costs of this greatly lowered, to the degree that there is a shared "culture" at the level of how collective choice units are to relate to each other—or, to put it in the terms of the original IAD framework, a constitutional understanding. That shared value may be understood a type of shared culture among collective choice units, or as a norm that is facilitate by shared culture. A polycentric order that lacks this shared value is likely to fall apart into suboptimal collective bads. In other words, cultural homogeneity within decision units is likely to facilitate governance. At the level of "institutional collective action," that is, collective action between collective choice units, some shared understanding—a second-order shared "culture"—is probably helpful.

Bloomington school scholars continue to discuss possible meanings of "polycentricity" (e.g., "Thinking Polycentricity" Workshop 2015). A frequently cited early definition of polycentricity associated with the Bloomington school comes from Ostrom, Tiebout, and Warren's article on metropolitan governance:

> "Polycentric" connotes many centers of decision making that are formally independent of each other. Whether they actually function independently, or

> instead constitute an interdependent system of relations, is an empirical question in particular cases. To the extent that they take each other into account in competitive relationships, enter into various contractual and cooperative undertakings, or have recourse to central mechanisms to resolve conflicts, the various political jurisdictions in a metropolitan area may function in a coherent manner with consistent and predictable patterns of interacting behavior. To the extent that this is so, they may be said to function as a "system." (Ostrom et al. 1961, 831)

This widely cited definition distinguishes a polycentric "system" from simply the joint presence of multiple decision units. Part of the constitution of a polycentric system is the shared understanding between decision units about how to take each other into account.

A critical issue for liberal assumptions about autonomous subjects has been the question of what anthropologist Saba Mahmood calls "life-worlds"—groups in whom individual meaning requires a set of collective arrangements, especially apparent when they diverge from the norms prevalent elsewhere in society. Retaining individual rights while recognizing and affirming groups continues remains a key challenge in constitutional arrangements. Political philosophers Will Kymlicka (1989) and Chandran Kukathas (2003) point to different possibilities for accommodating such diversity—the former in a multicultural liberal order, the latter in a libertarian arrangement. Neither use religious covenant as a starting point. In contrast, Daniel Elazar, emphasizes the covenantal religious origins of federal arrangements, and asserts that federalism potentially protects cultural integrities while working with the realities of power and political arrangements (Elazar 1987).

A polycentric order may be understood as an arrangement of mutual acceptance of the autonomy and integrity of different collective choice units. To the degree that each collective choice unit contains within it a distinct culture, a polycentric order might be a way to maximize cultural diversity—or, as Aliciga and Tarko (2013) suggest, to have greater potentials for normative heterogeneity. In contrast to monocentric models of deliberative democracy, which suggest a central state and a single public arena within which obtaining a normative consensus or convergence of public values ought to be of chief concern, "the polycentric approach is concerned with *the possibility of creating valued states of affairs from as many normative perspectives as possible*" (Aligica and Tarko 2013, 738 [italics in original]). That version seems to suggest that polycentric order is compatible with great cultural diversity—if we understand cultures as normative perspectives. To the degree that polycentricity is understood as a system that maximizes value heterogeneity, it can be said to be accommodating of cultural diversity. But that value heterogeneity has limits and bounds—namely, that the component decision units must respect the integrity of other jurisdictions. This is tricky to capture outside of particular cases, because the shape and nature of the jurisdictions is also subject change over time.

In the above view, polycentricity maximizes the potential for cultural diversity in a society by allowing different collective choice units the possibility of self-governing according to the rules their members find appropriate. As a general proposition, this seems to be appealing and possible, but the devil is in the details: what polycentricity, where, when, and how, and for whom? All these specifics are defined and negotiated in context-embedded, path-dependent ways. A certain basic mutual understanding—call it a shared culture of rules of the game—is needed in order to permit the flourishing of polycentric potentials. In other words, there must be a "culture of cultural diversity," shared understandings about permissible differences, for polycentricity to accommodate cultural differences.

POLYCENTRICITY AND COVENANT

Among Vincent Ostrom's significant contributions was an exploratory discussion of the nature of "covenant"—a premise for self-governing social orders—and how it might be expressed in different cultural settings. Covenant is a foundational affirmation of open-ended mutual obligation that is difficult to break even if it is not consistently reciprocated. Vincent initially emphasized monotheism and the Golden Rule as common denominators for covenants, outlining these in Christian, Jewish, and Muslim contexts, but his work does not exclude the possibility of other types of functioning covenants, in Confucian and other settings.

During the 1990s, Vincent was concerned with the vulnerability of self-governing orders that came about from the loss of intersubjective understandings. This happened with such phenomena as the manipulation of language, with "boss rule," and with the erosion of habits of heart and mind that sustained self-governing orders. Taken together, these might be considered a cultural shift, a cultural change over time. The key shared understanding underlying healthy self-governance was covenant: an open-ended obligation, not easily broken unilaterally, to continue to engage the other in the civic artisanship activities that made for productive relations. That way of thinking about it makes it sound like the health of the polycentric arrangements depended on maintaining covenant (or covenant-like) understandings, that is, primarily about performance. But there's something definitional too: the root of federal, *foedus*, means covenant, suggesting that a federal system is one based on covenant. One question this raised was about cross-cultural viability of polycentric orders. The title of Vincent Ostrom's book *The Meaning of Democracy and the Vulnerability of Democracies* (1997) gets at both the meaning and the performance aspects.

Yet there's a piece of this that continues to be difficult, possibly because of the disciplinary divides it crosses. One reason Vincent was so occupied with covenant—and with the root of usually religious language around covenant—was that it moved people (or legitimated their decision to move) in the direction of abiding by commitments. This has an ethical aspect to: why should be people be bound to act in certain ways? Rather than take this in the direction of infinite regress of prior institutional understandings, Vincent also talked about certain understandings as foundational. The Golden Rule was a pivotal understanding. To make sense, the Golden Rule had been grounded in another understanding—really an understanding of the cosmos and our place in it, in such views as the monotheistic traditions, but also other possibilities.

I recall that Vincent faced significant resistance when he first aired these ideas—partly because some social scientists found this to be a nonfalsifiable hypothesis or at least empirically difficult, but also, as a subtext, due to the disciplinary and societal presumptions of the separation of the metaphysical from discussions of the physical and the social. Yet it's worth remembering that the habits of a polycentric order are not only of the mind (what we tend to emphasize, sometimes based on an implicit logical positivism) but also the heart—an ethical and attitudinal orientation that is learned and transmitted through language. The civic habits underlying polycentric order can be considered part of a shared constitutional understanding. The general label "shared constitutional understanding" leaves open further specification of the substance of shared meanings that help bind people, and thus undergird social orders.

In this regard, the language of norms and first-person enforcement seems inadequate or partial, or at least demands some more explicit connection with the "classical" language of virtue and ethics, which seems more the domain of the humanities. To me, breaking that barrier helps in appreciating and comprehending some of Vincent's views. It was partly the reason for his interest in Ibn Khaldun, who wrote about the evolution of social solidarities predicated both on social-ecological settings (nomads vs. settled areas; rise, decline, and disruption processes) but also how this interacted with virtues.

That culture can serve to enable self-governance does not necessarily imply a functionalist or consequentialist understanding of the origins of culture. In my view, neither functionalist nor consequentialist logic fully captures the origins of the deep trust and reciprocity that allows decision units to interact in a way that resolves their institutional collective action problems. In other words, how that trust originates could just be from prior interactions where transactions are resolved—but they could also be from a sense of meaning and intersubjective understanding based on a presumed shared transcendent absolute, that shared transcendence being a reference point for covenant.

People's motivations as they understand them in this deeply embedded sense are not articulated in terms of transactions costs purely. Rather, they are articulated as emerging from moral obligation. That is where the sense of nonzero sum relations becomes important—although this dry label does not do justice to the inner meaning. Note that this does not mean that the pragmatics and the material self-interest portion of viable arrangements should be neglected.

Moral psychology has to do with meaning that is imputed to the arrangements. Our current use of "shared understanding" is often glossed over without substantial attention to content. The loss of this moral psychology of shared meaning will render polycentric arrangements fragile and brittle, not robust or resilient, and likely to fail altogether under conditions of substantial price shifts under which the bargaining power of decision units changes. This thesis has the potential to be investigated with qualitative comparative analysis, although it runs into the challenge of non-tautological or ex ante identification of covenant (discussed below), as well as the broader disciplinary hurdle placed by the "critical realism of logical positivism" wherein "the concept of normative inquiry makes no sense" (V. Ostrom 2011 [1982], 314).

SO WHAT?

Why does explicit attention to covenant matter? One reason is pragmatic: if polycentricity is an approach to governance and if it is to be relevant for our time of heavy cultural intersection and interaction, we must pay particular attention to the cultural and religious undergirdings. Our collective cross-community cross-cultural challenges demand some basis for intentional civic artisanship. The Golden Rule seems to be one that various theorists and faith communities (including humanists) have highlighted as a basis for productive interrelation. One can note its central position in Hobbes' path to peace, Kantian ethics, the grand moral theory of the Quran described by Draz (Abdelgawad 2014), and the principles of the Muslim-Christian outreach document called "A Common Word Between Us" (Malik 2013).

Another reason is semantic, and more broadly related to the problem of meaning, which became a major focus for Vincent Ostrom in his last major work (V. Ostrom 1997). In the Orwellian extreme, for example, the loss and alteration of meaning can lead to the same words being mobilized in support of almost the exact opposite social choices. How we understand the term federal has evolved—and with that evolution, have we lost something of the primacy of covenant? If so, to what extent to the concerns raised by

Tocqueville and others continue to be relevant for how we use the term today?

Yet another reason is epistemological: do we start from a pragmatist standpoint (which seems to be Paul Aligica's thoughtfully-articulated position (Aligica 2013)), or can a similar structure be generated from ordoliberal underpinnings, or from neoPlatonist or middle Platonist starting points (an area that I'm interested in exploring, specifically in relation to the work of the medieval philosopher Al-Farabi)? We may also consider what a historical-sociological or a postmodern historicist starting point would suggest. Covenant seems to play a different role in each epistemology. Thus the question of covenant can illuminate the diverse possible philosophical foundations of polycentric governance.

Additionally there is the normative question of why polycentricity should be considered good or desirable. There are different possible rationales from the different ontological and epistemological starting points. The Thomist (Thomas Aquinas' Catholic Aristotelianism) and a broader Christian preference for subsidiarity seems to fit rather well with polycentric arrangements-but does not square as well with liberal or postmodernist assumptions. Thus there might be parallel or competing normative arguments for or against polycentricity. The emphasis on efficiency and transactions costs seems to gloss over the key question of efficiency for what purpose. These normative clarifications may help specify that well.

DEFINING COVENANT

The moral psychology of Golden Rule covenants can be defined as an understanding of obligation to consider the well-being of the other as one would want done for oneself. It involves a leap of faith—and typically, repeated leaps of faith—rather than a purely egoistic strategic calculus. For convenience, I use "covenant" as short-hand for "moral psychology based on a Golden Rule covenantal shared understanding." Covenant is a specific type of constitutional-level shared understanding that promotes the trust and reciprocity needed in self-governing orders. The section below referring to Daniel Elazar's contribution is adapted from Malik (forthcoming a).

The term federalism can be traced to a "federal theology from foedus, or covenant, referring to the grounding of all human relationships in the original covenant between God and man described in the Bible and subsequent subsidiary pacts" (Elazar 2008, xii). "Covenant" may be defined as

> a morally informed agreement or pact based upon voluntary consent and mutual oaths or promises, witnessed by the relevant higher authority, between peoples

> or parties having independent thought not necessarily equal status, that provides for joint action or obligation to achieve defined ends (limited or comprehensive) under conditions of mutual respect which protect the individual integrities of all the parties to it. Every covenant involves consenting, promising, and agreeing. Most are meant to be of unlimited duration, if not perpetual. Covenants can bind any number of partners of partners for a variety of purposes, but in their essence they are political in that their bonds are used principally to establish bodies political and social. (Elazar 1998b, 8)

To Elazar, covenants are usually religiously grounded: at its core, a covenant is "an agreement in which a transcendent moral force, traditionally god, is a party" (Elazar 1998c, 7).

Elazar's work is tied to the Judeo-Christian tradition, and seems to have missed comparable Islamic contexts. This may have to do with the lineage of scholarship on covenant. Several covenant thinkers, including Martin Buber, Mordecai Kaplan, and Daniel Elazar, were Jewish; others, like William James and Reinhold Neibuhr, came from a reformed Protestant tradition. Kaplan suggested that all people had a covenanting bond (Elazar n.d.). To Elazar, a federal consociational polity starts with the Bible.

Premodern confederations emphasized defense and had few economic ties (Elazar 1998e, 44). Ancient premodern confederations featured constituent units were integral polities wherein all citizens were expected to follow the same religion and cultivate the same virtues; these were often amphictyonies, being formally united by religion, often around a central shrine (Elazar 1998e, 44). The Adat Bnai Yisrael, an Israelite polity from the thirteenth century BC (as described in the Bible) saw people and tribes united in pursue of a common virtue: living a God-fearing life under the terms of God's covenant with them" (Elazar 1998e, 45).

My own recent scholarship has explored the covenantal tradition in Islamic contexts. In his list of "Exemplary Premodern Federal and Protofederal Systems," (Elazar 1998e, 43, Table 2.1) Elazar does not list a single Muslim arrangement, although the Medina covenant appears to fit. Moreover, his list of premodern polities misses the Muslim empires that incorporated those of other religions, most prominently the Abrahamic faiths, and, in the Mughal case (although not consistently or uniformly), Hindu and other populations.

Vincent Ostrom wondered whether Islam had something similar to the image of Jacob wrestling with the Divine command, which he considered important to defining the covenanting, problem-solving society (V. Ostrom 1996). Muslim religious scholars typically depict Islam as a continuation of the Abrahamic tradition (to which the Judeo-Christian tradition also belongs). Further, the fallibilist premises of much of the Islamic jurisprudential tradition, in which scholars of religious scholars offer verdicts on legal questions while acknowledging the existence or possibility of alternative legal positions, presupposes contestation in the religious traditional approach to rule-giving. Describing prominent covenants in the Islamic sacred history period suggests that there is basis for identifying covenants within the normative Islamic religious tradition, and Vincent Ostrom came to recognize Islam's commonality with Judaism and Christianity (V. Ostrom 1997, 228–29).

Elazar distinguishes between covenant, compact, and contract. "Compact" and "contract" are both derived from covenant, but are sometimes (confusingly) used interchangeably. Covenants and compacts are both constitutional and public; contracts are private and express private law, and are accordingly "interpreted as narrowly as possible so as to limit the obligation of the contracting parties to what is explicitly mandated by the contract itself" (Elazar 1998c, 7). Covenants and compacts are both about reciprocal obligations, but in a covenant, the "morally binding dimension takes precedence over its legally binding dimension" (Elazar 1998c, 7). In a compact, moral force is only indirect; "rather than the guarantees of a higher authority, [a compact] rests more heavily on a legal though still ethical grounding for its politics" (Elazar 1998c, 8;[1] Malik forthcoming b). Sabetti (2000) offers a set of helpful questions addressing Elazar's view of covenant:

> As a mode of political association, covenant contains a strong primordial element of kinship and communitarianism. Does this rule out of the constitutional order people who do not share these kinds of covenants? Does the covenantal base have to apply to all considerations and all values of life, or can there be a limited covenantal base that allows diverse communities to share in more general communities of interest and a common political nationality? In fine, what understanding and considerations apply to the covenantal base of plural societies? (Sabetti 2000 [1982], 259–60)

Sabetti's questions summarize central issues in the discussion of covenant and polycentricity. This chapter can be seen as a close fellow traveler to these questions, informed by my own trajectory.

One approach to addressing whether covenants require grounding in a traditional religion is to have a broad, big-tent notion of what precisely defines covenant. Covenants "imbue the citizen with the responsibility and moral commitment to struggle with others in recognizing and solving commonly confronted problems" (Shivakumar 2005, 8; cites Allen 2005). In Sujai Shivakumar's expansive view, covenants are common to all civilizations, although different in cultural expression (Shivakumar 2005, 8; cites a study on covenanting indigenous African societies). Prominent recent efforts at generating a global interreligious covenant include the Common Word document and several related and allied initiatives (Malik 2013; Malik forthcoming a).

To Tocqueville, civil associations—if exclusive enclaves—promote an "insularity" that undermines liberty (Allen 2005, 136). Tocqueville was suspicious of mass rallies, and concerned that they were prerevolutionary fervor rather than demonstrative of democratic attitudes (Allen 2005, 136). This raises the centrality of covenant: "Institutions are animated by ideas as well as interests, Tocqueville maintained; where federations lacked covenantal thinking, institutional arrangements might not encourage constructive forms of civil and political association" (Allen 2005, 132).

One way to read Tocqueville is to ask whether the democratic revolution of the past 1000 years contains within it the mechanisms and energies to sustain the social order. This is one point where religion, the first political institution in Tocqueville's view, carries significance: it provides the community with motivation to persist in the covenant in the face of challenges, as well as the practical training and mores needed for enacting the covenant.

Vincent Ostrom (1990) elaborated on Tocqueville's concern that a "cognitive bias" in democracies will make people increasingly infantile and unable to more rigorously address themselves to common problems or hold rulers to account, producing a democratic despotism. Self-governing habits and the moral psychology that drives these can combat this tendency. Thus, a key problem is how covenanting values that undergird civic associations can be transmitted across generations, and how a culture of covenant may be preserved and replenished over time.

BUILDING AND MAINTAINING COVENANT

Vincent Ostrom criticized the tendency to reduce political science to who gets what when and how, and the gradual focus on regularities over the process of conscious deliberation in constituting orders. In Vincent's words, from his essay on normative context of community: "What was conceptualized by the Hebrews, renewed in the organization of European religious communities in the sixteenth century and used to launch a new venture in civil communities in the early seventeenth century may seem to have very little to do with the contemporary world . . ." (V. Ostrom 2011 [1982], 313). After pointing out that the God references sound quaint to many modern ears, Vincent Ostrom goes on to assert that in rejecting the concept of God,

> People may be incapable of yielding themselves to the appropriate presuppositions for conducting an inquiry into the grounds for human community. The presumption that human beings share a basic similitude of thoughts and passions may also be abandoned. No basis would then exist for developing a common idea of right as Tocqueville would express it, a moral philosophy as Hobbes would express it, or a concept of natural justice as Smith would express it (V. Ostrom 2011 [1982], 313)

In other words, the intersubjective affirmation of God provides a basis for shared understandings on why community is founded. Whether this is a necessary or a sufficient basis (or some joint version of necessary or sufficient) remains unclear, at least in my reading of Vincent Ostrom's work to this point. Indeed, the very presumption of necessity and sufficiency as propositions to be verified empirically in the social scientific mode are limited in addressing a metaphysical question. The above quote seems to suggest that the necessary condition is a "presumption that human beings share a basic similitude of thoughts and passions"; this logically follows from a belief in God.

Vincent's essay on normative context skips over the Islamic period in an all-too-common blind spot, one due mainly to the Eurocentric nature of many modern educational curricula. Unusually though (for American scholarship), Vincent became very interested in the fourteenth-century pioneering Muslim sociologist Ibn Khaldun. Vincent came to believe that Tocqueville, in seeking a "science of culture," was at least a clear fellow traveler to (if not directly or indirectly influenced by) Ibn Khaldun.

Tocqueville and Ibn Khaldun both saw a version of solidarity or group-feeling as essential to the health of societies. The social order would become increasingly brittle and vulnerable as its institutional forms became further relegated to third-party enforcement. Eventually the settled/civilized order would be displaced and undone, too administratively top-heavy to flexibly adapt to new challenges- and would be displaced or replaced by another community with great solidarity and group feeling; over time that community would settle, and eventually face the same challenges of loss of group feeling. To Ibn Khaldun this was a cyclic phenomenon.[2]

W. Cantwell Smith's comment in reflecting on the potential for an Islamic democracy captures the theme of an ethical basis well. In Smith's view, an Islamic democracy

> Has both a political and an ethical element: it cannot exist without the concurrence of both a governmental form and a popular ideal. [. . .] A democrat must believe not only in the democratic structure of the state; he must believe also in the fundamental significance and value of the other persons in his society. An association of cynics, or of misanthropes, or even of mutually contemptuous groups, could not run a democracy. [. . .] The members must [. . .] have a certain commitment to man, a certain trust in each other. (Smith 1951, 47)

This quote, in its emphasis on an inner conviction about the similitudes between persons, and the related affirmation of the value of the other, is closely complementary to Vincent Ostrom's understanding of some Enlightenment philosophers.

Keeping the covenantal outlook alive requires the transmission of virtues through education, and virtue in this view requires a shared understanding regarding the transcendent. Education can mold a shared culture, socializing students into logics of appropriateness. Consider the quote ascribed to Thomas Jefferson on education:

> No people can remain free unless they are properly educated. Education consists of teaching and learning virtues. And no people can remain virtuous unless both the personal and public lives of the individual person are infused with awareness and love of Divine Providence. (Crane 2012)

It is a pressing question whether humanism, or conceptions of human dignity not "infused with an awareness of the divine" as Thomas Jefferson put it, can provide the common basis for virtue. My own initial view is that this is quite possible, indeed likely, insofar as it retains a humility rather than a tyrannical or totalitarian monocentric, supremacist attitude—a grand pitfall that formed a critical concern for Tocqueville and George Orwell, as Vincent Ostrom's last major work *The Meaning of Democracy and the Vulnerability of Democracies* (V. Ostrom 1997) suggests.

POLYCENTRICITY AND ENLIGHTENMENT EPISTEMOLOGY: SOME FOUNDATIONAL QUESTIONS

As a graduate student, I was struck by the energetic reaction against Vincent's focus on the theology of covenant and particularly the virtues of monotheistic foundations. Vincent was drafting and presenting portions of the manuscript *The Meaning of Democracy and the Vulnerability of Democracies* and he was trying to take the theo-centered understanding of covenant seriously. One problem he sought to articulate was that of the role of monotheism in providing a foundation for social order. At the time he emphasize a particularly Christian and Jewish sense of this. His presentation was challenged by very competent younger social scientific faculty at the Workshop as being non-falsifiable, and therefore not a tenable avenue for further exploration in a social scientific context. Vincent, who remained intellectually curious and read expansively, took the criticism in stride, and stuck to his guns—but the further dialogue on this element of his exploration was stalled.

In my view, Vincent faced opposition during our Workshop meetings in the late 1990s because he went against a rule of how governance and social order was to be investigated—it was to be done without going into the substance of religious thought on its own terms. His transgression was to cross the boundary from "normal" (normatively defined) social scientists criteria of falsifiability and empiricism into the deep theological and philosophical foundations of culturally specific worldviews, which cannot be subjected to the rules of appropriateness that have guided much social scientific research. At another level, this was a discussion of claims about absolute Truth, rather than claims about the empirically verifiable social regularities that prevail in social scientific discussions. It also raised an uncomfortable and uninterrogated premise that some social scientists carry—"scientism," a philosophical view, often implicit, about the truth emerging from scientific inquiry:

> Scientism adds to science two corollaries: first, that the scientific method is, if not the *only* reliable method of getting at truth, then at least the *most* reliable method; and second, that the things science deals with—material entities—are the most fundamental things that exist. (Smith 2000, 233)

The scientific method, particularly the ideal of the controlled experiment as a way to separate true from false hypotheses, has preeminent station in the world-views of many social scientists, and yet this method does not and cannot get at the dimensions of inquiry into cultural diversity.

Thus, a principal challenge from a social scientific perspective is the difficulty in generating a falsifiable, testable proposition regarding covenants. Since this is a matter of the heart, the outward manifestations of covenant are possibly deceptions and self-deceptions; they represent less the Golden Rule as a rule-in-use than a claim, one that may be made in order to cover up gaps in other—regarding behavior in particular contexts. If the presence of covenant is only apparent in outcomes, then it cannot be tested. If covenant is identified semantically with good outcomes in resilience and adaptability, then it is a tautology and not a proposition relating two variables. Additionally, there is the persistent difficulty of strategic representation, that is, instrumental use of covenant and other symbols representing shared understanding, the erosion of which can undermine meaningful communication and with it the potential for shared understanding.

My view is that these questions cannot be addressed unless we better articulate our own culture of knowledge around the inquiry; in other words, how we understand and articulate "covenant," "self," "polycentricity" and "cultural diversity." In brief, my sense is that we in the Bloomington school community are largely embedded in a world-view that separates the "science" from the "humanities," the physics from the metaphysics, and as a result have difficulties or complications in trying to address the question of diversity in an integrated way. A fuller assessment of cultural diversity and polycentricity must go beyond the culturally specific assumptions about knowledge and culture itself. Without that, we cannot begin bridge the divide between different foundational understandings and their consequences.

The Enlightenment can be interpreted in different ways, as seen in the essays titled "An Answer to the Question: 'What is Enlightenment?' by

Immanuel Kant (2016 [1784]) and the essay with the same title written by Michel Foucault (1984). Despite divergences, according to the famous evaluation of Theodore Adorno and Max Horkheimer (2002), our "modern" culture is a child of the Enlightenment, and it tends to discredit claims that are not measurable, especially in quantitative ways: "For the Enlightenment, whatever does not conform to the rule of computation and utility is suspect" (Adorno and Horkheimer 2002 [1944], 6).

A common implicit metaphysical claim in the era since the Enlightenment period is the scientistic notion that the full reality can be grasped through empirical investigation with scientific methods. Certain paradoxes in empirical and theoretical explorations appear to pose difficulties for the scientistic perspective. For example, experimental science depends on a separation of the "zone of measurement" from the "zone of experiment." This was challenged most memorably by the double slit experiment, in which light behaves as a wave until a detector is put in place-at which point the light acts as a particle. The presence of the observer appears in a mysterious way to change the nature of the object. Heisenberg's uncertainty principle suggests limits to empirical determination. Godel's Incompleteness Theorem suggests that a perfectly self-enclosed system of logic is impossible. These are ways that modern scientific and theoretical investigations have pushed us to apparent boundaries of the knowable within the existing ways of knowing, leading to a variety of conjectures about alternative premises, some of which touch on the metaphysical.

Whether we are intentional about it or not, we bring metaphysical assumptions to our inquiry. In effect, we make truth-claims from metaphysical premises, hence why not incorporate the metaphysical more explicitly into the study of culture? At this juncture, it may be helpful to distinguish the intersubjective from the transcendent and the metaphysical. The subjective is that which is perceived and felt by the subject, and is dependent on the mind of the individual for its existence. The intersubjective is what two or more subjects have agreed upon or tacitly arrived at as a shared understanding. The transcendent, in contrast, is that which is beyond physical experience, and exists irrespective of the subjective understanding of it. Metaphysics is the branch of knowledge dealing with the nature of reality, being, and knowing—famously, the question of whether reality lies beyond what can be experienced, or whether the objects of experience form the only reality.

It seems to me that the underlying issue raised through Vincent's transgression was beyond the capacity of the social scientific method to resolve. Simply put, observations could themselves not be the basis or the assertion that the only reality was the observable. Why this matters for our discussion is due to the question of whether polycentric orders rely for their success on specific metaphysical claims. It strikes me that this is an area for significant additional inquiry. A truly alien metaphysics would probably render a polycentric order irreconcilable to the point of producing severe dysfunction or a split. A shared metaphysics is important. This is the basis for civic virtue that provides a motor for the order.

The presumption of separation between subject and object is also not strictly tenable in real-life situations for the most part, without artificial segregations. There's the paradox of predictability (Engel 2005, cited in Aligica 2014), wherein any prediction about future behavior is undermined by reflexivity, as agents update their knowledge and thus, behavior, having considered the prediction. The researcher is part of the experiment. The act of measurement changes things, as does the report and the dissemination of findings. Perfect predictability is impossible because strategic actors can take the previous findings into account and adjust their behavior accordingly, thus creating new outcomes.

THE ENLIGHTENMENT SPLIT

Vincent's Ostrom's repeated emphasis on artisanal intent in the deliberative effort to create and adjust social rules seems to require thinking about more than the efficient and material conditions alone—it seems to require thinking about formal and final causes too.[3] Yet our social scientific disciplinary thinking repeatedly pushes us away from formal and final causes in favor of an exclusive emphasis on efficient and material causes.

The modern scientific focus on efficient and material causes was expressed by the influential Francis Bacon, who asserted that physics inquires only into the material and efficient causes of natures, whereas metaphysics investigates the eternal, immutable forms:

> Let the investigation of forms, which are (in the eye of reason at least, and in their essential law) eternal and immutable, constitute Metaphysics; and let the investigation of the efficient cause, and of matter, and of the latent process, and the latent configuration (all of which have reference to the common and ordinary course of nature, not to her eternal and fundamental laws) constitute Physics. And to these let there be subordinate two practical divisions: to Physics, Mechanics; to Metaphysics, what (in a purer sense of the word) I call Magic, on account of the broadness of the ways it moves in, and its greater command over nature. (Bacon 1620)

The "practical divisions" Bacon refers to have influenced our disciplinary structures. Other influential figures, such as Giambattista Vico, thought the Cartesian method was valuable but could not be applied to the civic sphere.

This translated into the focus on efficient and material causes for the natural and observable, and final and formal causes for the civic sphere. And it is precisely at this juncture that tensions become apparent in the Bloomington school between considering covenant as a source of meaning and metaphysical postulate as well as an enabling shared understanding, a kind of metaconstitutional foundation for social order.

The full encounter with cultural diversity should consider a culture of knowing that takes other forms of knowledge seriously. The formal and final causes are a valuable point of entry to this conversation. I emphasize that this is not necessarily an "answer" partly because my training is as a social scientist rather than as a philosopher, but also because the spirit of the Bloomington school emphasizes a polycentric approach to addressing scholarly problems.

One argument is that the health of self-governing polycentric understandings depends on the quality of the underlying covenant. The quality of the covenant depends on its operation and manifestation in all four types of causes. In particular, there is its role in "exemplary cause": a subtype of formal cause, the idea in a mind that gives rise to a thing. This appears to connect closely to citizen artisanship that to my knowledge has not previously made explicitly in the Bloomington school scholarship. And yet it provides one promising element in a broader strategy for integrative understanding of the foundations of polycentric orders, and their potentials and limits in diverse cultural contexts.

Consider the terms "intersubjective," "transcendent," and "metaphysical," and the overlaps between these, as well as shared starting points-epistemological and ontological starting points. Most social scientists in the Bloomington school seem comfortable with asserting that intersubjective understandings vary between (and often, within) cultures. But there are some perspectives that treat "cultures" or "true religions" as subsets of one grand central wisdom, one mountain with many paths of ascent, as in the perennialist view. Others take the extreme opposite, where every essentializing attempt does violence to marginalized other views, and a person even marginalizes other aspects of their own self when they impose a single understanding. So one extreme insists that no generalization is possible, while the other interprets varied cultural experience according to a general metaphysics of being.

TOWARD CONTINUING EXPLORATION AND DIALOGUE

Our present approach to inquiry on covenant, culture, and polycentricity is dominated by an Enlightenment epistemology that emphasizes efficient and material causes and divorces these from formal and final causes, and in the process, impedes our explorations. Bloomington school scholars can enrich their inquiry by revivifying the eclectic style and multidisciplinary openness of Vincent Ostrom in approaching such questions, particularly when it comes to reading in the humanities.

Getting at cultural diversity more fully requires attention to inquiry in both humanities and social scientific arenas. This may be well served by systematic inquiry into not just into the material and efficient conditions of culture, but also the formal and final causes of culture. An emphasis on exemplary causes presents a key link between artisanship (a core self-governance activity in the Ostroms' approach) and the realm of formal and final causes so little considered by the "scientific" side of the school. The Enlightenment-influenced bifurcation into realms of inquiry has made this difficult within one "school" of research. Vincent Ostrom's work increasingly bridged this divide, particularly in *The Meaning of American Federalism*, and especially in *The Meaning of Democracy and the Vulnerability of Democracies* (1997). His eclecticism met with some resistance, and certain key strands of his thinking, particularly those related to covenant and the metaphysical roots of human similitude and sympathy, need further exploration. Vincent's fascination with Ibn Khaldun can also be understood not solely in terms of the remarkable parallels between Ibn Khaldun and Tocqueville's inquiry (and the possible direct influence of Ibn Khaldun's work on Tocqueville's) but also because Ibn Khaldun draws on a philosophical foundation that, while premodern, tries to systematically consider all types of cause in explaining culture and outcomes.

While much work remains to be done in exploring definitions of culture and polycentricity, a major area of continuing inquiry should be to go beyond the Vico-exemplified Enlightenment era fissure between efficient and material causes on the one hand and formal and final causes on the other hand. This division presumes that the scientific realm has little connection to the civic realm. Part of the strong emphasis of Vincent Ostrom's work in particular was on covenant, and the human connection and similitude that promoted self-governing orders. A major step for research in the Bloomington school must be to consider ways of knowledge that are not locked into the specific cultural lineage of one path from the Enlightenment era.

NOTES

1. For those familiar with the Islamic context, the Aqaba pledge, and the Medina covenant, would both fit Elazar's definition of covenant. The Hilf ul Fudul would more likely be characterized as a compact, unless we treat the principle of justice as a

transcendent. The general action required in taking baiyat involves voluntary consent and a mutual oath, as seen in Abu Bakr's pledge as Khalifa, which likely fits covenant too.

2. Ibn Khaldun, a fascinating polymath of the fourteenth century CE, continues to attract scholarly attention; interested readers can find some starting points in the earlier works of Issawi (1987) and Mahdi (1971).

3. The distinction between final, formal, material, and efficient causes can be traced to Aristotle. Proper knowledge of a thing, Aristotle claimed in the *Posterior Analytics*, required that we have grasped its cause—the "why."

> In *Physics* II 3 and *Metaphysics* V 2, Aristotle offers his general account of the four causes. This account is general in the sense that it applies to everything that requires an explanation, including artistic production and human action. Here Aristotle recognizes four types of things that can be given in answer to a why-question:
>
> - The material cause: 'that out of which,' for example, the bronze of a statue.
> - The formal cause: 'the form,' 'the account of what-it-is-to-be,' for example, the shape of a statue.
> - The efficient cause: 'the primary source of the change or rest,' for example, the artisan, the art of bronze-casting the statue, the man who gives advice, the father of the child.
> - The final cause: 'the end, that for the sake of which a thing is done,' for example, health is the end of walking, losing weight, purging, drugs, and surgical tools.
>
> All the four (types of) causes may enter in the explanation of something" (Falcon 2015).

REFERENCES

Aliciga, Paul and Vlad Tarko. 2013. "Co-Production, Polycentricity and Value Heterogeneity: The Ostroms' Public Choice Institutionalism Revisited." *American Political Science Review* 107(4): 726–41.

Aligica, Paul. 2014. *Institutional Diversity and Political Economy: the Ostroms and Beyond*. Oxford University Press.

Bacon, Francis. 2016 [1620]. *The New Organon*. Book II, Aphorism 9. Accessed May 8, 2016. http://www.constitution.org/bacon/nov_org.htm.

Crane, Robert. 2012. "Justice as Grand Strategy: The Missing Dimension in American Foreign Policy Toward the Muslim World." August 25. Accessed May 8 2016. http://www.tikkun.org/nextgen/justice-as-grand-strategy-the-missing-dimension-in-american-foreign-policy-toward-the-muslim-world.

Elazar, Daniel. 1987. *Exploring Federalism*. Tuscaloosa: University of Alabama Press.

Elazar, Daniel. 1998. *Covenant and Civil Society: the Constitutional Matrix of Modern Democracy*. New Brunswick, New Jersey: Transaction Publishers.

Falcon, Andrea. 2015. "Aristotle on Causality." *The Stanford Encyclopedia of Philosophy* (Spring 2015 Edition), edited by Edward N. Zalta. Accessed March 9, 2016. http://plato.stanford.edu/archives/spr2015/entries/aristotle-causality/.

Feiock, Richard C., and John T. Scholz, eds. 2009. *Self-Organizing Federalism: Collaborative Mechanisms to Mitigate Institutional Collective Action Dilemmas*. Cambridge University Press.

Foucault, Michel. 1984. "What is Enlightenment?" in *The Foucault Reader*, edited by Paul Rabinow, 32–50. New York: Pantheon Books.

Huntington, Samuel P. 1993. "The Clash of Civilizations?" *Foreign Affairs* 72(3) (Summer 1993): 22–49.

Issawi, Charles. 1987. *An Arab Philosophy of History: Selections from the Prolegomena of Ibn Khaldun of Tunis*. Darwin Press.

Kant, Immanuel. 2016 [1784]. "An Answer to the Question: 'What is Enlightenment?'" Accessed June 2, 2016. http://philosophy.eserver.org/kant/what-is-enlightenment.txt.

Kukathas, Chandran. 2003. *The Liberal Archipelago: A Theory of Diversity and Freedom*. Oxford University Press.

Kymlicka, Will. 1989. *Liberalism, Community, and Culture*. Oxford: Oxford University Press.

Mahdi, Muhsin. 1971. *Ibn Khaldun's Philosophy of History: A Study in the Philosophic Foundation of the Science of Culture*. University of Chicago Press.

Malik, Anas. 2013. "Reconciliation between Muslims and Christians: Collective Action, Norm Entrepreneurship, and 'A Common Word Between Us.'" *Journal of Religious Ethics* 41(3): 457–73.

Malik, Anas. Forthcoming a. *The Polycentric Islamic Polity*. Lanham, MD: Lexington Books.

Malik, Anas. Forthcoming b. *Islamic Interreligious Covenants: Pathways to Peace and Prosperity?* London: Palgrave.

Ostrom, Elinor. 2005. *Understanding Institutional Diversity*. Princeton, NJ: Princeton University Press.

Ostrom, Vincent. 1990. "Problems of Cognition as a Challenge to Policy Analysts and Democratic Societies." *Journal of Theoretical Politics* 2(3): 243–62. Reprinted as Chapter 17 in Michael McGinnis. ed. 1999. *Polycentric Governance and Development: Readings from the Workshop in Political Theory and Analysis*. Ann Arbor: University of Michigan Press.

Ostrom, Vincent. [1982] 2011. "The Normative Context of Community," in *The Quest to Understand Human Affairs: Natural Resources Policy and Essays on Community and Collective Choice (Volume 1)*, edited by Barbara Allen, 291–317. Lexington Books.

Ostrom, Vincent. 1997. *The Meaning of Democracy and the Vulnerability of Democracies*. Ann Arbor: University of Michigan Press.

Sabetti, Filippo. [1982] 2000. "Covenant Language in Canada: Continuity and Change in Political Discourse." In *The Covenant Connection: From Federal Theology to Modern Federalism*, edited by D. J. Elazar and J. Kincaid, 259–84. Lanham, MD: Lexington Books.

Said, Edward W. 1979. *Orientalism*. Knopf Doubleday.

Said, Edward W. 2001. "The Clash of Ignorance." *The Nation*, October 4. Accessed June 1, 2016. http://www.thenation.com/article/clash-ignorance/.

Shivakumar, Sujai. 2005. *The Constitution of Development: Crafting Capabilities for Self-Government*. New York: Palgrave Macmillan.
Siedentop, Larry. 2014. *Inventing the Individual: The Origins of Western Liberalism*. Cambridge: Harvard University Press.
Smith, Huston. 2000. *Why Religion Matters: The Fate of the Human Spirit in an Age of Disbelief*. San Francisco: Harper.
Smith, W. Cantwell. 1951. *Pakistan as an Islamic State*. Lahore, Pakistan: Ashraf Press.
Various Participants. 2015. "Thinking Polycentrically." Workshop on Polycentricity, December 14–18 2015, Ostrom Workshop. Bloomington: Indiana University.
Wolterstorff, Nicholas. 2013. "Is it Possible and Sometimes Desirable for States to Forgive?" *Journal of Religious Ethics* 41: 417–34.

Chapter 6

Social Learning and the Bonds of Self-Governing Communities

Dario Castiglione

A cake can be cut in many ways, and so can politics. We can "cut" politics by distinguishing different modes or levels of political action and decision making, such as constitutional politics (about the general rules) and normal politics (about the allocation of roles and resources). We can cut it by opposing different conceptions of where the real and/or legitimate core of politics lies; whether, for instance, in the exercise of power, or in the development of autonomous forms of organization, or in the protection of personal liberty. We can also cut politics by focusing on different styles and scopes of political activity: politics as mainly a problem-solving exercise, or as a more transformative process through which individuals and communities shape their identities and environment, make their commitments, and try to control their future. None of these ways of cutting politics exclude the others, and the different distinctions, as we shall see, may overlap in interesting ways. In this chapter, I wish to focus on the latter distinction in particular, as a way of exploring the institutional theory underlying the work of Elinor and Vincent Ostrom, and the kind of direction they gave to the Bloomington research programme. My strong intuition is that they clearly belong, by both training and vocation, to the camp that conceives politics as people coming together to find solutions to their separate and joint problems. Some of their insights on how such solutions are arrived at, however, make their vision of politics receptive to a more "transformative" style of it. From a more substantive perspective, I want to focus on how their conception of the institutionalized forms of collective action and social learning, often applied to local communities and to both the organization and administration of common services and resources, connects to a more general understanding of the nature of self-governing political communities.

The distinction between problem-solving and transformative politics is not categorical in a strict sense, but, as already suggested, a matter of *style* or an assumption about what politics do, or should do. It often comes with epistemological and ideological commitments that may reflect and reinforce that particular view of what politics is about. This is also the case with the Ostroms. Part of my argument, however, is that the "openness" and at times declared eclecticism of the Ostroms' research program pose questions and address issues that transcend politics as problem-solving. There is an obvious sense in which their intellectual and academic journey took them from an early interest in public administration and metropolitan reform to forms and principles of political governance in general (Aligica and Boettke 2009, 7–29). There is a particular way in which their approach was interstitial, between empirical, analytical and normative research, multi-methods and multi-disciplinary, using evidence from anthropology, history, sociology, law, as well as economics and politics. Such an open-minded attitude inevitably produces questions and puzzles that push the boundaries of one's chosen outlook and approach.

There is also, in the Ostroms' work, a certain academic "marginality" (McGinnis 2011; Aligica and Boettke 2011, 45; Castiglione 2014, xiv–xvii) to those research traditions, such as public choice, political economy, rational choice institutionalism, and federal constitutionalism, which they themselves contributed to establish, and to which their research is often associated. Such marginality is partly the result of the interstitial and eclectic nature of their work and approach, which has not prevented them from being generally recognized as important contributors to those traditions, but has perhaps clouded the appreciation of the innovative elements of their research programme.[1] Nonetheless, both Elinor and Vincent Ostrom have on occasion vindicated such marginality, as Elinor did in her 1997 Presidential Address to the American Political Science Association (APSA), when she provocatively started by arguing that what "our ancestors" have long learned in solving social dilemmas "is not, however, understood by the extant theory of collective action" (Ostrom and Ostrom 2014 [1998], 121). Notice that this was 1997. If anything, Vincent Ostrom's vindication of that marginality was even more self-consciously provocative toward standard approaches: "work on the periphery is where important advances at the frontier are most likely to occur" (Ostrom and Ostrom 2014 [1997], 244). There is an echo here of a Kuhnian conception of paradigm change in scientific revolutions, something also hinted at in Elinor Ostrom's introduction to a volume recommending a move "beyond positivism" in political science at the start of the 1980s (Ostrom and Ostrom 2014 [1982]; see also V. Ostrom 2008a, 11–15).

The originality of the work that the Ostroms did on the periphery of some of the dominant research paradigms of political science has been well illustrated by Aligica and Boettke (2009, 2011; see also Aligica and Sabetti 2014) in their discussion of the underlying social philosophies (in the plural, and occasionally in tension with one another) of the Ostroms' own brand of institutionalism. It has also been painstakingly documented by Barbara Allen's editorial work for the two volumes of Vincent Ostrom's miscellaneous writings on different kinds of choice, rules and institutions (V. Ostrom 2011; 2012). Both sets of works provide the intellectual contexts within which the Ostroms' understood their own way of doing political analysis, even though they were pushing at the boundaries of such intellectual traditions. In this chapter I wish to move beyond the boundaries, in enemy's territory, so to speak, and assess how the issues raised by the Ostroms resonate when politics is looked at from a more transformative perspective. My contention is that the issues of social interconnectedness and meaning, specifically of shared meaning, are the terrain where the somewhat mobile boundaries between the two styles of politics lie.[2]

SOCIAL LEARNING AND COLLECTIVE ACTION

In her already mentioned presidential address to APSA, Elinor Ostrom stated unequivocally that *the* central topic of political science is "the theory of collective action" (Ostrom and Ostrom 2014 [1998], 121). Both theory and empirical research must grapple with it in almost all situations in which political issues arise, from the general justification of the state to international dealings, from decisions about public policies to administrative implementation, from civil society mobilization to citizens' control of democratic government. The view that politics consists in bringing together a multitude of people is nothing new, but the introduction of modern economic thinking into political analysis changed the terms of the problem. Political economy, rational choice and game theory offered both a technical vocabulary and a way of framing the problem of collective action, mainly rejecting the historical, holistic and legal (descriptive) normativism that dominated the positive study of political institutions and behavior in the first half of the twentieth century. As Kenneth Shepsle has suggested, "the great success story (. . .) of the rational choice institutionalism programme is the logic of collective action" (2008, 30). Rational institutionalism, and the related research programs from which it emerged, offered three main tools for discussing the logic of collective action and political institutions: a broad philosophical anthropology of human agency and motivation roughly based on the vision of *homo economicus*, the related view that rationality as utility maximization can explain the process of political choice and action, and the graphic use of abstract (often game-theoretic) models in order to capture the situations in which agents find themselves when trying to solve social dilemmas and collective action problems. These were assumptions that the Ostroms shared in, at least in the first instance.[3] In combination, such assumptions also supported the Ostroms' declared commitment to methodological individualism.

The Ostroms' adherence to this set of theoretical and methodological assumptions was partly reinforced by more practical and normative considerations, which they broadly shared with other authors in the economistic rationality tradition. On the more practical and policy side, the Ostroms were critical of the dominant position during the mid-decades of the twentieth century, that free-rider problems and market-failures could only be solved by external intervention, and by the state in particular; and that efficient public administration was tantamount to increased centralization and state-driven regulation.[4] Normatively, they put great store on individual liberty and how this required both taking seriously the human capacity for self-government, and implementing more systemic forms of protection such as bottom-up polycentricity, separation of powers, rights and the rule of law (issues discussed by Oakerson and Malik in this book). So far, so mainstream within the economistic tradition. But once we start looking more closely at the positive analysis of the logic of collective action offered by the Ostroms and further developed by other exponents of the Bloomington school, the picture that emerges becomes more distinctive in both intellectual and institutional terms. In this section, I shall mainly focus on the work of Elinor Ostrom, though some of the key ideas I discuss emerged as part of the life-long collaboration between her and Vincent.

A decisive element of Elinor Ostrom's push beyond the "extant theory of collective action" was her deep engagement with empirical reality. In absence of such an engagement, she argued, political scientists were "hand waving" at the logic of collective action rather than grasping it (Ostrom and Ostrom 2014 [1998], 121). There was no suggestion that empirical research could do without theory, or that theory could only follow from empirical analysis. Theory, instead, had to be informed by an appreciation of real-world solutions to collective action problems. In a sense, she suggested to upend the economistic approach to the logic of collective action by taking as her starting point not the impossibility, or extreme difficulty of cooperation, as the three main models of the "tragedy of the commons," the "prisoner dilemma," and Olson's free-rider tended to do; but by taking seriously the fact that, even though with different degrees of success, most of the time, social dilemmas are resolved without the necessary intervention of "external" and third-party agents (E. Ostrom 1990, 2–7). Ostrom admitted that, in their pessimism, the three models were powerful ways of capturing some of the conditions for collective action, but that social theory needed to explain *how* social dilemmas are or could be solved. As the title of her most famous book graphically shows, she proposed a shift from the *static* of the tragedy of commons, where the constraints to collective action "are assumed to be fixed," to the *dynamic* of governing the commons, which investigates the ways and capabilities through which the people involved "change the constraining rules of the game to lead to outcomes other than remorseless tragedies" (E. Ostrom 1990, 6–7).[5] The shift is not so much to a more optimistic view, but to one that includes social learning—individuals' ability to learn from their interactions with the environment and others, hence adapting and changing their behavior—and the recognition of the situational complexity within which human beings operate (E. Ostrom 2005, 118). Such a shift in perspectives has important consequences for the three main assumptions of the economistic paradigm of collective choice and action mentioned above: the philosophical anthropology of the political agent, the rationality of political choice, and the analysis of the situational context relevant for the solution of social dilemmas.

The Ostroms were not the only ones to argue for a revision and expansion of the economistic paradigm of the rational agent, criticizing both the self-interest and maximization assumptions from an internal choice-theoretic perspective. Kenneth Shepsle, for example, while still vindicating that "abstraction, simplification, analytical rigor, and an insistence on clean lines of analysis from basic axioms to analytical propositions to empirical implications" are important virtues of rational choice institutionalism, admits that there are a number of ways in which the clear line on rationality gets blurred (Shepsle 2008, 33). He mentions bounded rationality, behavioral economics, transaction costs, and analytical narratives (or historical case studies) (Shepsle 2008, 33–35). The first three play an important role in Elinor Ostrom's own correction of the rational agent paradigm, the latter is functional to getting at the complexities of the structure of the action arenas in which agents operate. In the rest of this section, I offer a brief outline of the kind of revisions that the three standard assumptions about rationality, agency and context in collective action situations may require, trying to chart the Ostroms' own contribution to such a revised research program.

Let's start with the issue of rationality as utility maximization. This is vulnerable to three fundamental objections, each of which refers to important limits of human rationality, which can be corrected by taking a less calculative and more deliberative (i.e., open to verification, communication, and reflection) view of how human beings reason in social contexts (see also Weale's distinction between rationality and reason in his contribution to this book). The first is a more internal, or cognitive, limit of our reasoning capacities, and to the way in which we make rational decisions. Bounded rationality (Simon 1983), for instance, points at both informational and predictive constraints in decision making, which make satisficing, rather than maximizing strategies both more likely and cost-effective. Experimental psychology and economics have developed other non-canonical theories of the relationship between rationality and behavior, such as Prospect theory (Kahneman 2011, 278–88), challenging expected utility conceptions of rationality from a number of perspectives, like asymmetric perceptions of losses and gains; the way in which cognitive issues such as "framing" and "understanding" may determine our preferences, thus producing, for instance, value reversal; the importance of heuristics and related choice biases, and the role of ex ante expectations and ex post valuations in assessing choices and states of affairs (cf. Elster 2007, 214–31). Elinor Ostrom regarded the recognition of a more behaviorally accurate picture of agents' reason as essential to "second-generation models of rationality" (Ostrom and Ostrom 2014 [1998], 136–37). As she argued in Chapter 4 of her *Understanding Institutional Diversity* (E. Ostrom 2005, 99–133), such models are needed in all those situations that are neither simple nor competitive, and where there is no complete information—that is, the vast majority.

The second limit of rationality is its defeasibility.[6] Human rationality is not infallible: agents cannot be certain of the outcome of theirs or others' action, nor can they be sure of the best way of pursuing their ends, nor finally can they fully rely on their own rational capacity to draw correct consequences from given premises. Both Vincent and Elinor Ostrom put great store on human fallibility not as a limit to the possibility of knowing, explaining and predicting social action, but as a fundamental condition of human knowledge and action, of what they considered the "artifactual" nature of social arrangements and the way in which these were the products of trial-and-error processes and of both intended and unintended forms of social learning. As Vincent Ostrom put it: "learning and the generation of new knowledge are themselves marks of fallibility. (. . .) Fallible creatures need to accommodate their plans to changing levels of information and knowledge" (1980, 311); while in a joint piece, they extended the epistemological point by stating that "human rationality is *grounded* in the condition of fallibility, with potentials for learning" (Ostrom and Ostrom 2014 [2004], 86, emphasis added).

There is a more technical sense in which we can talk of the defeasibility of rationality, which applies to non-monotonic forms of logic, as when we analyze everyday life inferences based on forms of reasoning that are only tentative, relying on most likely types of explanations (like abductive reasoning), default kinds of logic, and taxonomic generalizations, all of which can be subverted by new information giving rise to belief revision. While classical logic is *monotonic*, in the sense that its logical conclusions cannot be preempted by the addition of new premises; the inferences of non-monotonic logic are *defeasible* in the double sense that they can be overturned (i.e., defeated) by new evidence and that they are formulated according to a tentative, fallibilist logic (i.e., defeasible in principle), and therefore may require correction mechanisms that are already built in the process of knowing. Although defeasibility is due to the open-textured nature of theoretical knowledge, which continuously challenges the closed world assumption on which we rely for most of our common inferences; practical reasoning must deal with a more specific sense in which the knowledge of intentional human action is open-textured. This is a function of the creativity that characterizes human agents (V. Ostrom 2011 [1988], 456). Such capacity needs to be factored in when we try to understand human actions and their consequences. The twin characters of fallibility and creativity have important consequences for the logic of collective action. For instance, contrary to the more economistic paradigm, it is possible that collective arrangements subsist at a suboptimal level, but that such arrangements are still supported by the people involved for reasons that are valuable to them (E. Ostrom 1990, 56, 182–83). More importantly, the Ostroms considered "fallibility and the capacity to learn . . . as assumptions of a more general theory of the individual," as *homo sapiens*, in opposition to the traditional view of *homo economicus* (Ostrom and Ostrom 2014 [2004], 70; see also V. Ostrom 2012 [1997a], 92–94). Rather than considering decisions as following from "mechanical calculation processes," one should consider them as "informed judgements about uncertain benefits and costs" (E. Ostrom 1990, 208). Moreover, human creativity (and fallibility) is closely related to the way in which human beings operate within and adapt to their social and environmental conditions by interpreting them through language, ideas and a variety of values;[7] so that, from a more normative perspective, it may be important to reflect on how "maximizing utility without attention to the way that ideas shape deeds leads people to trample civilization underfoot" (Ostrom and Ostrom 2014 [2004], 65).

The third challenge to economistic rationality is more closely related to the assumption that the rational agent should be considered as mainly self-interested. Both Elinor and Vincent Ostrom quoted Amartya Sen's criticism of the self-defeating logic of the "rational fool" (Sen 1977; 2002, 3–64; see E. Ostrom 2005, 111–12 and Ostrom and Ostrom 2014 [1997], 244). There are two aspects to this criticism. One is more analytical, and questions the usefulness of a "formulaic view of preference and choice" that fails to distinguish different ways in which an individual may make reasonable choices: for one's well-being, for narrow self-interest, in view of one's chosen goals and objectives, because of a commitment to some values (or to values about values) (Sen 2002, 6). The second comes from experimental research and evolutionary studies of cooperation, suggesting that most people are not simply concerned about themselves but also about others, and that they therefore may subscribe to norms of reciprocity and fairness (Taylor 2006, 134–54; Bowles and Gintis 2008; Elster 2009). Both aspects play an important role in Elinor Ostrom's analysis of the way in which individuals "animate" institutions (2005, Chapter 4), since she assumed that in any action arenas there are different types of agents such as rational egoists, norm-users and conditional cooperators. Depending on the contexts in which these agents operate, and the institutional incentives available to them, the interactions between them may facilitate adaptive strategies, while contributing to changes in sets of preferences and their own modus operandi. Social learning, and self-reflection on one's actions, strategies, and payoffs therefore help shaping the very agents' self-understanding within the social context. Communication and language are of crucial importance in this context. While in situations represented as noncooperative games, communication is considered as "cheap talk," Elinor Ostrom maintained that in most social dilemmas, face-to-face communication plays several roles, by facilitating common understanding of joint problems, by providing useful information on the normative stances of the various agents and on levels of trust (2005, 65), by "creating and reinforcing norms, and developing a group identity" (Ostrom and Ostrom 2014 [1998], 133).

The transformation in question does not simply concern the preferences and behavior of the agents, but also their beliefs, expectations, and ability to make credible commitments. This has transformative effects on the very nature of the situation that the agents face and of their own perception of it. The economistic paradigm tended to portray such situations through game-theoretic models. In *Governing the Commons*, Elinor Ostrom warned against the "metaphorical" use of such dominant models, since these describe situations in a highly stylized form, where agents act entirely independently, with no communication, and where the cost of changing rules or incentives is high (1990, 18 and 182–84). Social dilemma situations are often more complex and it is easy to misrepresent them. The emphasis in her later work was not just on complexity, but on the dynamic way in which social learning, communication, and deliberative reasoning can make it possible for agents to re-model the collective action problem that they are facing (Ostrom and Ostrom 2014 [1998], 144–46). Furthermore, a communicative and deliberative form of rationality, one based on language and ideas (Aligica and Boettke 2009, 93–94), is capable of articulating reasons for action, hence providing agents with normative self-direction, and contributing to a Tocquevillian "self-interest rightly understood," which, according to Vincent Ostrom is a proper understanding of both the "individual and joint interests of people living with one another and tending to the affairs of everyday life" (V. Ostrom 2012 [1997b], 391–92; see also V. Ostrom 2012 [1997a], 92–94 and Weale 2013, 107–8). Such an enlightened form of prudence contributes to stabilize one's behavior in relation to both one's desires, and the desires one has for one's future, giving assurance to others about one's own commitments. In game-theoretic terms, one could suggest that what we are witnessing is not a simple move within a game (a change in the payoffs), but a change to an entirely different game. Elinor Ostrom alerted us to the importance of re-describing situations according to different models, or to the presence of different underlying structures in a situation, so that agents may face a variety of game-theoretic problems and not a simple social dilemma in each particular situation (E. Ostrom 1990, 46–47; 2003, 246–48). The deeply transformative implications of re-describing situations according to different models is something that, in other contexts, others have also observed. For instance, in *Justice as Impartiality*, Brian Barry claims that contractarian, mutual advantage conceptions of social justice and cooperation, are unstable because they have the structure of a prisoner's dilemma, while the greater stability of a more impartialist view of just cooperation derives, in his view, from it having an assurance game structure (Barry 1995, 51). Reflecting on the "difficulties of *acting together*" in the circumstances of politics, Jeremy Waldron suggests that such circumstances are captured neither by prisoner's dilemma nor by coordination games, but by "partial conflict coordination problems" like the battle of the sexes (Waldron 1999, 103–4).

These various observations and the whole thrust of the revision of the logic of collective action as illustrated in Elinor Ostrom's work on common pool resources, and supported by a number of Vincent Ostrom's theoretical insights, point to the fact that in order to understand both the fragility and the resilience of social cooperation, we need to go beyond the rationality of self-interested actors and dig deeper into the working of trust, reputation, reciprocity, credibility, mutuality, and norms. These "core relationships," which are supported by social and communicative interaction between agents (Ostrom and Ostrom 2014 [1998], 143–46), are game changing, in so far as they facilitate both the production of operational rules intended to solve social dilemmas, and the creation of shared meanings and understandings that provide more stable conditions for social cooperation across time and activities. Through social learning and the production of shared meanings, fallible and creative individuals devise rules and institutions that are both fit for problem-solving, but (as we shall discuss further in the next section) also make sense of their life as social beings (see Offe 1996, 201). As Charles Taylor has argued, "mutual respect and mutual service of the individuals who make up society" (2004, 12 and passim 3–22) are at the basis of the "moral order" that in the modern imaginary has supplanted that of the hierarchical complementarity of traditional societies. In this respect, modern mutuality is egalitarian and mainly directed toward our ordinary goals in life: security and prosperity. But it comes in different shades. We would have a distorted view of it, if we simply read it in strictly individualistic and economistic terms, while modern individualism has as "its inevitable flip side a new understanding of sociality, the society of mutual benefit, whose functional differentiation are ultimately contingent and whose members are fundamentally equal" (Taylor 2004, 18). For Taylor too, the problem is to move from Hobbes's prisoner dilemma to the more nuanced social psychology of Tocqueville. As we have seen, part of this move depends on how social learning contributes to the solution of collective action problems by a process through which agents transform themselves, their rational commitments and the situation within which they operate. However, this is only one level of action and choice, since they also give themselves rules on how to make choices and establish institutional settings within which to pursue different cooperative ventures and activities. Choice about choices pertains to the logic of constitutional politics, which was a central part of the Ostroms' conception of institutionalism. It remains to be seen whether the kind of tension between problem-solving and transformative styles of politics that I have tried to illustrate applies there too.

CONTRACTS, COVENANTS, AND CONSTITUTIONS

I started the previous section with the observation that the Ostroms regarded the theory of collective action as *the* problem of political science. But an equally distinctive feature of their approach to politics and institutional analysis was the conviction that addressing collective actions problems and social dilemmas takes places at different levels. Such levels, though analytically distinct, are importantly related to each other both empirically and normatively. In *Governing the Commons*, Elinor Ostrom observed that when assessing collective action and cooperation within smaller social units one "must overtly take the activities of surrounding political systems into account in explaining behaviour and outcomes" (1990, 190). The logic of collective action is therefore nested into a more general second-order logic (a meta-level of analysis) connecting different levels of choice, action and rules, and their reciprocal influence. In this way, *the* problem of political science can be reformulated as the logic of nested and connected social orders (Ostrom and Ostrom 2014 [2004], 61). The formulation of the "constitutional" level, as distinct from what the Ostroms regarded as the "collective" and "operational" levels, is an essential move in discovering such logic and its underlying principles (Ostrom 2012 [2002], 550–52; E. Ostrom 1990, 50–55). While in their approach to the logic of collective action the Ostroms were influenced by the political economy paradigm at large, they acknowledged a particular indebtedness to the public choice paradigm for the study of the constitutional logic: "in our effort to understand the logical foundations of constitutional democracy, we both found that the *Calculus of Consent* . . . gave us basic tools for acquiring . . . analytical leverage . . . The principle of conceptual unanimity gave meaning to what we had observed and what was accomplished." (Ostrom and

Ostrom 2014 [2004], 61; see also V. Ostrom 2012 [1997a], 81–110).[8] In the rest of this section I wish to explore how, particularly in the work of Vincent Ostrom, constitutional choice is able to establish the "authority and limitations" of political power (2012 [2002], 551), and whether this also evokes a more socially transformative understanding of the enterprise of politics, as we saw in the previous section.

The kind of constitutional politics outlined in *The Calculus of Consent* (1962) was mainly aimed at denying legitimacy to the majority principle as the foundational element of democracy, while undermining a "romanticized and idealized" view of politics and of the state as the embodiment of the common good (Buchanan and Congleton 1998, xi). Accordingly, James Buchanan has presented public choice theory as "politics without romance," as a "theory of governmental failure," which borrows the tools and methods of modern economic theory and applies them to politics (1999 [1979], 45–59). He considered such a theory, not only entirely consistent with "political reality," but "a wholly positive theory, wholly scientific and *wertfrei*" (*ibid.*, 46–47). We have already seen how the Ostroms departed both from a narrow positivist conception of political science and from the standard vision of the rationality of the economic agent when applied to collective action. But they still shared in the more analytical and implicitly normative move that distinguished between constitutional and post-constitutional politics. For Buchanan, both levels deal with politics as a form of "exchange" between more than two parties. Post-constitutional politics offers a positive and predictive theory of how political institutions (electoral systems, political parties, bureaucracies) work within an already established constitutional framework. Constitutional politics, on its part, deals both with the positive assessment of the robustness of constitutional arrangements, and with the normative principles of the constitutional framework itself. This very last point is what Buchanan considers as the foundational logic of constitutional politics, which at its most abstract level "becomes the complex exchange among all members of a potential political order, who personally and separately enter into relationship because of shared expectations of mutual gains" (Buchanan and Congleton 1998, 16). The normative principle guiding the constitutional level, as Buchanan and Tullock argued in the *Calculus of Consent*, is the Wicksellian criterion of unanimity, which is also the starting point for social contract theories in so far as they assume that the legitimacy of the coercive power of the political community lies in the voluntary agreements of all parties to the contract (Buchanan and Congleton 1998, 16–18 and Buchanan 1999 [1979], 51).

Buchanan's version of the contractarian logic of constitutional politics, however, is only one possible interpretation of a two-level logic of social order. There are several ways in which constitutional politics can be both characterized and justified. More to the point, the version to which the Ostroms adhered, and which informs Vincent Ostrom's constitutional writings, is quite distinctive, embracing, as we shall see, a more "covenantal" conception of constitutionalism. This, in combination with his related views about federalism, polycentricity and self-governance, go far beyond the standard public choice conception of politics and of the political community. I shall first sketch different contract-based justifications of constitutional politics, before returning to Vincent Ostroms' particular understanding of it.

There is an immediate sense in which constitutions and contracts can be compared. There are logical and empirical similarities between them. Their natural evolution as social practices show signs of reciprocal influence. Historically, constitutions often developed from, and took the functions of other forms of agreement either between individuals or among the community as a whole (Lutz 1988, 16–22). The comparison between constitutions and social contracts, as *theoretical constructs*, is partly dependent on the general meaning given to a "constitution" as the act of establishing a political community: that is, its more constitutive rather than regulative meaning. If we stick to such constitutive function, there is a sense in which we can compare the kind of justifications used in social contract theory with the justification for a two-level politics, where constitutional, or second-order politics fixes the general rules of the game. In the case of contracts, justification is normally based on the value of choice and of consensual (unanimous) agreement. But there are different forms of social contract theories, which, though all based on choice, consent, and some credible commitment to reciprocity, offer differing constructions of them.

Broadly speaking, we can distinguish three different versions. The first, economic contractarianism, which is closer to the Buchanan's and public choice version, is mainly based on the idea of mutual advantage, which rational chooser find compelling either because the natural conditions in which they are placed makes them vulnerable to others (*negative* advantage, cf. Kymlicka 1990, 127–31), or because they see the possibility of "cooperative surplus" (*positive* advantage, cf. Sudgen 1993, 3 and 20–21). Since from such a perspective, morality is the artificial product of the coordination of irreducible subjective preferences, the conditions of choice, consent (and subordinately of reciprocity) are empirically determined. In such cases the social contract takes the transparent form of bargaining between separate individuals, who need to be convinced that "over the whole set of political actions that may be taken under the operation of the chosen rules, benefit would exceed costs," and that this would apply to each single one of them, satisfying Pareto optimality (Buchanan and Congleton 1998, 18).

The other two versions of social contract theory can be grouped under the label of "contractualism."[9] One is more political in nature, resting on the actual agreement of participants, who are open to reasoned agreement. Its paradigmatic institutions are those where public discussion is enacted; and, as it is normally the case in public discussion, appeals to the parties' separate interests carry no great conviction, unless such particular interests are reconciled with, and ultimately subordinated to, the concerns of the public as a whole (Kukathas and Pettit 1990, 32–33) This form of contractualism is particularly sensitive to the *ideal* preconditions of choice and consent, such as Habermas's ideal-speech situation (Habermas 1990), or the absence of gross differentials in bargaining power. The place of reciprocity, in this theory, is at its most abstract, as the general maxim "doing unto others as you would have them do unto you." The other version of contractualism is normally formulated in a hypothetical form, as a heuristic device used to uncover more direct principles of legitimation. In this version both the contract and consensual agreement have an evaluative more than legitimating role, since strictly speaking the hypothetical contract rests on intuitive notions of fairness and moral obligation, whose standing do not depend on the empirical conditions of choice and consent. Such intuitive moral notions can only be determined ideally and constructively (Rawls 1993, 89–96), while reciprocity is conceived as a complex idea, mid-way between impartiality (other-mindedness) and mutual advantage (self-mindedness), underlying a morally charged conception of social cooperation (Rawls 1993, 15–17).

Each of these versions has its appeal, but also important limits as a way of explaining and justifying social order and political power. Hypothetical contractualism, for instance, fails to consider the situatedness of choice and consent, which in this version are ultimately subordinated to more basic moral intuitions (fairness, impartiality, the moral standing of persons) as justifying principles. On the other hand, the hypothetical formulation, graphically captured by Rawls's (1971) and others' idea of the "veil ignorance" or basic uncertainty, has the advantage of highlighting one important analytical element in the idea of constitutional politics. This lies in the fact that the definition of the general rules of the game presents a different decision-structure (in terms of knowledge, temporal framework, and object of choice) from the one applying to normal politics, where direct allocation and distribution of power and resources are at stake. Because of such differences, decisions can be taken according to different principles of decision making, which may be more demanding on the one hand (for instance, unanimity instead of majority rule); but more open to agreement on the other, in view of the uncertainty about one's future position and about the effect that rules may have on the substantive patterns of allocation and distribution of power and resources. This is a point that Buchanan makes also about his own version of constitutional politics (1999 [1986], 23–24). In comparison to hypothetical contractualism, the political version has the advantage of offering more solid grounds both in terms of motivation and autonomous justification for the establishment of a constitutional setting within which normal politics can take place. Where it fails is in its circularity, since it seems to presuppose conditions of impartiality and ideal speech, which can only be conceived as the product of an already well-established political community, where such values and conditions are nurtured and promoted.

Economic contractarianism is less prone to the kind of criticisms moved to the two versions of contractualism, since it relies on actual consent and has a less moralized and idealized view of the precontractual conditions, taking into account differences in the agents' bargaining power. However, its imperviousness to reasons, other than those suggested by advantage over the status quo, subject to the strict requirements of unanimity and Pareto optimality, makes the application of its principles to constitution making exceedingly demanding. Besides, depending on the status quo conditions, gross bargaining differentials can produce unjust constitutional arrangements, as it is the case with unfair contracts. Indeed, bargaining may be an inappropriate way of characterizing the internal logic of constitutional politics, where the main object is the establishment of general social order and a viable political community. In such instances, one may assume that for the rules of the game to be generally recognized and considered acceptable, they need to be seen at some remove from the parties' power differential.[10] The limits of instrumental rationality in such situations may be even more evident than the limits we discussed in the previous section in relation to collective action; since the costs of failing to agree the constitutional basis for social and political order (*negative* disadvantage) is too high to be considered, so that no one individual or group has real bargaining power in this instance. Bargaining power is relevant only if and when failure to establish a political community can be realistically judged in terms of forfeiting cooperative surplus (*positive* disadvantage); but for this to apply one needs to draw the conditions of noncooperation in such a way that a sustainable (even minimal) life is possible in isolation.

I think that the implicit a-sociality underlying economic contractualism is where the Ostroms' own conception of constitutional politics departs from the public choice version. Some of the differences have to do with the conception of the rational agent discussed in the previous section, but there is also a more general vision of constitutionalism and polycentricity as a philosophy of politics that I think makes their position distinctive. The Ostroms embraced the idea of constitutional politics both as an analytical tool to understand the nature of social choice and social order, as these are dependent on rule-ordered relationships across all levels of social action; and as a normative paradigm, to assess how individuals can meaningfully self-govern themselves.[11] The analytical/normative distinction partly overlaps with the two senses of constitution. There is a regulative meaning of constitution that applies to any institutional context organized according to de jure or de facto rules. In this sense, constitutional politics takes place in any domain of social organization, from states to public and private institutions, from municipal authorities to voluntary associations and clubs, from formally regulated consumers' or producers' regimes to informal (even tacit) arrangements between them. In each of these domains, constitutional choices involve second-order decisions about rules and about the fixing of deontic operators: what is forbidden, what is required ad what is permitted, which in turn enable and constrain collective and operational choices. This regulative sense of constitutional politics is analytically important. But regulating practices and activities through second-order choices is tantamount to *constituting* them. Such constitutive meaning has a special significance for those complex, all-encompassing institutions that play an important role for the security and well-being of peoples, and that have strong powers for enforcing their own rules, up to the use of force. It is in these cases in particular that the normative dimension of constitutional politics matters, since it involves problems of jurisdictional disputes, ultimate authority, and the legitimate use of force. Vincent Ostrom was fully cognizant that social order is dependent on forms of coercion, with opportunities for domination and exploitation. He called this the inescapable "Faustian bargain" of using "evil to do good" (V. Ostrom 1982, 35; cf. Aligica and Boettke 2009, 60–63). Hence he thought that the terms and conditions for what he described as the "rule-ruler-ruled" relationship "is the most critical problem in the constitution of order in human society" (V. Ostrom 2011 [1988], 466). His reflections on the normative dimension of constitutional order provide an answer that, though strongly relying on ideas of choice and consent, does not fit neatly in any of the three models of contract theory outlined above. Moreover, in its own way it combines both the constitutive and regulative meanings of constitutional politics in order to give and answer to the problem of legitimate power and good government.

In spite of his recognition that Buchanan's and Tullock's contribution was paradigm-changing, Vincent Ostrom's constitutional theory grew out independently, originating in his early research interests in public administration—as summarized in *The Intellectual Crisis in American Public Administration* (2008a [1973]). His theory matured and developed along quite different directions as part of his exploration of the logic of American Federalism in *The Political Theory of a Compound Republic* (2008b [1971]). The common thread of these two lines of research was the opposition between monocratic and polycentric conceptions of public administration and of the political order. Ostrom's work on public administration challenged what he took to be the dominant paradigm of centralized state bureaucracy in the public sector, which he associated with Woodrow Wilson and Max Weber (2008a, Chapter 2). Against this he argued for self-governing and multiorganizational arrangements in the public economy, through overlapping and fragmented authorities comprising public service industries (2008a, Chapter 3).[12] Contrary to the monocratic and centralising perspective, he thought that such arrangements were both feasible and efficient, and that they offered a full theory of democratic administration (2008a, Chapter 4). A number of these ideas have since been adopted and elaborated, though rarely acknowledged, in the specialized literatures on regulation, new public management, administrative accountability, and multi-level governance in transnational communities such as the European Union. One of the reasons for the lack of acknowledgment is perhaps that, while the thrust of these approaches is more akin to experts- and guardianship-based idea of democratic governance, Ostrom's view was insistent on bottom-up forms of self-governance. While there are formidable technical and empirical challenges to decentralized and polycentric conceptions of public administration, particularly when combined with strong democratic elements, the real normative issue in modern societies comes at the higher level of social organization, where political power and the force of law operate.

Ostrom took the central concept of the monocratic paradigm to be that of "sovereignty," as first elaborated in modern times by Bodin and Hobbes, and embodied in the dominant political form of the unitary nation-state. Rousseauian ideas of the social contract, forming a general will that rules over society, seemed to offer a democratic version of the same monocratic perspective. Ostrom thought that the American federal experiment provided not only a blueprint for democratic, decentralized administration, but also an alternative model for democratic governance—a different way of approaching the "Faustian bargain." He cited Tocqueville's suggestion that democracy in America was a distinct form of government from those vying in contemporary Europe, the one where the "state rules over society," and the old regime type of hierarchical power, based on division into ranks. In the United States, instead, in Tocqueville's own words, "society rules itself for itself" (cited in V. Ostrom 2008a, 70). From this perspective, federalism is not a different form of government, where power is dispersed through different authorities, which are, nonetheless, ultimately dependent on a unitary sovereign power. Federalism is the expression of a very different form of social order, which comes from the autonomous organization of society, where sovereignty cannot be located in a person, real or fictitious, outside society itself, but remains with the people. This is how Ostrom interpreted Tocqueville's chapter on "The principle of the Sovereignty of the People in America." Ostrom defined this broader, philosophical sense of federalism as "the efforts of people as communities of individuals to achieve self-governing capabilities consistent with requirement of liberty and justice in multiple communities of relationships" (V. Ostrom 2012 [2002], 547).

Ostrom's enquire on the American experiment in federalism was not so much a historical reconstruction of the Federalists' intention and of the politics of the time, though it was that too; but, as he said, it was primarily a search for a political theory: for the "logic" and the "spirit" of federalism as an alternative model of self-governance (V. Ostrom 2008b, 3; V. Ostrom 2012 [2000], 541). Eventually, Ostrom came to regard this federal constitutional philosophy as founded on "covenantal" principles, and therefore not exclusively American in origins (V. Ostrom 2012 [2000], 543–44). The idea of a covenantal constitution emerged from Ostrom's dialogue with and reflection on the work of other scholars who had taken a particular interest in the way in which the religious background of some of the New England communities had influenced constitutional thinking in revolutionary America. They particularly focused on the close relationship between federal thinking and the covenant theology of Puritan communities.[13] As Anas Malik argues in his contribution to this book, Ostrom himself came to regard the religious aspect of the tradition (in the broad sense of a set of beliefs in which the relationships between human beings are mediated by their own conception of a deity) as an important component of covenantal constitutionalism. But it is possible to consider the covenantal logic apart from religious beliefs, applying it "to the constitution of secular self-governing communities" (V. Ostrom 2012 [1992], 372).

As other covenant scholars, Ostrom understood the covenantal logic both as a normative principle of constitutional choice and an alternative model for political organization. How does such covenantal logic work, and how does it differ from the contract-based theories we examined earlier? On the face of it, covenant is another word for pact or agreement. If the distinction with contract theories is not just nominal (or a way of referring to specific religious or theological beliefs), there must be something more in the argument itself to suggest a distinctive way of founding constitutional orders. In a stylized way, we can highlight four elements which pertain to the covenantal logic, as I think it underpins Ostrom's and others' interpretation of it.[14] Firstly, the covenantal approach is less abstract and hypothetical in nature, coming closer in this to what I have described as political contractualism.[15] It insists on the importance of the social practice of covenants, or various forms of pacts between people, and the way in which they determine social life in associational terms. Hence, associational practices are not only important and diffuse, but also formative and educative, constitutive of human personality. This part of the argument links covenants to federalism by remarking that the latter's etymological origin is in the Latin *foedus*, which means pact or covenant. The point is not narrowly linguistic, but more substantive. It suggests that, at least in this context, one should take federalism not as an organizational structure, but as a true form of association between either nested or complementary associations.

Moreover, the federal way of constituting polities suggests a bottom-up process, where the coercive power of the state results from the sovereignty of the people and from its capacity of progressively aggregating into wider circles of territorial communities (cf. V. Ostrom 2008b, 139).

The second element of the covenantal logic is its strong voluntarism. By grounding its very logic in the historical and empirical practice of pacts and constitution making, the covenantal approach takes actual consent seriously. In this, it is more akin to economic contractarianism, with which it shares a strong emphasis on the liberty of the individual in willingly entering into agreements with others, and the fact that agreements must be in some relevant way mutually advantageous. However, this more individualistic and freedom-based element is strongly qualified by the other two elements of the covenantal approach, which point instead toward more moral and communitarian features. With respect to the former element, the covenantal position is much closer to both versions of contractualism, since they subscribe to ideas of reasonableness and right reason, which imply moral principles that are independent from the actual agreement between people. Daniel Elazar suggested that, both theologically and politically, "covenant is informed by a moral or ethical perspective," linking power and justice as two faces of politics (2000, 13). Ostrom agreed on this point, suggesting that the original religious conception of the covenant with God as a way of honoring the deity, had its natural extension in the way in which we treat others, according to "the Golden Rule of 'do onto others as you would have others do unto you'" (V. Ostrom 2012 [1992], 372). Ostrom saw the Golden Rule as a fundamental normative principle, which he associated to Hobbes' conception of the laws of nature as prescriptions of reason to search peace over war, and which he thought informed Adam Smith's ideas of propriety and the impartial spectator, Kant's categorical imperative, and other later formulations of the same impartialist view (V. Ostrom 2011 [1982], 293–97). Such principle makes one reconsider "one's own preferences in relation to the preferences of others when interdependent interests require *impartiality* in arriving at a judgment pertaining to joint interests" (Ostrom and Ostrom 2014 [1997], 247, emphasis in the original).

The final element of the covenantal logic is the way in which its conception of association contains a communitarian character. Filippo Sabetti has rightly remarked the presence of such a character, and of how historically this has also manifested itself through strong kinship ties (2000, 260). This character is problematic in more than one sense, posing the question of how much diversity of values and commitments can a covenantal constitution sustain particularly in modern societies, while highlighting the inner tensions of the covenantal logic between individual and community values, between voluntarist and naturalist forms of obligation. However, it is possible to look at such tensions in a more positive way, not as opposite perspectives, but as elements to be reconciled through constitutional politics. One way of doing this is perhaps by taking a broader, more secular view of the covenantal tradition, as well as by looking beyond the American experience. This gives us a less neat, more mixed empirical and ideological picture of discourses of governance than one captured by the simple dichotomy between two philosophies of governance. Indeed, Vincent Ostrom was clearly aware of the many intellectual sources and versions of the federal and anti-sovereigntist political theory he was searching for.[16] Arguably, his own interpretation of the American federal experiment, and of its underlying covenantal logic, was shot through with his reading of Tocqueville on democracy. If one looks at Europe in the nineteenth and early twentieth century, one does not find a single dominating model of the centralized state. Intellectually, the tradition of Althusius, with his alternative view of sovereignty, as located in the people, and not the ruler, who only administers power (1995, 66), was never entirely dormant. Federalists, pluralists, corporatists, and anarchists of different hues were active throughout the nineteenth and twentieth centuries (cf. Laborde 2000). All of them developed views critical both of the organization of political societies and of where the legitimacy of the use of coercive force should lie. Moreover, they were not without influence in both the organization of the concrete administration of the constitutional state, and the interplay between the political and the various legal systems. In spite of the checked history of the European states throughout the nineteenth and twentieth centuries, and many authoritarian experiences, it would be an oversimplification to say that they all followed a monocratic and centralist model. It would also be mistaken to think that the centralized tradition of the state was tantamount to an organic view of it. On the contrary, Hobbes's conception of sovereignty and the state was based on a more individualist view, with the state being considered "persona fictia," distinct from the persons who administer state affairs, yet capable, as an artificial, not a natural "person," of acquiring obligations (cf. Skinner 2009); while those like Otto Gierke who at the end of the nineteenth century wanted to revive the tradition of communities, associations, and of fellowship (*Genossenschaft*) embraced a much stronger communitarian and organic view of those collective non-state forms of association, whom they regarded as natural persons that could not be subordinated to state authority (Black 1990, xvii–xix).[17] On the other hand, as Ostrom was well aware, American federalism in itself was no natural defense against more unitary and centralized developments, nor was an absolute guarantee against dominion and exploitation.

From this historically broader and intellectually more mixed perspective, the two main models that Ostrom often opposed to each other, Hobbes and Madison (Ostrom 2008b, xxix), were probably too sharply drawn. But if we return to the central theoretical question of the normative basis for constitutional politics and social order, we may see that the Tocquevillian reading of the covenantal logic animating the Ostroms' research program, with its focus on self-governing associational life,[18] instead of papering over the tensions highlighted above, it tried to offer a way of dealing with them. The key element would seem to be the way in which associational life deals with the interdependency of the human condition and the intersubjective nature of social life and social learning. In *Governing the Commons*, Elinor Ostrom talked of a "lattice of interdependence" (1990, 38) in which collective action takes place. In a passage already cited, Vincent Ostrom talked of the way in which one ought to adopt an impartial perspective because there are "interdependent" and "joint" interests (Ostrom and Ostrom 2014 [1997], 247). The way in which people associate, and the associational spirit in general, is therefore not just an instrument through which separate individuals achieve security and prosperity, but the very way in which those individuals understand their own life, security and prosperity. It is a joint enterprise, not based on mutual, though separate, advantage; but a joint, interdependent activity involving mutual understanding, a sense of reciprocity, and a spirit of mutuality.[19] In an essay of critical appraisal of Buchanan's work, Vincent Ostrom clearly acknowledged how his own "covenantal approach" builds upon Buchanan's original contribution to the establishment of the constitutional paradigm, but it goes beyond Buchanan's own "contractual approach" (Ostrom 2012 [1997], 102). Not only Ostrom thinks that "*homo economicus* has the capacity to learn and achieve capabilities associated with an enlightened self-interest equivalent to Tocqueville's self-interest rightly understood," but also that, because of "speech, reflection, and choice," it is possible for *homo economicus* to transform into *homo sapiens* and achieve peace through associating in communities (102). A few lines later, Ostrom stresses how human societies "require complex cultural codes . . . common knowledge and shared community of understanding," how "methodological individualism is not the opposite of social bonds achieved through communicating with and relating to others" (103). In short, for the Ostroms, the normative basis of constitutional politics and social order lies therefore not so much on the capacity of autonomous and separate individuals to make contracts for mutual advantage, but in the fact that, given the lattice of interdependence, human beings develop the cognitive and moral resources and capacities to associate into communities of shared understanding. Constitutional politics is the very process of such transformation.

CONCLUSION: SHARED UNDERSTANDING AND SOCIAL BONDS

I hope to have showed how the Ostroms' conception of politics, starting from a focus on collective action as problem-solving, and from premises and traditions of economic rationality and public choice constitutionalism, push the boundaries of their research program toward a more transformative style of politics, where social learning through engagement with others fundamentally shapes both the rationality and commitments of the choices and actions of individuals, and where the logic of social order is determined by the very social capacity for association. In both instances, politics is a reflection of interdependence but also of intersubjectivity, an element well captured by the Ostroms' growing insistence on the importance of recovering cultural codes, shared meanings and norms, and linguistic communication as fundamental parts of the context for collective choice and constitutional order. This intrinsically intersubjective sense of the political association is bounded up with the human capacity for communication and language, and shares with language that very same quality of being a "public" or inevitably joint enterprise. This is a point that Charles Taylor has argued by describing a society, a culture, and a language as "irreducible social goods," which are not public goods in the economic sense, of joint supply and non-subtractability, like a dam can be, but in the more specific sense that there is no way in which we can make sense of them outside a social, intersubjective context, as Taylor say: "something is common when it exists not just for me or for you, but for *us*, acknowledged as such" (Taylor 1995, 139). This does not imply a community as a natural person, but the very specificity of intersubjective reality as manifested in the phenomenon of language. A point, more recently elaborated by Charles Taylor himself in his recent book on *The Language Animal* (2016), where he defends a "constitutive" conception of language, as one that produces shared meaning, and not simply as designative, an instrument to transmit privately internally produced signs to others. According to the constitutive conception, language "evolves always in the interspace of joint attention" (Taylor 2016, 50). The importance of the constitutive jointness of language is also remarked by Vincent Ostrom in many of his writings. He addresses the issue of the constitutive dimension of language in particular in *The Meaning of Democracy and the Vulnerability of Democracies* (1997, 171). In another place he maintained that linguistic meaning depends on "communities of shared understanding" (Ostrom and Ostrom 2014 [1997], 263). And this is also true for political associations, since they are always the product of joint choice and action, within the context of communities of shared understanding.[20]

> Human communication and human transactions depend upon the existence of common languages. Communication and transactions cannot occur without reference to the common understanding that is inherent in a common language. In a similar way, democratic self-governing communities depend upon a common understanding among the person comprising such communities regarding the terms and conditions for tending to the affairs of such communities. (Ostrom 2011 [1978], 276–77)

NOTES

1. For glaring omissions of any mention of the Ostroms' work, see the personal contributions of James Buchanan's and Douglass C. North to the *Oxford Handbook of Political Economy* (Buchanan 2008; North 2008). Given the issue discussed in their reflections on the discipline, one would have expected some reference to Vincent's and Elinor's work in their respective contribution.

2. This is a question also explored by other contributors in this book, particularly by Albert Weale in his discussion of the importance of language and the distinction between rules and regularities. My own take is more focused on the way in which meaning provides an important insight for the understanding of the nature of political association.

3. In *Understanding Institutional Diversity*, Elinor Ostrom said that "individual actors are the animators of an institutional world" and that she was happy to use rational choice and game theory to explain behavior (2005, Chapter 4); while Vincent Ostrom explicitly subscribed to methodological individualism as part of his discussion of epistemic choice (Ostrom and Ostrom 2014 [1997], 257–58).

4. The Ostroms were also critical of the "market" alternative as the only other solution. Something will be said later on this issue, but in this chapter I cannot make justice on their position on this issue. Three brief points can here be mentioned. One is that their analysis rejected a simplistic view of the alternative state vs. market. The other is that, as other institutionalists also recognized, market transactions require specific institutional contexts, which are often of a "political" nature, and that involve transaction costs, which need to be considered. The third is that the dominant dichotomy of state and market contributes to the oversimplification of the kind of bundles of rights involved in the provision and appropriation of different goods, resources, and services. The combination of such bundles (access, withdrawal, management, exclusion, and alienation) may produce a variety of property regimes, which cannot be reduced to the simple state/private property distinction (E. Ostrom 2003, 248–52).

5. Vincent Ostrom makes the same point: "Perhaps the important challenge for Public-Choice scholars is to address how basic anomalies, social dilemmas, and puzzles can be resolved in human affairs, rather than to apply economic reasoning, narrowly construed, to nonmarket decision making" (Ostrom and Ostrom 2014 [1997], 244).

6. For this point, I partly rely on Albert Weale (2013, 101–11); see also my comments on Weale's discussion in Castiglione (2015, 167–69).

7. On the role of ideas in the Ostroms' research programme, see Aligica and Boettke 2009, 76–98; on the way in which Vincent Ostrom imaginatively combines value pluralism and some insights of cybernetics, see Barbara Allen's "Introduction" to V. Ostrom 2011, xxv–xxvi and endnotes 14 and 15 at p. xxxv).

8. For a discussion of the influence that Buchanan's and Tullock's work exercised on the Ostroms, see Aligica and Boettke (2009, 124–31), and Barbara Allen's "Forward" to Ostrom (2008a, xiv–xv) and her "Introduction" to Ostrom (2011, xx–xxi). These authors also notice, however, how the Ostroms went beyond the public choice approach.

9. By contractualist theories are here meant those broadly of Kantian inspiration, which ground the social contract on an appeal to the reasonableness of the contracting parties. Contractarian theories are those more directly influenced by Hobbes where rationally prudent agents try to achieve an agreement to their mutual advantage. On the distinction, see Ashford and Mulgan (2012) and Cudd (2012).

10. This is a point that is clearly made by Vincent Ostrom: "The constitutional decision maker is concerned about the essential conditions of justice and fairness that apply to the rig of the game for collective decision making" (2008a, 198).

11. This is what Vincent Ostrom called the Hamilton's query: whether societies are capable of establishing good government on choice and reflection rather than force and accident (2012 [2011], 632).

12. On the Ostroms' particular conception of ideas of "industry" and "public economy," cf. Aligica and Boettke (2009, 41–46).

13. For some of the background information on some of the influences on Vincent Ostrom's thought on this subject, see Daniel J. Elazar, "Foreword" to Ostrom (2008b), and Barbara Allen, "Introduction" to Ostrom (2012, xxviii–xxix and note 18 at p. xxxv).

14. I am not here trying to offer an accurate synthesis of either Ostrom's own discussion of the covenant tradition, or of other authors,' such as Daniel Elazar (1995–1998), for instance (see also Lutz 1988 and Allen 2005). My intention is simply to highlight the conceptual points that I take to be distinctive of this body of works, in the same, stylized form that I have used to sketch the different families of contract theories.

15. Ostrom links covenanting societies with the open public realm and public deliberation (2014 [1997], 264). This aspect, discussed in Oakerson's contribution in this book, links well with recent deliberativist theories of democracy, which can be seen as supportive of political contractualism.

16. The awareness of other experiences (even those that have turned in a very different direction, or those that had not fully succeeded, but whose memory and influence was still relevant) and Vincent Ostrom's intellectual engagement with them is particularly evident in V. Ostrom (2012 [1992] and [1997b]).

17. Vincent Ostrom (2008b, 9) reads the distinction between *Hersschaft* and *Genossenschaft* as another manifestation of the monocratic and polycentric political philosophies, but glosses over the strongly organicist element that the latter has in the corporatist tradition, also challenging the Weberian conception of the state.

18. Vincent Ostrom's idea of a science of associations (also discussed in Sołtan's contribution to this book) and the normative importance that associations have for the social and political order could be linked (also via Tocqueville) to the critical revival of the idea of civil society in the second part of the twentieth century (cf. Castiglione 1998).

19. I think "mutuality" should here be distinguished from mutual advantage, implying a more generalized, and not particular or calculative, conception of reciprocity. Mutuality and general reciprocity capture a greater social awareness and sense of sympathy and support between people. If one considers this aspect, a certain "anarchic" element in the Ostroms' position (in the sense of the principle of

individual self-governance and spontaneous aggregation against top-down sources of power) is probably nearer to some form of late nineteenth-century form of anarchist and syndacalist pluralism in France and Proudhon's federalism (Laborde 2000, Chapter 2). Where mutualism comes together with forms of contractual individualism and anti-statism. In these traditions, mutualism tempers extreme individualism. With reference to such "anarchism," I diverge from Aligica and Boettke (2009, 104), otherwise always very perceptive assessment of the Ostroms' intellectual lineages, who link them to the "analytic anarchism" of Buchanan and Nozick. My own interpretation is also supported by the way in which Vincent Ostrom himself made a connection with the anarchic positions of people like Proudhon and Kropotkin (2012 [1992], 372–73).

20. An implicit part of my argument is that the Ostroms' declared adherence to "methodological individualism" is not all the way down. I think this is another example of them pushing the boundaries. Although I think they always adhered to what one can perhaps call "normative individualism," a principled conviction about the separateness of persons, and of their dignity; methodologically their view challenges the strictly individualist position, which tends to reduce all explanations to individual components. Significantly, Elinor Ostrom made reference to the idea of "holons" in her book on institutional analysis (2005, 11–13); and similarly there are many places in Vincent Ostrom's writings, where he considers collectivities to have an artifactual, but distinctive character, which cannot be reduced to simple individual users and components, as it is the case for languages.

REFERENCES

Aligica, Paul D. and Peter J. Boettke. 2009. *Challenging Institutional Analysis and Development. The Bloomington School*. London and New York: Routledge.

Aligica, Paul D. and Peter J. Boettke. 2011. "Two Social Philosophies of Ostroms' Institutionalism." *The Policy Studies Journal* 39, 1: 29–49.

Aligica, Paul D. and F. Sabetti. 2014. "The Ostrom's Research Program for the Study of Institutions and Governance. Theoretical and Epistemic Foundations," in Ostrom and Ostrom (2014), pp. 1–19.

Allen, Barbara. 2005. *Tocqueville, Covenant, and the Democratic Revolution Harmonizing Earth with Heaven*. Lanham: Lexington.

Althusius, Johannes. 1995. *Politica*. Abridged edition, Edited and Translated by F. S. Carney. "Foreword" by D. J. Elazar. Indianapolis: Liberty Fund Press.

Ashford, Elizabeth and Tim Mulgan. 2012. "Contractualism." *The Stanford Encyclopedia of Philosophy*. E. N. Zalta (ed.). Accessed 1.07.2016. http://plato.stanford.edu/archives/fall2012/entries/contractualism/.

Barry, Brian. 1995. *Justice as Impartiality*. Oxford: Oxford University Press.

Black, Antony. 1990. "Introduction," in Otto von Gierke. *Community in Historical Perspective*. Edited and selected by A. Black. Cambridge: Cambridge University Press, pp. xiv–xxx.

Bowles, Samuel and Herbert Gintis. 2008. "The Evolutionary Basis of Collective Action," in eds. B. R. Weingast and D. Wittman. *The Oxford Handbook of Political Economy*. Oxford: Oxford University Press, pp. 951–68.

Buchanan, James M. 1999. *The Logical Foundations of Constitutional Liberty*. Indianapolis: Liberty Fund Press.

———. 1999 [1979]. "Politics Without Romance: A Sketch of Positive Public Choice Theory and its Normative Implications," pp. 45–59.

———. 1999 [1986]. "Better than Plowing," pp. 11–27.

Buchanan, James M. 2008. "Politics and Scientific Enquiry: Retrospective on a Half-Century," in eds. B. R. Weingast and D. Wittman. *The Oxford Handbook of Political Economy*. Oxford: Oxford University Press, pp. 980–95.

Buchanan, James M. and Roger D. Congleton. 1998. *Politics by Principle, not Interest: Towards Nondiscriminatory Democracy*. Cambridge: Cambridge University Press.

Buchanan, James M. and Gordon Tullock. 1962. *The Calculus of Consent: Logical Foundation of Constitutional Government*. Ann Arbor: University of Michigan Press.

Castiglione, Dario. 1998. "Civil Society," in *The New Palgrave Dictionary of Law and Economics*, P. Newman (ed.). Houndmills: Macmillan Press.

Castiglione, Dario. 2014. "Foreword," in Ostrom and Ostrom (2014), pp. xi–xvii.

Castiglione, Dario. 2015. "The Logic of Social Cooperation for Mutual Advantage—The Democratic Contract." *Political Studies Review*, 13: 161–75.

Cudd, Ann. 2012. "Contractarianism." *The Stanford Encyclopedia of Philosophy*. E. N. Zalta (ed.). Accessed 1.07.2016. http://plato.stanford.edu/archives/fall2012/entries/contractarianism/.

Elazar, Daniel. J. 1995–1998. *The Covenant Tradition in Politics*. 4 vols. New Brunswick, NJ: Transaction Publishers.

Elazar, Daniel. J. 2000. "From Biblical Covenant to Modern Federalism: The Federal Theology Bridge," in Elazar, D. J., Kincaid, J. eds. *The Covenant Connection: From Federal Theology to Modern Federalism*, pp. 1–14.

Elster, Jon. 2007. *Explaining Social Behaviour*. Cambridge: Cambridge University Press.

Elster, Jon. 2009. *Le Désintéressement*. Paris: Éditions du Seuil.

Habermas, Jürgen. 1990. "Discourse Ethics: Notes on a Program of Philosophical Justification," in *Moral Consciousness and Communicative Action*. Cambridge: MIT Press, pp. 43–115.

Kahneman, Daniel. 2011. *Thinking Fast and Slow*. London: Penguin Books.

Kukathas, Chandran and Philippe Pettit. 1990. *Rawls. A Theory of Justice and its Critics*. Cambridge: Polity Press.

Kymlicka, Will. 1990. *Contemporary Political Philosophy. An Introduction*. Oxford: Oxford University Press.

McGinnis, Michael D. 2011. "Elinor Ostrom: Politics as Problem-Solving in Polycentric Settings," in eds. D. Campus, G. Pasquino and M. Bull, *Maestri of Political Science*, volume 2. Colchester: ECPR Press, pp. 137–58.

Laborde, Cécile. 2000. *Pluralist Thought and the State in Britain and France, 1900–25*. Houndmills: Macmillan Press.
Lutz, Donald S. 1988. *The Origins of American Constitutionalism*. Baton Rouge: Louisiana State University Press.
North, Douglas C. 2008. "What is Missing from Political Economy," in eds. B. R. Weingast and D. Wittman. *The Oxford Handbook of Political Economy*. Oxford: Oxford University Press, pp. 1003–8.
Offe, Claus. 1996. "Designing Institutions in East European Transitions," in ed. R. E. Goodin, *The Theory of Institutional Design*. Cambridge: Cambridge University Press, pp. 199–226.
Ostrom, Elinor and Vincent Ostrom. 2014. *Choice, Rules and Collective Action. The Ostroms on the Study of Institutions and Governance,* edited by F. Sabetti and P. Aligica. Colcester, UK: ECPR Press.
———. 2014 [1982]. Elinor Ostrom. "Beyond Positivism," pp. 213–225.
———. 2014 [1997]. Vincent Ostrom. "Epistemic Choice and Public Choice," pp. 243–69.
———. 2014 [1998]. Elinor Ostrom. "A Behavioral Approach to the Rational Choice Theory of Collective Action," pp. 121–66.
———. 2014 [2004]. Elinor Ostrom and Vincent Ostrom. "The Quest for Meaning in Public Choice," pp. 61–93.
Ostrom, Elinor. 1990. *Governing the Commons: the evolution of institutions for collective action*. New York: Cambridge University Press.
Ostrom, Elinor. 2003. "How Types of Goods and Property Rights Jointly Affect Collective Action." *Journal of Theoretical Politics*, 15, 3: 239–70.
Ostrom, Elinor. 2005. *Understanding Institutional Diversity*. Princeton NJ: Princeton University Press.
Ostrom, Vincent. 1980. "Artisanship and Artifact." *Public Administration Review*, 40, 4: 309–17.
Ostrom, Vincent. 1982. "The Human Condition," in Workshop Archives, Workshop in Political Theory and Political Analysis. Bloomington, IN: Indiana University.
Ostrom, Vincent. 1997. *The Meaning of Democracy and the Vulnerability of Democracies*. Ann Arbor: University of Michigan Press.
Ostrom, Vincent. 2008a. *The Intellectual Crisis in American Public Administration* (3rd edition), Foreword by Barbara Allen. Tuscaloosa: University of Alabama Press.
Ostrom, Vincent. 2008b. *The Political Theory of a Compound Republic. Designing the American Experiment* (3rd, augmented edition with a co-authored chapters with Barbara Allen), Foreword by Daniel J. Elazar. Lanham: Lexington.
Ostrom Vincent. 2011. *The Quest to Understand Human Affairs. Natural Resources Policy and Essays on Community and Collective Choice*, edited by B. Allen. Lanham: Lexington.
———. 2011 [1978]. "Language, Reason, and Discourse: A Comment on Thomas Sowell's 'Institutional Advantage and State Action Concepts,'" pp. 271–89.
———. 2011 [1982]. "The Normative Context of Community," pp. 291–317.

———. 2011 [1988]. "The Foundations of Institutional Analysis and Development," pp. 451–75.

Ostrom Vincent. 2012. *The Quest to Understand Human Affairs. Essays on Collective, Constitutional, and Epistemic Choice*, edited by B. Allen. Lanham: Lexington.

———. 2012 [1992]. "Democracy and Self-governance," pp. 372–380.

———. 2012 [1997a]. "Buchanan's Opening to Constitutional Choice and Meta Levels of Analysis," pp. 81–110.

———. 2012 [1997b]. "The Inevitability of Democracy," pp. 381–93.

———. 2012 [2000]. "The Spirit of Federalism," pp. 541–45.

———. 2012 [2002]. "What is Federalism? A Search for Meaning," pp. 546–57.

———. 2012 [2011]. "Citizens-Sovereigns: The Implication of Hamilton's Query and Tocqeville's Conjecture about the Democratic Revolution," pp. 632–52.

Rawls, John. 1971. *A Theory of Justice*. Oxford: Oxford University Press.

Rawls, John. 1993. *Political Liberalism*. New York: Columbia University Press.

Sabetti, Filippo. 2000. "Covenant Language in Canada: Continuity and Change in Political Discourse," in Elazar, D. J., Kincaid, J. eds. *The Covenant Connection: From Federal Theology to Modern Federalism*, pp. 259–84.

Sen, Amartya. 1977. "Rational Fools: A Critique of the Behavioural Foundations of Economic Theory." *Philosophy and Public Affairs*. 6: 317–44.

Sen, Amartya. 2002. *Rationality and Freedom*. Cambridge, Mass: Harvard University Press.

Shepsle, Kenneth A. 2008. "Rational Choice Institutionalism," in eds. R. A. W. Rhodes, S. A. Binder and B. A. Rockman. *The Oxford Handbook of Political Institutions*. Oxford: Oxford University Press, pp. 23–38.

Simon, Herbert A. 1983. *Reason in Human Affairs*. Oxford: Basil Blackwell.

Skinner, Quentin. 2009. "A Genealogy of the Modern State." *Proceedings of the British Academy*. 162: 325–70.

Sugden, Robert. 1993. "Rationality and Impartiality: Is the Contractarian Enterprise Possible?" in D. Gauthier and R. Sugden eds. *Rationality, Justice and the Social Contract: Themes from "Morals by Agreement."* New York and London: Harvest Withsheafer, pp. 157–75.

Taylor, Charles. 1995. "Irreducible Social Goods," in *ibid*. *Philosophical Arguments*. Cambridge, Mass.: Harvard University Press, pp. 127–45.

Taylor, Charles. 2004. *Modern Social Imaginaries*. Durham and London: Duke University Press.

Taylor, Charles. 2016. *The Language Animal: The Full Shape of the Human Linguistic Capacity*. Cambridge, Mass.: Harvard University Press.

Taylor, Michael. 2006. *Rationality and the Ideology of Disconnection*. Cambridge: Cambridge University Press.

Waldron, Jeremy. 1999. *Law and Disagreement*. Oxford: Oxford University Press.

Weale, Albert. 2013. *Democratic Justice and the Social Contract*. Oxford: Oxford University Press.

Chapter 7

Civic Theory, Bloomington, and a Republican Renewal

Karol Edward Sołtan

When Paul Dragos Aligica published his *Institutional Diversity and Political Economy* (2014) Elinor Ostrom wrote in the blurb on the back cover: "It is simply a fantastic book. Paul Dragos Aligica brought together aspects of our work that I knew about but had not yet linked together in the way that he has. The overwhelming reaction I have had is that he has taken our work many steps into the future." The importance of the book lies mainly in its details, the many fronts along which he develops the Bloomington program. But the book is also striking in the two ways it locates the Bloomington program in an intellectual context. First, as part of an effort to develop "the art and science of association" and to elaborate the perspective of a citizen. And, second, as a work within the pragmatist tradition.

This chapter reflects a partial dissent. I treat the Bloomington School as part of an emerging interdisciplinary discipline of civic studies, developing the perspective of citizens. But I believe it is fruitful to also see it as part of a broad renewal of the republican tradition, not of pragmatism. Instead of making my case through a text based argument, matching Bloomington and republican texts, I outline in the chapter a form of moderate republicanism transformed into social science, that seems to me to have strong Bloomington affinities. But it is not all Bloomington. Civic theory requires a robust normative theory, which has not been fully developed in Bloomington. And moderate republicanism should be in many ways law centered, more so (I believe) than has been common in Bloomington.

CIVIC STUDIES AND BLOOMINGTON

In September 2007 a group of scholars called for the development of a new field, a new interdisciplinary discipline, which we might call a new civics, or civic studies. Their statement was signed (in alphabetical order) by Harry Boyte, Stephen Elkin, Peter Levine, Jane Mansbridge, Elinor Ostrom, Rogers Smith and myself.[1] Many others might have signed it, but were not present at the meeting that formulated the idea.

We can describe the goal of this new field in a variety of ways. It is the development of ideas and skills supportive of the "art and science of association" or of the "art and science of self-government and self-organization," or the development of ideas helpful to citizens understood as cocreators of their worlds. The idea of human beings as creators, and a conception of human creation with a significant social dimension (cocreation), seem to be central to this new civics (Sołtan 2014).

Civic accounts of the mind, of human interaction, of human ends and ideals are accounts that take human creative capacity as a fundamental fact. Allowing for this in social science has been a difficult task, often resulting in unproductive complex discussions of agency and structure, and not much progress in our understanding. Much of mainstream social science builds causal models without worrying about this, secure in the knowledge that the models will be sufficiently incomplete and inadequate that the underlying issue of determinism can be swept under the rug. The new civics takes a different tack. Instead of simply allowing for the capacity of human beings to be cocreators, it aims to develop ideas that would actually strengthen that capacity.

After the 2007 meeting we organized yearly Summer Institutes of Civic Studies, so we needed to identify, however tentatively, a canon of civic theory. It includes most prominently the Ostroms (2014), Jürgen Habermas (1984; 1987; 1996), Roberto Mangabeira Unger (1987; 2007), Brent Flyvbjerg (2001) and Philip Selznick (1992; Krygier 2012). In some ways the central debate in civic theory is the debate between the Bloomington School and the various followers of Habermas, including a range of proponents of deliberative democracy (Levine and Sołtan 2014). We can also see a tension between two powerful influences, between various forms of pragmatism on one side, and various forms of republicanism on the other. And, finally, we have our own version of the famous German Methodenstreit in social science between the followers of Newton and Newton's enemies, between "naturalism" and "anti—naturalism," between "positivists" in the loose sense commonly accepted in social science, and "anti-positivists."

A civic theory must have a serious normative component. It must be able to distinguish action that is civic from action that is a narrowly self-interested manipulation. It must be able to identify improvements, and distinguish them from changes that are not improvements. This suggests that civic theory cannot be "naturalistic" or "positivist" in the usual sense. And in fact many civic theorists (such as Habermas (1984; 1987), Unger (1987; 2007) or Flyvbjerg

(2001)) elaborate alternatives to naturalism. This is not the choice of the Bloomington School. In the Bloomington School, however, the issue of normative theory is mostly sidestepped. There are some notable discussions by Vincent Ostrom (2011), but they do not feature prominently. The central value of polycentricity, for example, is promoted mostly as an instrument. It is not usually presented as valuable in itself.

Paul Aligica describes the main commitments of Ostroms' work as "realism, fallibilism, pluralism of method, recognition of the role of reasons and ideas in social action, robust empiricism and a focus on practice and the applied level" (Aligica 2014, 197). He formulates the Bloomington program as "an institutionalist political economy framed from a pragmatist perspective" (Aligica 2014, 197). He, too, does not leave much room for normative theory. If we seriously aim to elaborate a civic perspective, this seems problematic.

In this chapter I outline a form of civic theory that belongs to the party of Newton, and with strong affinities to the Bloomington School, with its roots in rational choice institutionalism, and its concern with polycentricity. But as an alternative to rational choice institutionalism I propose a civic account of the human mind in interaction, with room for incentives, ideas and institutions. And instead of pragmatism I propose a reformulation of the republican tradition, including a civic and polycentric form of natural law. And I embed the ideal of polycentricity in a larger project of moderation (Sołtan 2008; 2010; 2011; see also Craiutu 2012). In this account there is no ambivalence about normative commitments. I propose an alternative that goes beyond the Bloomington School, as it is understood by Aligica, in three ways. It goes beyond rational choice institutionalism, it goes beyond pragmatism, and it aims to reconstruct a deeply moderate form of republicanism.

But what I propose can also be read, I think, as one (perhaps unorthodox) *elaboration* of the research program of the Bloomington School. And since the Ostroms did not seem very keen on maintaining orthodoxy, I will leave it to the reader to decide how the alternative I elaborate in this chapter relates to the ongoing program of the Bloomington School, when the latter is construed as a school of civic theory.

BEYOND RATIONAL CHOICE INSTITUTIONALISM

If we adopt in a serious way the idea of a new civics as a social science, we ought to take as a starting point the work of the Bloomington School. We begin, as a first approximation, with rational choice and game theory, and we add the significance of institutions, ideas and human fallibility. But it is easy to underestimate the intellectual transformation that is required to do this in depth.

We should build a micro-civics while taking seriously two constraints: First, rational choice and game theory should emerge as an approximation to a special case of the models of micro-civics, as they do (in principle at least) in both the work of the Bloomington school and in Habermas. Second, these models should allow appropriate room for both the influence of ideas and of institutions.

Working within these constraints I will outline a micro-civics that can be seen at one level as an account of situation-specific structures of power (or fields of power). At another level it can be seen as an account of human interaction or of cooperative games. One can start by noting that the process of negotiation consists of two kinds of events. First, human minds attempt to modify the existing structure of power (field of power) within the negotiation by making new threats, new promises, new arguments, new commitments and so on. And second, human minds respond to those structures of power by conceding at various speeds.

So, as rational choice would have it: human minds respond to incentives. But they also respond, for example, to arguments. And human minds also create incentives, and they create and entrench structures of reasons for action (institutions among them). Human minds are both made by these structures, and they are makers of them.

It is central to a civic conception of the mind that human beings are creators, responsible agents, capable of initiative, authors of their actions, producers, capable of bringing new things into the world. They are cocreators of the structures of power (fields of power) within which they act.

In developing this kind of civic conception of the mind, I suggest we follow four rules.

Rule 1: Social science (and civic theory) should explore the microstructure of human action, as does rational choice and game theory. A superficial version of this rule leads to some form of methodological individualism. Groups are composed of individuals, so individuals are the microstructure of groups. A deeper alternative begins not with groups but with human interaction, with bargaining, negotiation, deliberation, and with tacit forms of all three. We search for the microstructure of these processes, and we find it (I would suggest) composed of fields of force created by power resources brought to bear on a situation (through threats, promises, arguments, and so on).

Rule 2: Social science (and civic theory) should adopt the internal point of view, as does rational choice theory. Rational choice and game theory are usually developed with a distinctive kind of internal point of view on action. They are not an effort to see action as the agent sees it, adopting the reasoning of the agent, and requiring a sympathetic understanding of the perspective of the agent. This has been one form of "adopting the internal point of view," often labeled with the German word "verstehen." For rational choice, the internal point of view is something different. It represents a perspective that can be a source of *advice* to the agent (it can be helpful to the agent, it can be part of the education of the agent). So in game theory we ask how the players should play, and we can use the answers to advise the players, to tell players how to play, or to teach them how to play. This is not necessarily the agent's *actual* perspective.

We can think of game theory as articulating a canon for teaching how to play, or an account of player competence, as against actual player performance. We will see actual performance, then, as a combination of this competence and errors. Actual decision making is in part errors and in part the following of heuristics designed to diminish error rates. And these heuristics are something we could teach.

To look at human actions and human decisions in this way, from the internal point of view, is to combine normative and descriptive tasks. It is to do precisely what Kahneman and Tversky criticize and try to avoid in developing their prospect theory (1979). But prospect theory lacks a strong sense of internal logic. It presents human decisions as a product of a sequence of moves, using seemingly ad hoc devices. The internal point of view, by contrast, provides a coherent logic to theory, precisely because it provides a canon of what we should teach.

Like rational choice theory, a civic theory is an account of human action, of cocreation, from the internal point of view. It can be the basis of advice helpful to cocreators, it can be seen as a rational reconstruction of the canon of cocreation, or as an account of civic competence, a combination of competence in the choice of means (or instrumental competence) and competence in the choice of ends, or in the choice of first principles, of human ideals and purposes.

The concept of "internal point of view" is also familiar in legal theory. In his classic reformulation of the positivist theory of law H.L.A. Hart (Hart 1961) contrasted the external and the internal point of view on rules. From the external point of view, rules and laws can be identified with regularities of behavior. We can predict the behavior of judges when they follow rules, and when we can, we understand the law from the outside. But "prophecies of what a court will do in fact" (Holmes 1897, 461) do not help judges, who must understand the law from the inside, because they take part in the law. A judge's understanding of the law takes a form that can be used to advise judges about how to act, and it can be used to teach judges how to be judges. That is an understanding of law from the internal point of view. And so it would be for institutions in general, and for structures of power within which these institutions are embedded.

Rule 3: Explanation of action is not and should not be the goal of social science (or of civic theory). The goal (or at least one goal) should be to explain *changes* in actions. In economics we explain changes in the behavior of consumers or producers in response to changes in prices, that is, changes in incentives. And in the social sciences more generally the task ought to be to explain "minds in motion," to explain how minds change in response to the structures of power. We can put this in a strikingly simple way. We follow the example of Newtonian physics. Where physics explains the motion of matter as a product of fields of forces, we explain the motion of minds as a product of fields of power, which can also be seen as force fields. Systems of incentives are often key components of such force fields.

Our window on such force fields is an analysis in detail of negotiation and deliberation grounded in a spatial theory of politics. All human interaction takes the form of minds in motion under the influence of power fields build up of incentives, reasons for action and other resources. Minds are in motion in the fields of power, in spaces akin to those familiar from spatial models of politics. And we can see some of the microstructure of those power fields through a detailed analysis of the microstructure of negotiation, with attention to power at each point in the space of human interaction, and with attention to the speed of the movement of minds at each point (empirically, that would be the speed of concession).

In attempting to explain the sources of mind change, the sources of the motion of minds in the spaces of human interaction, we have a better hope of deeper understanding of human action. But we cannot in this way actually explain any human action. Human action occurs when people make up their minds, when their minds stop.

Rule 4: "People respond to incentives" is the fundamental axiom of economics and of rational choice. It is best seen as one among a number of axioms in a more inclusive theory of power, or a theory of human capacities to influence outcomes. People also resist incentives. And people respond to arguments, to reasons for action and to reasons for beliefs, including reasons in the form of rules. Some of those reasons for action are entrenched in situations, or entrenched in individual and collective actors, or entrenched in actions. The microstructure of human interaction, or the microstructure of power, is composed of all these elements. Some of these entrenched reasons for action (or rules) correspond to what we would call institutions (in the sense of "rules of the game"), some constitute the goals and preferences of agents, others define action types. Some of the entrenchment enhances predictability of social life, but some does the opposite, it expands the range of meaningful alternative actions available to agents. Entrenchment only sometimes produces social order, but it more reliably produces meaningful forms. I elaborate on some of this in the next section, when I discuss the social varieties of "morphogenesis."

Let me reiterate: human minds move in response to fields of power, which include incentives, and more. But human minds also help create and modify those fields. They respond to incentives, and they modify incentives. They choose strategies within games, and they modify those games. They concede in light of threats, and they make those threats.

Or let us put it in the language of citizenship: human beings are both rulers and ruled. There is a kind of tacit citizenship in much of human interaction. And there is a dualism in the civic perspective. Human beings both obey and create the rules and power structures within which they live.

HOMO CREATIVUS

A key distinctive feature of civic theory must be to accept human creativity, and to go beyond acceptance. The goal is to help this creativity, or to develop ideas that make creation *easier*, so difficulty is the central concept, and the central variable, of civic theory.

The Realm of the Difficult

If we develop ideas that are helpful to cocreation (e.g., helpful in overcoming the problem of collective action) we are—simply by being helpful—participating in cocreation. Our ideas are a part of cocreation, they ought to be part of the canon of cocreation. We can say that we are developing an internal point of view on cocreation. The internal point of view is a helpful perspective, the perspective of a friend, a loyal advisor, a teacher. This is, or should be, the perspective of civic theory.

The realm of human cocreation is an alternative to the realm of necessity and of accident. In a world of nature, entirely governed by settled laws, human actions could only be either inevitable or impossible or accidental. There would be no room for human initiative and agency. We need a fourth concept, and for the purposes of the new civics the best candidate is the idea of *difficulty* (Sołtan 2014). An action is impossible if it reaches the extreme value of difficulty. An action is inevitable if *avoiding* it reaches the extreme value of difficulty. But between these extremes we live in the realm of difficulties that can be overcome, we live in the realm of human creativity. To study human creativity in a way that is meant to be helpful to that creativity, we study impediments (what strengthens difficulty, the sources of difficulty, the sources of resistance). Human cognitive limits or the problem of collective action are examples. Or we study what we might call civic resources, or assets that weaken or overcome difficulty (here certain institutions or skills may be examples).

An excellent exemplar of such research is the work of the Bloomington School on the problem of collective action, and on the "tragedy of the commons." In that research the tragedy is transformed into an impediment that can be diminished or overcome, "a drama of the commons" (Ostrom et al. 2002). It is a source of difficulty, but there are strategies, heuristics and institutions that can diminish or overcome this difficulty.

To create is to bring into existence something new that did not exist before. Any action is at least marginally an innovation. But some actions are more unprecedented and unpredictable. They contain more novelty, and require more creativity. They are also more difficult.

We can go further in our analysis of human beings as creators. Consider as an example, familiar in an academic setting, the writing of a paper. We begin with some vague ideas, and maybe an incomplete outline. But by the time we are finished, the vagueness has been much diminished and the outline has been replaced with a completed text. The paper has been given *form.* And we have achieved this (most likely) by writing multiple drafts, each an *improvement* over the previous one. We could describe in roughly the same way the creation of laws and institutions, or the creation of actions.

The process of bringing something new into existence will have (at least) two features (which we can see most clearly if the process is extended over time): we *give form* and we *improve*. First, to create is to give form. It is morphogenesis. It is some combination of composition and articulation. And, second, to create is also to improve. Writing papers in multiple drafts is an excellent example. Let me consider these two features in turn.

Creation as Morphogenesis

Two processes are central to morphogenesis in social and institutional life. The first (let us call it composition) works through "gluing" elements together, attaching together through entrenchment (for example) actions and reasons for action, entrenching them in agents, in situations or in actions themselves. The second is a process of articulation.

Morphogenesis through composition requires attaching together elements. Here the metaphor of glue seems appropriate. You glue together different components *through entrenchment*, and you create relations among those components. You create structures; you entrench reasons for action in agents and in situations, but also in actions. The more general problem is not design and creation of institutions, it is the design and creation of forms, physical and mental forms, forms that exist in a world of matter, and forms that exist in mental worlds, in spaces in which minds move.

The question arises: what do we entrench, and in what? In my example of an academic paper, we entrench words in a text. But here let me limit myself to cases in which we entrench actions and reasons for action. *In what* do we entrench? First, we entrench in situations: reasons for action entrenched in situations are institutions in the sense of rules of the game. We also entrench in individual and collective agents. These then constitute action guiding systems of practical reasons which can form preferences. And we entrench in actions. We determine, for example, what you have to do in order to make a legally binding promise. Actions can be components of actions. Such entrenchment gives form to situations, to institutions, to agents and to actions; it constitutes various types of morphogenesis. Sometimes it also improves predictability, but sometimes not. Sometimes it expands the range of available options, and can reduce predictability. Morphogenesis has a complicated relationship to social order.

Entrenchment is achieved through a variety of instruments, notably through enforcement (using incentives) and through education (which we often misleadingly call socialization). Education can be in the form of tacit learning, or in the form of explicitly designed program of teaching, which requires the design and creation of a canon.

Some actions and some reasons for action are easier to entrench than others. Some are easy to agree on, they have Schelling's conspicuous uniqueness, they are "focal points" (Schelling 1960). Others are better or more nearly right. Here we encounter a window from the realm of reasons for action that are simply entrenched, and in this sense conventional, toward what we might call a post-conventional morality. We can find here, or build, a view out of the cave, to invoke a somewhat tired Platonic metaphor.

Morphogenesis also occurs through articulation, a process that begins in vagueness, chaos and confusion, and proceeds to clarity and distinctness. It can be the process of codification or of rational reconstruction. It moves away from the fused and the confused, away from the tacit to the explicit. We see it in legal codifications, in reasoning in common law, in the creation of job evaluation schemes (Sołtan 1987), in various forms of rational reconstruction of human competence, and in the methods of ethics, such as the Rawlsian method of reflective equilibrium (Rawls 1971). More on this below.

Creation as Improvement

A civic theory that is helpful to cocreators of their worlds should help in the selection of means, but it should not limit itself to means. It should be responsive to the critique of instrumental reason, so prominently featured in the Frankfurt School tradition (Jay 1973), and in the work of Habermas (1984; 1987). We must take very seriously the task of elaborating a civic conception of ideals, of ends and goals of development. To be helpful to citizens we must develop a way of distinguishing better from worse ideals and ends, real improvement from apparent improvement, and we must do so in a way that is both civic and credible in a modern world for which science is the prime exemplar of reliable knowledge. A civic theory of ideals for the modern world ought to be distinctly practical, and distinctly rooted in, and testable by, empirical evidence.

I would suggest we treat the methodological writings of Rawls as a kind of halfway point from the treatment of ideals traditional in philosophy to a more empirical and practical framework. As I see it, a *civic* approach to ideals must be helpful to the task of making the world better. Let me use as an illustration the ideal of justice, where the contrast with Rawls can be more fully developed. A theory of justice must be helpful in making the world more just. This may sound obvious, but it is not widely accepted as a goal, and has some serious consequences for the formulation of the ideal of justice.

First, the ideal of justice must be as inspiring as possible, and it must be formulated in a way that is as inspiring as possible. To evaluate different accounts we ask the question: how attractive and inspiring are they for those open to inspiration. The ideal test would be in the form of deliberation among philosophically informed Gandhian satyagrahis (who show themselves open to inspiration by being willing to sacrifice for the satyagraha). It would not be deliberation among academic philosophers. And it would not be deliberation in a Habermasian ideal-speech situation, or in the original position.

Second, the ideal must be embedded in a promising project for reform. So it is reasonable to take as a starting point ideas and considered judgments found in the cultures of such promising projects.

In light of these considerations, we can construct a three step method that takes Rawlsian ideas as a starting point, but gives them a more practical and more empirical turn.

Step 1: Within the public and the tacit political cultures of promising projects of reform we identify a central idea for an account of justice (the equivalent of Rawls' s "fair terms of cooperation among free and equal citizens" (Rawls 2001, 5) but demonstrably, empirically, found in the relevant political culture) and a set of authoritative judgments (equivalent to Rawls's "considered moral judgments"). In the contemporary world the best candidate for a promising setting is the global project of human rights. Its central idea is the principle of inviolability of human dignity. The evolving lists of human rights in various declarations and treaties can be taken as the authoritative judgments (Nickel 2007; Clapham 2006).

Step 2: We articulate an account of justice broadly consistent with the authoritative judgments identified in Step 1, and formulated to do well in the tests identified in Step 3. Coherence is not here the highest value, and reflective equilibrium is not the goal.

Step 3: We test the account. To do this, we develop a conception of the ideal test, which can be used to construct a variety of different tests, and which can be also used to improve tests. I would suggest deliberation among satyagrahis as something close to an ideal test, and multiple experimental approximations and thought experiments as parts of a program of testing.

This method is not limited to the exploration of the ideal of justice. We can also use it to construct an account of legitimate goals for human development. Here too we begin with the empirical identification of goals contained in the global public political culture, but also in the tacit culture of human ideals. We begin with the goals of peace, development and sustainability, which are easily found in the global public political culture. We note that from within the global subcultures committed to these goals there have been efforts to break out to a more inclusive formulation of goals. Those who struggle for peace introduce the notion of positive peace as a complement to negative peace, which is the absence of war (Galtung 1996). Those committed to development propose conceptions of development (as in the capabilities approach) that include more than the growth of per capita income (Sen 1999; Nussbaum 2011). Finally, those committed to sustainability hope to abandon environmentalism and ecologism as distinctive programs, and embed them into a more encompassing project (Speth 2008; Nordhaus and Shellenberger 2007; Ophuls 2011).

I believe that the most attractive formulation of the project they all aim for would identify it as a project of deep moderation. In this project, development is understood as development toward maturity, more than simply development as emancipation (Sen 1999). Development is also seen as a struggle against human destructiveness (for peace, against ecological destruction, against the use of threats of harm as a basis of power, in favor of renewal as a reversal of destruction). And the code of goals of human development incorporates harmony, or unity in diversity, or polycentricity.

So with the global political culture as a starting point, we can sketch a project of deep moderation, with a distinctive code of ideals and purposes. We aim to formulate it in a way that will make it competitive in the necessary tests in step 3 of the method I outlined. The articulation of a code of deep moderation must be taken as the beginning of research, not its endpoint. It is the stage of articulation, prior to the stage of testing.

This method allows us to construct normative theories rooted in existing social settings and embedded in existing promising projects of reform. It is consistent with understanding ideals as real forces, with real (inspiring) effects on human minds, and hence as resources in the fields of power in which human minds move. The normative theory emerges from the conception of the human mind and of human interaction, a generalization of the models of rational choice and game theory, which I discussed in the previous section. But the conception of the ideal test is also based on a deeper normative idea, a kind of civic reformulation of natural law, which I discuss in the next section, when I address the issue of pragmatism in civic theory, and move toward an alternative: civic theory as part of a republican renewal, invoking Cicero, not Dewey.

BEYOND PRAGMATISM

Civic theory sometimes seems dominated by pragmatism, and by Dewey's pragmatism in particular. We can see this in Paul Aligica's development of the Bloomington School (Aligica 2014), but also in the romantic radicalism of Unger (Unger 2007), and in the humanistic social science of Selznick (Selznick 1992). Habermas's critical theory is also indebted to Dewey and the pragmatists (1986), although it does provide something of an alternative. Is it possible to resist this powerful attractive force of pragmatism? Let me suggest some ways.

Pragmatism is a good candidate for a "public philosophy" of modernity, and that may explain its pervasive influence. So we need alternative candidates for a public philosophy of modernity. Pragmatism is also an attractive candidate for a public philosophy of a modernity *in crisis*, lacking self-confidence, reduced to small thinking and a preoccupation with its own exhaustion. An alternative to pragmatism would propose a better public philosophy of modernity, or a better alternative to public philosophy. Perhaps it could be a public philosophy with the potential of taking modernity out of its crisis, capable of helping it to recover its nerve, and to discover new potential of the modern transformation.

From within the domain of the new civics we can suggest a civic theory of modernity, within a framework of what we might call the civic conception of the human mind. And in the modern spirit, we can make it as scientific as possible, taking Galileo and Newton as our intellectual heroes. We build on the strongest developments in the social sciences so far, in micro-economics and rational choice theory. In the next section I will suggest this can be best achieved through a reformulation of the republican tradition.

Some forms of pragmatism provide a good way to express what is now a common attitude, reflecting the sense of exhaustion of the modern project (Lyotard [1979] 1984; Rorty 1989). When we no longer find any large projects credible for humanity, when we find such projects only a source of danger, then a small minded form of pragmatism may seem appealing. In practical matters we insist on ad hoc problem-solving, avoiding the formulation of large-scale, long-term, inspiring projects. In theoretical matters we advocate problem driven research, contrasting it with what we call method driven research (Shapiro and Green 1984). Both in intellectual and in political matters we prefer the small and the ad hoc. This petty pragmatism is the kind of pragmatism Unger complains about in the opening to his recent book in which he embraces pragmatism, while simultaneously attempting to liberate it (the subtitle of the book is: *Pragmatism Unbound*).

For purposes of civic theory we can say that pragmatism centers on two commitments. First, a commitment to "naturalism," taking modern science as a model for reliable knowledge and for action. And, second, a commitment to experimentalism, and democratic experimentalism in particular, as a model for action and for politics.

Unger (2007) notes that the usual form of the commitment to modern science as a model for knowledge actually conflicts with a serious commitment to experimentalism in politics, and he urges the rejection of the first in order to take the latter to the hilt. But we can, and should, take both these commitments even more seriously than does pragmatism. If we do, I suggest, we will arrive at a form of civic theory that can only be described as an alternative to pragmatism.

Let us start with science. Many thinkers, perhaps Polanyi (1951) and Popper (1963) most famously, urged us to take modern science as a model for the production of reliable knowledge, but also for the organization of society. We now understand more deeply how science works than in the time of Polanyi and Popper, so we need to modify how we use it as a model. Science makes progress through a sequence of research programs that build on each other, but also involve profound reformulations of goals, concepts and theories. This is the sequence of paradigms according to Kuhn ([1962] 1970), of research programs according to Lakatos (1978), of research traditions according to Laudan (1977). Accepting this feature of scientific progress does not require the common relativistic misinterpretation of Kuhn (see Godfrey-Smith 2003).

Outside science we take this to be a pattern of human cocreation over time, cocreation working on ongoing projects, which we can understand as forms of shared creative capital, allowing contributions of different people to extend over time, and to build on each other. We create a project as a form of capital, then we use that project for a sustained period of cocreation, until the project is exhausted. Some projects are renewable, or turn out to be renewable when they become exhausted. Cocreation using nonrenewable projects follows approximately the familiar logistic curve. Cocreation using renewable projects gives us a pattern of cycles of creation. Because of the fame of T.S. Kuhn, science is here a familiar example. But in many ways a more elaborate example is the sequence of what Carlota Perez calls "techno-economic paradigms," which drives global economic development over the last two centuries, and drives the business cycles as well (Perez 2003).

If we take science as a model and as a window on human development, then we will expect such cycles. And we can adopt different civic strategies for different stages of the cycle. What is to be done in the crisis of exhaustion, and working toward the breakthrough of a new stage of a project (a new paradigm) will be different from what is required when the paradigm is at its full creative speed. Perez also identifies another distinctive moment in the development through projects, the moment of turbulence, when the new paradigm begins to threaten the old, which it might not initially. This moment of turbulence would require a distinctive approach as well.

If development proceeds in projects then the Deweyan pragmatist model seems doubly inadequate. It does not allow room for different perspectives at different stages of development. And more generally it does not allow for the significance of continuity in cocreation, the importance of tradition and of the past.

The second commitment of pragmatism in civic theory is to democratic experimentalism. But democratic experimentalism takes neither democracy nor experimentalism far enough. Democracy, for example, requires a certain rigidity in the way we understand the principle of equal respect, reflected in the rigidity with which we insist on the principle of one-person/one-vote. The project of democracy is also driven forward by the aspiration to expand the sphere of human creativity which cannot be identified with, or reduced to, experimentalism.

Experimentalism should not be reduced to a trial-and-error process; it should not be identified with the crudest possible form of experiments. It is better to see testing and exploration more generally as a project, in which we find better and worse windows on reality, we distinguish better and worse tests, we develop a diverse set of tests, and aim to improve them. By what standards should we make such distinctions? One of the key innovations of the scientific revolution is the development of carefully designed and executed tests (or experiments), and the development of instruments to be used in testing. So, in the spirit of modern science, we need to translate simple democratic experimentalism into an effort that develops tests for the various projects through which we strive to improve the world.

Finally, if we are going to be serious about science as a model for knowledge and for practice (as pragmatism appears to be), we need to transform the science of humanity in response to three fundamental challenges. The first challenge is determinism. A science that is serious about explaining human actions, or changes in actions, will show them to be products of causes and thus will put in question human agency and human responsibility. In fact, in multiple settings, this has been happening for a long time. The second challenge is the marginalization of ends. Modern science is insistent that it can be the basis for a choice of means, but not for the choice of ends. And the result is that the authority and credibility of ends has been undermined, even as instrumental reason triumphs. The third challenge is to the meaning and purpose of human lives. The more we understand the world, and humanity in it, scientifically, the more difficult it is to sustain meaning and purpose for human lives. In this way a culture based on modern science, as modern culture largely is, seems to undermine itself.

The scientific world view, when it is applied to the understanding of humanity, as it must be in a culture committed to it, produces inevitable pressure against any belief in the possibility of human initiative, human creativity, human agency and human responsibility. Humans and their actions will be seen ultimately as products of causal processes, and our belief in ourselves as actual agents will be revealed as an illusion.

The scientific world view helps in the improvement of means, but it claims not to be helpful in the choice of ends. So cultures under the influence of the scientific world view will be increasingly dominated by instrumental reason, and will increasingly undermine the authority of ideals. They will see them as merely subjective, or as arbitrary products of natural selection, good perhaps for the survival of the species or of its genes, but certainly not something that deserves our loyalty. Why should mere products of natural selection deserve our loyalty?

The scientific world view, finally, undermines systematically a broad range of sources of meaning and purpose in human lives. "The more the universe seems comprehensible, the more it also seems pointless," as Steven Weinberg said (1977, 154). And our lives in that world seem similarly pointless.

Perhaps the most common way to avoid these three challenges, is not to think about the subject enough to arrive at any conclusions. Or we can be content in the fact that the scientific understanding of humanity is in any case so deficient, we need not worry. Or we can try to separate somehow the realm of human freedom from the realm of natural necessity. Or in the social sciences we can attempt to articulate increasingly complex and convoluted views that attempt to reconcile human agency and the constraints of mental and social structures.

Alternatively we can reject the scientific world view and the broader legacy of the Enlightenment. This has been, if one can paint in broad strokes, the choice of the romantic Counter-Enlightenment. In the study of humanity it has been the choice of those who reject the model of science, and argue we should think about humanity in a different way.

I suggest we have an opportunity in civic theory to develop an alternative, but the alternative will not embrace pragmatism. We should take seriously the plain fact of everyday experience that human beings are capable of initiative, creativity and agency, and also that human beings are a part of reality. So reality contains within it what we can call reality's process of self-creation, and it is a process we can investigate in human beings. We will find traces of this process within the fields of power, within structures of human interaction, to the extent we can identify in them the effects of power resources belonging to reality's process of self-creation.

To suggest such a possibility is to propose a way of thinking with clear roots in the natural law tradition. But it is a very distinctive form of natural law. It is a strong form, in so far as it contains more than just law. It is a modern form, because we aim to investigate it scientifically. It is a civic form because it does not govern matters that are settled. It is embedded rather in a process of creation.

Pragmatism is notoriously hard to define, but surely it does not allow such ideas! Yet I suggest this is a place we arrive when we push our commitments to naturalism and to practical experimentalism to the hilt, as Unger would say. So if we take pragmatism's commitments more seriously than pragmatists do, we arrive at a position that is altogether different, and—I suggest—more promising as a response to the three great challenges facing the scientific world view, and hence facing also modernity whose culture is to a large degree built on the scientific world view.

What does this alternative look like then? We begin with a speculative empirical hypothesis: reality contains within it a process of reality's self-creation. Human beings as creative agents are our best window onto this aspect of reality. Exploring this aspect of humanity, their creative agency, from the inside, is our best chance to understand this process. We can develop a strategy for this exploration within the framework of the civic conception of the mind. Minds move in fields of power, but minds also cocreate those fields of power. Power resources (bases of threats, promises, arguments, commitments) create force fields in those fields of power. What people do, and what people believe, is a product of those force fields. In the language lately popular in the social sciences and beyond: human actions and human beliefs are socially constructed.

But if we take this view seriously as the basis of a scientific perspective on human action and human beliefs, then we have to say that scientific theories themselves are socially constructed. In the form of the strong program of the sociology of science (Barnes and Bloor 1982; Barnes et al.1999), this view seems self-undermining. Our understanding of science and our critique of ideology are themselves socially constructed. As indeed on this view they must be. But this conclusion is not self-undermining if reality itself is a source of influence in the fields of power. Then we can say, reasonably enough, that scientific theories are socially constructed, with variable influence from reality. Some theories are more open to the influence of reality than others. It is the business of science to enhance this openness, to look for windows on reality, to construct analogues of telescopes and microscopes.

By increasing openness to reality we reduce the *arbitrariness* of scientific beliefs.

If reality contains a process of self-creation, a creative component, we can also attempt to explore the influence of that component of reality in the various processes of social construction through fields of power. We look for situations where reality is the most creative, as it is in human beings, and we look for situations where it is plausible to attribute this creative process to an objective reality, not to individual animals of the species homo sapiens. We look for settings where reality is creative through us, through the power fields in which human minds move.

Such exploration requires a search for windows onto this reality; it requires some equivalent of instruments and tests. It should guide our methodology for the exploration of the world of ideals, including the specification of what would constitute ideal tests (a topic I discussed in Section 3 above). But it is also helped by the development of some guiding hypotheses about the nature of this process, hypotheses to be elaborated and tested. I propose as such a guiding hypothesis the idea that the project of moderation, including a strong and transformative component, is the project whose adoption reality demands. The project elaborates on a simple code, consisting of, first, a commitment to pluralism, the ideal of unity in diversity, the idea of polycentricity; second, a recognition of human cognitive and moral limits and a commitment to determine the precise shape of those limits; and, third, an opposition to human destructiveness. According to this hypothesis of moderation the idea of polycentric cocreation is built into reality's process of self-creation.

The exploration of reality's process of self-creation is combined with a normative command: Take part in this process, take part in reality's process of self-creation. One reason for us to explore this process, in addition to a simple desire to discover a largely hidden, and little understood aspect of the world, is to help us act in accordance with this command, to help us take part in reality's process of self-creation.

To make progress in this participation we will need to advance on two fronts. First, the principles and institutions that govern our actions will need to be improved. To the extent they are means they will have to be made into better means. To the extent they are ends they will have to be made into better ends. The first will require instrumental expertise, and deliberation among those with the relevant instrumental expertise (which in general will require a balance of general and local knowledge). The second, I would suggest, will require deliberation among those who take human ideals and purposes seriously, those open to being inspired by them. Hence I have suggested above that deliberation among something like Gandhian satyagrahis will come close to being an ideal test, more so than general democratic deliberation, or deliberation in philosophy departments.

The second front consists of progress in implementation, including the development of institutions that constitute effective instruments of implementation, such as courts of law, sovereign territorial states, markets or civic social movements.

This alternative to pragmatism can be best seen as a reformulation and extension of a strong and modern form of the natural law tradition. Our exemplar of scientific knowledge is not Aristotle, as it was for Thomas Aquinas, but Galileo and Newton. And we restate natural law, abandoning features that historically have been seen as defining features of that tradition.

Those who invoke natural law love to quote Cicero:

> True law is right reason in agreement with Nature; it is of universal application, unchanging and everlasting; it summons to duty by its commands, and averts from wrong-doing by its prohibitions. . . . It is a sin to try to alter this law . . . and it is impossible to try to abolish it entirely. We cannot be freed from its obligations by Senate or People. . . . And there will not be different laws at Rome and at Athens, or different laws now or in the future, but one eternal and unchangeable law will be valid for all nations and for all times . . . (Cicero, *De Republica*, III, xxiii, 33).[2]

But if principles and projects are based not in settled nature, but in reality's process of self-creation, then we will expect what they demand of us to vary over time. And since these demands are not derived from a universal human nature, they do not need to be universal. Reality may make distinctive demands on humanity as a whole, but also distinctive demands for different groups and situations. For each individual human being, it may demand that we be true to ourselves, that we become who we are. We may have then a polycentric natural law, containing some universal elements but also some local ones. This would be one way to interpret the notoriously ambiguous thesis of value pluralism put forward by Isaiah Berlin (1990). I would suggest we take this alternative as a plausible and attractive interpretation of the language of Gandhi, when he speaks of his work as the search for truth, and of similar reliance on the language of truth in the struggle against communism. This is not a conceptual framework, nor a system of claims, that can be fit into a pragmatist perspective. But the invocation of Cicero suggests an alternative. We have here, I would argue, a contribution to the renewal of the republican tradition.

REPUBLICANISM RENEWED

The common formula for the goal of the new civics, to develop ideas helpful to citizens understood as cocreators of their worlds, sounds vaguely pragmatic. We are interested in useful ideas. Ideas are to be tested in a particular form of practice.

In light of the above discussion, we can add a deeper goal: we aim to develop ideas that help us take part in reality's self-creation, ideas that help us understand the process of reality's self-creation from the inside. Doing so takes to the hilt (to use again Unger's favorite expression) the idea of human being as creator (homo creativus) and it takes to the hilt *opposition to arbitrariness*. It can best be seen as a contribution to the ancient republican tradition. We develop this tradition not by repeating its old claims, but by diversifying, generalizing and enriching it. We take its central concepts to a higher level of abstraction. And we construct from within the republican tradition an answer to the legacy of Hobbes (including rational choice), that incorporates that legacy, rather than rejecting it.

Contemporary mainstream rational choice theory can be seen as elaborating an important part of the intellectual legacy of Hobbes. And we can also develop a civic theory (or a public philosophy) of modernity, in a Hobbesian style, committed to modern science and to the more austere forms of rational choice. I do not read the Bloomington School as part of this line of thought, although some might. Paul Aligica's suggestion of pragmatism as a guiding framework for Bloomington seems to me deeper and more interesting. But there is a third alternative, which I have begun sketching in the previous sections. I believe it is a promising framework for civic theory, and arguably to be found as well in the Bloomington tradition. The path I suggest is to reformulate the republican tradition in the spirit of modern science, and to generalize it.

Such reformulation can and should include a scientific framework for exploring human action, with its roots in the republican tradition. And it should incorporate a normative theory and a conception of liberty with their roots in a republican alternative to Hobbes (Pettit 1997). And we can elaborate an alternative solution to "the Hobbesian problem of order" by way of codifying the classics of social theory (Parsons 1937). Actually, we can go deeper, and explore republican alternatives to the Parsons-influenced preoccupation with "the Hobbesian problem of order," as I do in my discussion of morphogenesis in Section 3.

The alternative I have sketched above is a broader intellectual framework which is inspired by modern science, as is Hobbes. It is inspired even in a parallel way by the idea of a science of motion governed by fields of forces. But to build on the rational choice tradition we make it a science of minds in motion, subject to fields of forces created by bringing to bear power resources (i.e., by making threats or promises, or making persuasive arguments). We add a fundamental "civic" element. These fields are cocreated by human beings. We are both governed by them and cocreators of them. In this manner we are like citizens of them (both rulers and ruled). Within the fields of power we can distinguish the public resources from the private ones, so we can develop a more general concept of a res publica as a distinctive form of a field of power. And we can reformulate within this framework the ideal of the reduction of arbitrariness.

To make it a good alternative to pragmatism, we not only reformulate republicanism in the spirit of modern science, but construct from its elements a civic theory for the project of modernity, and in particular for the next stage of modernity. Inspired by civic humanists of the fifteenth century, we incorporate a proposal for a reform of education, not simply of how we teach, but of the content of what we teach, and how we organize the teachable knowledge. So we call for a reorganization of the disciplines, including adding a new civic studies. Inspired by the Enlightenment we incorporate a multi-level proposal for an institutional and constitutional reform, featuring a distinctly moderate form of the call for a deeper democracy.

The alternative ought to be a modern reformulation of the moderate form of republicanism. If we care about this project as a universal project, however, it would be better to call it a republican form of a global project of moderation, the main Western form of the universal tradition of moderation. Outside the West, moderation elaborates on Confucian themes, or builds on the legacy of the emperor Asoka, or on the themes of ahimsa, or on the identification of Islamic civilization with "a middle community (*ummah wasatah*)" in light of a well-known Quranic verse (Quran 2,143; Nassr 2004, 162).

I would identify the following as the key aspects of this reformulation. First, we construct a new idea of res publica, defined in a framework of the fields of power: abstract and general, distinctly not state centered, building on the idea of public good and related ideas. Second, we identify two commitments as central for republicanism: promoting the idea and the practice of human beings as creative (homo creativus), and opposition to arbitrariness. Finally, we build the ideal of moderation on three pillars: first, a commitment to a realistic appraisal of human cognitive and moral capacities, and the shape of their limits; second, a commitment to balance, equilibrium and harmony, expressed in the ideals of unity in diversity and simplicity in complexity, elaborating the idea of polycentric cocreation; and finally opposition to the influence of human destructiveness.

The Spectrum of Republicanism

The contemporary renewal of the republican tradition takes a variety of intellectual and political forms. We have, first, a remarkable national diversity. Reading Elkin (2006) and Sandel (1996) gives us a sense of the range of US-centered republicanism. A very different French republicanism emerges from, say, the work of Ferry and Renaut (1992). Viroli's (2002) renewal of the Italian republicanism is quite distant in its central themes from Legutko's (Legutko and Kloczkowski 2002) or Krasnodębski's (2003) forms of Polish republicanism.

We have also a profound diversity of theoretical styles. For some, republicanism translates above all into support for participatory democracy, or citizens' authentic participation in the sovereign. For others republicanism should be identified with a commitment to a distinctive, neo-Roman conception of liberty. To be a republican is to love *aurea libertas*, and the central polemic between republicans and liberals concerns the definition of liberty. And there is a third style for whom what is central to republicanism is the love of the res publica, of the common good, a form of patriotism we can identify with civic virtue. These emphases are not mutually exclusive, but it is possible to weigh different aspects of the republican tradition differently. A theoretical and practical republican renewal is bound to create multiple republicanisms.

We also have a more profound divide between what we might call the moderate and the radical republicanisms. Moderate republicanism is especially at home with Aristotle, Polybius and Cicero, Montesquieu and the American founders. It is a republicanism that loves the law, aspires to make law king, and is open to the idea of natural law. It also loves complex systems of institutional balances, *res publica mixta* and the separation of powers. In Bloomington language we might say: it loves polycentric republics. It is moderate also in its reluctance to use violence as a basis of power, and in its willingness to be realistic about human moral and intellectual capacities. If by revolutions we mean the violent rejections of the institutional inheritance from the past, including cutting off the heads of monarchs and aristocrats, this republicanism is profoundly antirevolutionary. But of course there is also a revolutionary and radical republicanism famous for cutting heads, and for attempting to build a republic that consists in something entirely new. The Jacobins in love with the republic of virtue (and some of their English Puritan predecessors) were among prominent republicans, and outside Marxism, a great deal of the socialist tradition (certainly in France) can be counted among the republicans also. Ferry and Renaut cite Blum's identification of "Jaures's socialism [with] a 'deepening of the idea of a republic,' and 'a sort of deduction of the republican principles'" (Ferry and Renaut 1992, 117). Ferry and Renaut suggest that we return from this "deepening" to the republican idea itself. They want to return to republicanism in its moderate form; and they want it to reconnect to the project of human rights, now global in scope. For moderate republicans, the radical alternative will always seem suspect; it has the air of a republican façade.

Republicanism Reformulated

Our effort should be to reformulate, to raise to a higher level of abstraction and generalize the broad framework of the republican tradition. In saying this I am paraphrasing the famous opening paragraph of Rawls's *A Theory of Justice*. Rawls writes: "I . . . present the main idea of justice as fairness, a theory of justice that generalizes and carries to a higher level of abstraction the traditional conception of the social contract" (Rawls 1971, 3). Our reformulation of the republican tradition needs to go deeper, requiring both a framework for the empirical exploration of human action and a program for the transformation of the social world, including an account of both institutions and ideals. It defines the res publica within a framework of fields of power, and building on the distinction between public and private goods. I have sketched above both the empirical and the normative frameworks, but it is worth recapitulating to bring out more clearly the republican origins of some of the key features of this framework.

The republican tradition as part of political theory has been diverse, but consistent in its statism. The Greek polis, and the Roman res publica are seen as ancestors of the modern state. The state is seen as the only candidate for a res publica. Aristotle's zoon politikon is translated as political animal, with the quality of being political often understood in the statist way.

But there is a deeper alternative way to understand polis and res publica as parts of the republican project. A res publica may be understood minimally as an autonomous system of power or field of power, or field of human interaction. Or res publica may be understood more demandingly as a relatively autonomous field of power dominated by a distinctive form of power resources, which we can call public resources. Or more demandingly still we may require that the system of power not be *arbitrary*, so that a res publica is any relatively autonomous field of power to the extent it is not arbitrary. A zoon politikon is an animal that lives and feels at home in such fields of human interaction, with Athens, and some other Greek poleis, serving as early and very imperfect exemplars.

The framework allows a further elaboration of the distinction between public and private, begun in the political economy tradition, reconstructing the idea of a res publica. The focus of analytical attention up till now has been on goods, and the distinction between the private and the public has centered on the dimension of the capacity to exclude. This is work to which the Bloomington School has contributed so much: especially in identifying different local public goods, and stressing the practical and empirical contrasts between public goods and common pool resources.

The power field construct allows us to introduce a second key dimension of the contrast between res publica and res privata. If we consider now the diversity of power resources, or goods that create the capacity to influence outcomes, one of the key distinctions is between what we might call private resources and public ones. Public resources share the difficulty-of-exclusion property with other public goods. But they also have another crucial property: those who bring them to bear on a power situation cannot choose the direction in which the resource will influence outcomes. An example will clarify. A gun is a private resource in this sense: I can use guns to influence outcomes in many different directions, depending on what I happen to want. A policy argument is an example of a public resource. I can only use it to favor those alternatives which it supports. If I change my mind I can use a gun to support my new preferences. But the policy argument will still support my old preferences; I cannot use it for whatever preferences I happen to have.

A simple ideal type of private property involves the capacity to exclude others from using an object, and the capacity to use the object in whatever way we want. A public resource by contrast will fail on both counts. We will have trouble excluding others, and we will not be able to use it for whatever purpose we happen to want.

Once we have this distinction we can begin to reconstruct in a new way some crucial ideas from within the republican tradition, such as the idea of arbitrariness and the idea of the common good. A res publica is a field of power, a system of power, in which power is not arbitrary, it serves the common good and supports justice. The project of law is committed, as Selznick (1969) would have it, to the reduction of arbitrariness. The modern state can and should aspire to reduce arbitrariness and thus become a res publica. So can modern organizations, whether profit making or not for profit. Markets can be seen as incubators of entrepreneurial creativity as Schumpeterians would have it, and simultaneously as instruments for the reduction of arbitrariness.

Opposition to Arbitrariness

The idea of arbitrariness goes deeper than the usual accounts of it in social and political theory allow. We find opposition to arbitrariness not just in the republican idea of liberty or in conceptions of the ideal of law (such as Selznick's), we find it also in science and in art. One goal of science is the progressive reduction of arbitrariness in our knowledge. And the great artists also struggle against arbitrariness. The struggle is perhaps most simply expressed in Michelangelo's intuition that he *discovered* his sculptures in marble. It is hard to imagine a stronger form of opposition to arbitrariness in creation: creation is discovery. You discover the sculpture in the marble. Or you discover the song you are writing: like an archeologist you need to just brush away some of the surface dust to reveal the song that is there (I once heard a folk song writer describe his work in this way). You discover a beautiful and inspiring axiomatic system: Roger Penrose, for example, presents the system of complex numbers as full of magic (Penrose 2004).

Weberian Entzauberung has apparently not reached mathematics. The capacity to inspire, to be magical, could be taken as one sign that our creation is not arbitrary, that it is a form of discovery, or that our creation is a part of reality's process of self-creation.

If we leave now the domains of the arts and the sciences, in order to attend to the concerns of practical reason, we can still follow the example of Michelangelo: in making law, or in creating institutions more generally, we should be discovering them, we should allow them to emerge from human interaction, from the underlying structures of power, and beyond that, from reality's process of self-creation. And we will find, I would suggest, that opposition to arbitrariness is also at the heart of moderation. We find it in the ancient republican opposition to tyranny, and in the ideal of reduction of arbitrariness implicit in the project of the rule of law. In the West especially, the political and institutional form of this project of moderation is carried above all in the projects of law and of the republic. Its ancient Roman roots are visible in the venerable Latin formulae: *lex est rex* and *res publica mixta.*

Michelangelo's dictum seems to me best understood as an expression of a fundamental commitment that the sculpture not be a product of the arbitrary will of the artist. But how can the sculptor recognize that what he or she does is not arbitrary, that it is a discovery in stone? In art we do not expect an articulate answer to such questions; we do not expect artists to be able to effectively justify what they do. The beauty of the sculpture is the answer. But in the sphere of practical reason we can also find more articulate forms of nonarbitrariness. When law emerges from human interaction, when a judge makes a decision, especially outside the sphere of enacted law, we may be seeing something fundamentally the same, a kind of intuitive avoidance of arbitrariness. The great projects of law and of the republic (as well as the project of science) require more than such an intuitive search for nonarbitrariness, however. They require also articulate and well tested forms of justification.

This fuller articulated form of the struggle against arbitrariness we can see as a process in multiple stages. The first stage requires good justification. A decision, an action, or a belief are arbitrary to the extent they are not well justified. The second stage requires a nonarbitrary way to evaluate justifications. I suggest we may think of this as a requirement of good tests of quality of justifications. And this immediately suggests a third stage: a nonarbitrary way to evaluate the quality of those tests. Do we have an infinite regress? Not really, just a progressive deepening of nonarbitrariness, without ever eliminating arbitrariness completely. I suggest two starting points for building such a construction. The first is loyalty to reality, in a manner of modern science, a form of realism that is not to be identified with cynicism. The second is loyalty to modernity as a project (which in part determines the form of the loyalty to reality, in the spirit of modern science). The quality tests of justifications should be empirical tests to the extent possible. They should express loyalty to reality, the least arbitrary of loyalties. Loyalty to reality is the deepest and most general of republican loyalties. And reality is our ultimate res publica.

NOTES

1. The text can be found as The Framing Statement of the Summer Institute of Civic Studies at http://activecitizen.tufts.edu/wp-content/uploads/CivicsFramingEnglishandPolish.pdf.

2. Quoted after A. P. d'Entreves (1951, 25). It can also be found in William Ophuls (2011, 20–21).

REFERENCES

Aligica, Paul Dragos. 2014. *Institutional Diversity and Political Economy: The Ostroms and Beyond.* Oxford: Oxford University Press.

Barnes, Barry and David Bloor. 1982. "Relativism, Rationalism and the Sociology of Knowledge," in *Rationality and Relativism*, edited by in Martin Hollis and Steven Lukes, 21–47. Cambridge, MA: MIT Press.

Barnes, Barry, David Bloor and John Henry. 1996. *Scientific Knowledge: A Sociological Analysis.* Chicago, IL: University of Chicago Press.

Berlin, Isaiah. 1990. *The Crooked Timber of Humanity.* New York: Knopf.

Boyte, Harry et al. 2007. *Civic Studies Framing Statement* at http://activecitizen.tufts.edu/wp-content/uploads/CivicsFramingEnglishandPolish.pdf.

Chomsky, Noam. 1965. *Aspects of a Theory of Syntax.* Cambridge, MA: MIT Press.

Clapham, Andrew. 2006. *Human Rights Obligations of Non-State Actors.* Oxford: Oxford University Press.

Craiutu, Aurelian. 2012. *A Virtue for Courageous Minds: Moderation in French Political Thought.* Princeton, NJ: Princeton University Press.

Donnelly, Jack. 2003. *Universal Human Rights in Theory and Practice.* Ithaca, NY: Cornell University Press.

Elkin, Stephen. 2006. *Reconstructing the Commercial Republic.* Chicago, IL: University of Chicago Press.

d'Entrèves, Alessandro Passerin. 1951. *Natural Law.* London: Hutchinson.

Ferry, Luc, and Alain Renaut. [1985] 1992. *From Rights of Man to the Republican Idea* (*Political Philosophy*, vol. 3). Chicago, IL: University of Chicago Press.

Flyvbjerg, Brent. 2001. *Making Social Science Matter.* Cambridge: Cambridge University Press.

Galtung, Johan. 1996. *Peace by Peaceful Means.* New York: Sage.

Godfrey-Smith, Peter. 2003. *Theory and Reality: An Introduction to the Philosophy of Science* Chicago, IL: University of Chicago Press.

Habermas, Jürgen. 1984. *The Theory of Communicative Action*, vol. 1. Boston, MA: Beacon Press.
Habermas, Jürgen. 1986. *Autonomy and Solidarity*. London: Verso.
Habermas, Jürgen. 1987. *The Theory of Communicative Action, vol. 2*. Boston, MA: Beacon Press.
Habermas, Jürgen. 1996. *Between Facts and Norms*. Cambridge, MA: MIT Press.
Hart, H. L. A. 1961. *The Concept of Law*. Oxford: Oxford University Press.
Holmes, Oliver Wendell Jr. 1897. "The Path of the Law." *Harvard Law Review* 10: 457.
Jay, Martin. 1973. *Dialectical Imagination*. Boston, MA: Little Brown.
Kahneman, Daniel and Amos Tversky. 1979. "Prospect Theory: An Analysis of Decision Under Risk." *Econometrica* 47: 263–92.
Krasnodębski, Zdzisław. 2003. *Demokracja Peryferii*. Gdańsk: Słowo/obraz terytoria.
Krygier, Martin. 2012. *Philip Selznick: Ideals in the World*. Stanford, CA: Stanford University Press.
Kuhn, T.S. [1962] 1970. *The Structure of Scientific Revolutions*. Chicago, IL: University of Chicago Press.
Lakatos, Imre. 1978. *The Methodology of Scientific Research Programmes*. Cambridge: Cambridge University Press.
Laudan, Larry. 1977. *Progress and Its Problems: Toward a Theory of Scientific Growth*. Berkeley, CA: University of California Press.
Legutko, Ryszard, and Jacek Kloczkowski, eds. 2002. *Oblicza Demokracji*. Kraków: Ośrodek Myśli Politycznej.
Levine, Peter, and Karol Edward Sołtan, eds. 2014. *Civic Studies*. Washington, DC: Bringing Theory to Practice.
Lyotard, Jean Francois. [1979] 1984. *The Post-Modern Condition*. Minneapolis, MN: University of Minnesota Press.
Mikhail, John. 2011. *Elements of Moral Cognition*. Cambridge: Cambridge University Press.
Nassr, Seyyed. 2004. *The Heart of Islam*. San Francisco, CA: Harper.
Nickel, James. 2007. *Making Sense of Human Rights*, 2nd ed. Malden, MA: Blackwell.
Nordhaus, Ted, and Michael Shellenberger. 2007. *Breakthrough*. Boston, MA: Houghton Mifflin.
Nussbaum, Martha. 2011. *Creating Capabilities*. Cambridge, MA: Harvard University Press.
Ophuls, William. 2011. *Plato's Revenge*. Cambridge, MA: MIT Press.
Ostrom, Elinor, Thomas Dietz, Nives Dolšak, Paul Stern, Susan Stonich, and Elke Weber, eds. 2002. *The Drama of the Commons*. Washington, DC: National Academy Press.
Ostrom, Elinor, and Vincent Ostrom. 2014. *Choice, Rules and Collective Action*. Edited by Filippo Sabetti and Paul Dragos Aligica. Colchester (UK): ECPR Press.
Ostrom, Vincent. 2011. *The Quest to Understand Human Affairs*. Lanham, MD: Rowman and Littlefield Lexington Books.
Parsons, Talcott. 1937. *Structure of Social Action*. New York: McGraw-Hill.
Penrose, Roger. 2004. *The Road to Reality*. New York: Vintage.

Perez, Carlota. 2003. *Technological Revolutions and Financial Capital*. Cheltenham (UK): Elgar.
Pettit, Philip. 1997. *Republicanism: A Theory of Freedom and Government*. Oxford: Oxford University Press.
Polanyi, Michael. 1951. *The Logic of Liberty*. Chicago, IL: University of Chicago Press.
Popper, Karl 1963. *Conjectures and Refutations: The Growth of Scientific Knowledge*. London: Routledge and Kegan Paul.
Rawls, John. 1971. *A Theory of Justice*. Cambridge, MA: Harvard University Press.
Rawls, John. 2001. *Justice as Fairness*. Cambridge, MA: Harvard University Press.
Rorty, Richard. 1989. *Contingency, Irony and Solidarity*. Cambridge: Cambridge University Press.
Sandel, Michael. 1996. *Democracy's Discontent*. Cambridge, MA: Harvard University Press.
Schelling, Thomas. 1960. *The Strategy of Conflict*. Cambridge, MA: Harvard University Press.
Selznick, Philip. 1969. *Law, Society, and Industrial Justice*. New York: Russell Sage.
Selznick, Philip. 1992. *The Moral Commonwealth*. Berkeley, CA: University of California Press.
Sen, Amartya. 1999. *Development as Freedom*. New York: Anchor Books.
Shapiro, Ian, and Donald Green. 1994. *The Pathologies of Rational Choice Theory*. New Haven, CT: Yale University Press.
Sołtan, Karol Edward. 1987. *The Causal Theory of Justice*. Berkeley, CA: University of California Press.
Sołtan, Karol Edward. 2008. "Constitutional Patriotism and Militant Moderation." *International Journal of Constitutional Law* 6: 96–116.
Sołtan, Karol Edward. 2010. "The Project of Law, Moderation and the Global Constitution." *Maryland Journal of International Law* 25: 230–63
Sołtan, Karol Edward. 2011. "Le difficile projet de la modération globale," in *Comment Changer une Constitution?* Edited by Eugénie Brouillet and Louis Massicotte, 17–40. Quebec: Les Presses de l'Université Laval.
Sołtan, Karol Edward. 2014. "The Emerging Field of a New Civics," in *Civic Studies*. Edited by Peter Levine and Karol Edward Sołtan, 9–22. Washington, DC: Bringing Theory to Practice.
Speth, James Gustave. 2008. *The Bridge at the Edge of the World*. New Haven, CT: Yale University Press.
Unger, Roberto Mangabeira. 1987. *Politics: A Work of Constructive Social Theory*. Cambridge: Cambridge University Press.
Unger, Roberto Mangabeira. 2007. *The Self Awakened: Pragmatism Unbound*. Cambridge, MA: Harvard University Press.
Viroli, Maurizio. 2002. *Republicanism*. New York: Hill and Wang.
Weinberg, Steven. 1977. *The First Three Minutes*. New York: Basic Books.

Part III

FROM GOVERNING THE COMMONS TO THEORY BUILDING

Chapter 8

For a History of the Struggle to Constitute and Sustain Productive Orders

Lessons from Sicily

Filippo Sabetti and Rosolino Candela

The conventional wisdom in the literature on the history of Sicily emphasizes gross inequality of social, political and economic conditions between the rulers and the ruled, the use of force to settle disputes, and economic stagnation and lack of economic progress in the long transition from feudalism to modernity. We do not dispute this conventional wisdom where it is applicable. Nor do we wish to minimize opportunistic behavior, temptations to free ride, to shirk responsibility, to pursue ambition and dispensation of favor, and to break commitment among the dominating classes. What we argue is that there is more to Sicilian history than individualistic behavior, oligarchic tendencies, institutional weakness and stagnation. We suggest that it is possible to gain a more accurate, if more complex, understanding of Sicily's past if we take the struggle to constitute and sustain productive orders as the basic orientation used to frame historical inquiries. In fact, the title of the chapter is inspired by the title of a book honoring the intellectual contributions of Vincent Ostrom to politics and community living (Sproule-Jones et al. 2008). That book dealt with present-time public affairs. In this chapter we focus on institutions for collective action and economic growth in premodern times.

We are required to consider that alternative possibilities existed in designing, constructing and maintaining different social realities and the very nature of political and social phenomena over the course of centuries. This orientation to history draws largely on the epistemological perspectives that animate the Ostrom research programme, the civic theory presented in Sołtan's chapter (in this book) and the very orientation used by Carlo Cattaneo (1801–1869) in the nineteenth century to make sense of different historical periods in Italy's urban development (Sabetti 2010). This method of work was also followed by Tocqueville in dissecting the old regime in France. He approached the task "with a view to eliciting the laws of life" and "supply a picture that while scientifically accurate may also be instructive" (Tocqueville [1859] 1956, xii). He did not discount the gross inequalities of conditions and the political and economic hierarchies, but whenever he found, beneath the power of fixed social orders and monarchical administrations, a spirit of healthy independence and human creativity he threw them in sharp relief. We follow this method here. We first sketch the epistemological perspective that informs our understanding of what constitute productive orders. The rest of the paper shows how this perspective can be used as a guide to what to look for in providing a more reliable analysis of the history of Sicily than what is currently available in the scholarly and popular literature.

The process of economic development requires sustained increases in economic productivity. Such increases in real productivity come from investments and technological innovation that increase and improve physical and human capital. However, the formation of capital is an artifact of the human mind (V. Ostrom 1980, 311), which is the ultimate resource of economic development (see Cattaneo [1861] 2002; Simon 1981). Moreover, in order for individuals to exploit the gains from trade under the division of labor and the division of knowledge (Hayek 1937, 49), the extent of the market must be continuously extended to facilitate the transition from small-scale capital accumulation to large-scale capital accumulation. In theory, as the extent and complexity of the market widens, so does the complexity and specialization of knowledge within the market. These developments ought to permit individuals to "take ownership" and concentrate their particular talents and productive abilities in those activities where they exercise a comparative advantage, from which capital investment and technological progress emerges as a by-product of the incentives provided by an institutional framework of property rights (Alchian 1965, 825). Through this process, entrepreneurship can, then, be expected to effectively lead to greater productivity, higher real wages, an expansion of output, and an overall increase in human welfare.

Such manifestations of productive orders can be found in Sicily's past with some important differences. These differences involved three sets of factors: large landownership based on heredity, the difficulty of sustaining market arrangements over extended periods of time within the configuration of political and institutional arrangements, and closely connected, the vicissitudes of dynastic succession since Norman times exposed Sicily to the competing claims of European princes as Sicily became a province of successive European empires. There is no pretension here to do justice to a complex and rich history encompassing more than 700 years of developments since Norman times; that would be premature and beyond the confines of a single paper. The advantage of stretching the entire period before us is that it allows to spot variations, fluctuations and long-term trends better than a shorter time span. It also allows us to overcome a persistent problem in social inquiry. When a practice (good or bad) is found operating at any one point, one of two things happens: either it is assumed by implication that the practice lasts forever, or there is a tendency to project back that practice (or failings in the nineteenth century) without bothering to investigate earlier or subsequent periods. Still, the analysis stretching across such a long time and space carries its own constraints. We draw attention to the historical nature of social scientific knowledge across historical-time periods and offers a way to remove the shadows and false light that have obscured the practice of self-organization and self-governance, including relations based on contractual relations, extended to almost all forms of known collective activity and undertaking. In brief, the chapter suggests an agenda for comparative institutional and historical research and not necessarily definitive results.

BASIC CONCEPTIONS IN FRAMING THE INQUIRY

In framing the inquiry we are required to confront the nature of political and social phenomena over time. This may be understood as "the choice of conceptualizations, assertions, and information to be used and acted upon on in problem-solving modes" (V. Ostrom 1997, 91). There may be a fundamental contradiction between theoretical inquiry and making sense of the observed complexity of human affairs (E. Ostrom 1990, 24–25). Whereas the former privileges the search of regularities, the latter confronts diversity. As a result, too often many analysts in academia and beyond have been doing the equivalent of "'Forcing Squares, Triangles and Ellipses into a Circular Paradigm' by using the commons dilemma model without serious attention to whether or not the variables in the empirical world conformed to the theoretical model" (E. Ostrom 1990, 24). A chief strength of the Ostrom research program is that it has succeeded in meeting this challenge and in developing a method of analysis based on realistic assessments of human capabilities and limitations in a variety of situations.

We assume human beings to be creative agents in the world in which they live and use as a starting point the microstructure of human action in different field settings. This orientation can be extended to the study of the struggles to constitute productive orders in different historical periods and treating these periods as the laboratory for providing us with a history of institutions for collective action. That means offering an internal point of view on action as the agents see it, adopting the reasoning of the agents, and requiring a sympathetic understanding of the perspectives that move agents to action, as much as the historical record permits (Sołtan 2016, 4). The main point is less on imposing causal explanations of observed reality and more in explaining changes in actions. As Elinor Ostrom puts it:

> As an institutionalist studying empirical phenomena, I presume that individuals try to solve problems as effectively as they can. That assumption imposes a discipline on me. Instead of presuming that some individuals are incompetent, evil, or irrational and others are omniscient, I presume that individuals have similar limited capabilities to reason and figure out the structure of complex environments. It is my responsibility as a scientist to ascertain what problems individuals are trying to solve and what factors help or hinder them in these efforts. When the problems that I observe involve lack of predictability, information and trust, as well as high levels of complexity and transactional difficulties, then my efforts to explain must take these problems overtly into account rather than assuming them away. In developing an explanation for observed behavior, I draw on a rich literature written by other scholars interested in institutions and their effects on individual incentives and behavior in field settings. (1990, 25–26)

We take historical periods as a laboratory to study changes in the ongoing stream of events, with a focus on what problems in collective action people try to address and solve and what factors helped or hindered them in these efforts. It is hard to affix a beginning date but we know that the conceptual and computational logic necessary to form organizational arrangements that promoted growth and community governance was deeply rooted in the way of life of people by the twelfth century. For example, Sicilian cities were already vibrant with life as "sites of Roman law courts, municipal night-watch companies, armies of harbor officials, schools, tariff codes, almshouses and hospitals, more tax collectors, tavern, warehouses and urban magistrates endlessly copying, invoking, exercising, and seeking to expand their cities' cherished and obsessively guarded *consuetudines*. Each community followed its own customs but remained open to outside contact" (Backman 1995, 20).

The local multi-constitutional world thus included considerable diversity in organizational form and scope with common underlying principles of various forms of self-rule, joint rule and one-man rule. These undertakings covered almost all aspects of organized existence: work; goods that had private and public characteristics like food and health; and common pool resources ranging from woodland to churches and neighborhoods. In varying degrees, it was possible to find in almost any community a public space (*res publica*) that permitted problem-solving through the spontaneous creation of joint undertakings of all sorts. One of the best examples of this comes from the work of economic historian Stephan R. Epstein (1992).

He found that, contrary to the conventional wisdom, late medieval and early modern Sicilian economy achieved high levels of productivity in various sectors. His in-depth analysis started by detailing regional geographic and demographic differentiation, and then he moved to the organization of different economic ventures in local, regional markets and foreign trades. The capacity of many Sicilians to be active agents in the economic development and social change in late medieval Sicily is neatly conveyed by the book title of his research: *An Island for Itself.* This led him to question the epistemological basis of the received wisdom.

> Ever since the Enlightenment criticized the latifundia, large scale farming in Sicily and Southern Italy, has been given a major share of responsibility for the Mezzogiorno's agricultural "backwardness." Latifundism is supposed to have bred many social and economic ills, including landlord absenteeism, low investment, lack of innovation and peasant poverty and exploitation. So far no convincing explanations exists, however, as to why such backward and inefficient property rights survived apparently unchanged for nearly a millennium. It is a priori very unlikely that such an allegedly highly inefficient organization should have endured so long; empirical evidence confirms that this is so.

He continues,

> In fact, despite the use of seemingly "archaic" tools (oxen and scratch ploughs) both yields ratios and production per hectare in Sicily up to the eighteenth century seem to have been equivalent or higher than in the most advanced northern European countries (England, Flanders, the Netherlands) and subsequently better than in Northern Italy or the Baltic regions. Whatever Sicilian agriculture's failings during the eighteenth-century "agricultural" revolution further north, it thus seems that one cannot project such failings unquestionably onto previous centuries. (1992, 163; see also Epstein 2000)

Epstein's research challenges the presumption of failure that characterizes so much of the literature on the history of Sicily and directs attention to the importance of charting and surveying the configuration of institutions for collective action since medieval times.

INSTITUTIONS OF GOVERNANCE

The Norman landing near Messina in 1060 signaled the end of two hundred years of Muslim rule in Sicily and the establishment of a new and independent kingdom of Sicily. By the end of the twelfth century, however, the vicissitudes of Norman dynastic succession exposed Sicily to the competing claims of European princes and swept away its independence. The Sicilian realm became a province of successive European empires. Yet below the power of alternating vice-regal administrations, certain vestiges of Sicilian independence, although half—destroyed, were still distinguishable. Parliament, baronial jurisdiction, and local laws and privileges, commonly described as feudal, kept alive a spirit of independence and self—reliance as well as a sense of the Sicilian nation.

The succession of foreign monarchs ended in 1759 with the proclamation of the third son of the Spanish king as the new ruler of Sicily. While the new king established himself in Naples, his designation as Ferdinand the Fourth of Naples and Ferdinand the Third of Sicily indicated the relative independence of the island from Naples. The change from the Spanish Bourbons to the Neapolitan Bourbons attached Sicily to the Italian peninsula for the first time in more than four centuries.

The principal features of eighteenth-century vice-regal administration dated back to the sixteenth century when Spanish Hapsburg rulers brought to a successful end the efforts of the previous rulers, the Aragonese, to exclude Sicilian barons completely from royal councils. This was achieved by obtaining the consent of the Sicilian parliament[1] to a reform of the two Sicilian supreme courts, the Great Court and the Court of the Royal Patrimony. Too late parliamentary barons realized the implications of their consent. While holders of the great feudal offices of state were allowed to keep their ranks and titles, all effective authority was withdrawn from them and transferred to the viceroy and senior vice-regal officials. The extension of vice-regal authority was designed to harness Sicilian economic resources for the Hapsburg Empire and to insure sole imperial control over Sicilian defense. At that time the empire stretched from North Africa to the Baltic and Sicily was a critically important outpost in the defense of Christendom against the Turks and the Barbary states.[2]

The Court of the Royal Patrimony, while retaining some judicial functions, took over the Grand Chamberlain's supervision of public finance to become the viceroy's principal administrative agency for bringing under imperial direction, supervision and control all other central administrative agencies. For example, through the Master of the Harbor or Central Customs Office the viceroy came to regulate almost the entire domestic and foreign trade of wheat, one of the most important Sicilian commodities. The reach of the Patrimony over the whole field of government and economy ran, however, against several constraints interposed by other more or less independent political institutions.

First, the Sicilian parliament, smarting from its inability to revert the exclusion of Sicilian barons from royal councils, effectively blocked the recruitment of Spanish ministers and civil servants for the Patrimony by insisting upon the legal and customary practice of filling almost all the governmental positions with Sicilian citizens. Viceroys were thus forced to fill most of the administrative positions with Sicilians whom they regarded as unreliable. Second, the tradition of strong civic independence in the form of either baronial jurisdiction or communal liberties meant, in effect, that vice-regal edicts and writs ran at the pleasure of parliamentary barons and communal officials. Some parliamentary barons as well as some domanial towns still had tax-free privileges for wheat and other products (like sugar and silk) they exported; some city officials even had the right to reserve and disallow pragmatic sanctions or royal decrees in their jurisdictions. Third, the Spanish monarch enjoyed extensive ecclesiastical authority in Sicily through the Apostolic Legateship, originally conceded by the papacy to Count Roger in 1098, and through the Sicilian Inquisition, established in 1513, but these royal institutions also imposed limitations on the reach of the vice-regal administration.

In order to mitigate these constraints and to cope with the difficulties inherent in controlling the details of the entire central administration, successive viceroys resorted to several strategies. They concentrated all possible authority in the few offices, like that of the auditor general of the Patrimony, which could be legally held by Spaniards. They came to rely increasingly upon selected Sicilian civil servants who toured the island as vice-regal commissioners or inspectors. The consultor, or the viceroy's deputy, and the auditor general of the Patrimony became, as one viceroy suggested, "the pivots" on which hinged the entire central administration (Koenigsberger 1951, 101; see also Corrao 1991). These developments led to the transformation of the vice-regal household into a vice-regal secretariat—in effect, a duplicate chain of command to make the administrative agencies of the Patrimony work "as they should." Thus, by the second half of the sixteenth-century centralized administration was established among a crowd of autonomous, uncoordinated and lesser powers. But the protracted imperial wars in Europe during the seventeenth century exposed Sicily to extraordinary financial demands which soon undermined the very reorganization of vice-regal administration.

The two principal sources of imperial revenues in Sicily were parliamentary donatives or grants and export taxes on wheat imposed without the consent of parliament. Already by the end of the sixteenth century, as a result of rising expenditures for military actions in the Mediterranean, parliamentary taxation had reached the sum of almost 300,000 scudi a year. The tax revenue from the wheat trade had generated as much as 500,000 scudi in a good year (Titone 1955, 321–31). Soon, however, it became increasingly apparent that these two sources were inadequate in meeting increasing military expenditures for European wars (Koenigsberger 1971, 80–93; Petino 1946). As a result, viceroys in Sicily were ordered "to sell everything which can be sold and even which cannot be sold" (quoted in Mack Smith 1968 [1988], 220).

The practice of selling regalian rights, including the baronial obligation of knight services, was another source of income for the Spanish monarchy in Sicily. But in the course of the seventeenth century, it became "a predatory attack" on vice-regal administration itself (Mack Smith 1968 [1988], 139). Government offices, ranging from the Master of the Harbor to the Master Notary of the Great Court to the purveyor of coal to the royal mint, were either sold to the highest bidder or leased or pledged to creditors of the Spanish government. Even domanial towns with their taxes and profits of jurisdiction became marketable commodities, although the stiff opposition of local residents prevented the sale to reach the proportions it did under the Aragonese monarch in the early fifteenth century when some towns were sold seven or eight times. In 1621, the occasional sale of criminal and civil jurisdiction (the *merum et mistum imperium*) to individual barons became an established legal practice, further strengthening the local independence of the aristocracy and the seigneurial courts (e.g., Cancila 2008). Hence, if the financial and military demands of the Spanish empire stimulated the centralization of vice-regal administration, the changing nature of those demands undermined that very effort.

The "predatory attack" did not, however, exhaust Sicilian economic resources. Indeed, the seventeenth century was the period when not only new palaces and churches were built by private individuals but also vast public works projects were carried out by local officials and scores of new villages were established by old and new barons acting as economic and political entrepreneurs. But the secure investment of commercial profits in regalian rights served to reduce the availability of capital for the transformation of Sicilian technological inventions and patents into an industrial revolution.[3] Political simony not only took out of beneficial circulation large sums of money but also created additional economic difficulties for the vice-regal administration as holders of new posts and titles claimed exemptions from taxation or other privileges. The succession of Franco-Bourbons, Savoy and Austrian Hapsburg monarchs that followed the disintegration of the Spanish Hapsburg rule of Sicily did not put a stop to the sale of government posts—it simply increased their prices or made them into inheritable property.

By the second half of the eighteenth century, the administrative machinery of the Patrimony was still that fashioned by sixteenth-century viceroys. But the practice of political simony had built up year by year like so many non-vice-regal "pivots" within the Patrimony that vice-regal administration, while keeping its earlier form, had been drained of its substance (Brancato 1946–1947, 255–65; see Arnolfini 1962). Hence, though the viceroy of Sicily continued to represent and claim the power of sovereign, he enjoyed but a very small portion of it. The parliamentary barons could still flatter themselves, in the words of contemporary jurists, as being "associates of the sovereign" in governing Sicily (quoted in Pontieri 1943, 267; see also Santamaria 1881, 123). In 1770, their territorial jurisdiction extended to about 780,000 of the approximately 1,176,000 people living in villages and towns; some 280 of the 367 villages and towns were under baronial jurisdiction.

The claim of baronial jurisdiction was based on the argument that the original Norman barons had strictly been not feudatories of Count Roger, but rather his comrades-in-arms (*commilitones*) who, by helping him to conquer Sicily, had won for themselves a share of sovereignty in the land (Mack 1968, 291). In the thirteenth century, barons successfully pressured King Frederick III, the Aragonese monarch, to extend the primogeniture law of succession to permit the inheritance of fiefs to collateral branches of childless barons (*Si Aliquem* law) and the almost unrestricted alienation or sale of fiefs (*Volentes* law). These laws, which became part of the *Capitula regni Siciliae* or liberties of Sicily that succeeding viceroys swore to uphold, admitted, in effect, that fiefs could lapse to the crown only under exceptional circumstances. The opportunity to become a parliamentary baron was thus opened to anyone[4] with sufficient capital to purchase a fief, to pay for a royal license to people it (*licentia populandi*) and to organize the land under baronial jurisdiction as an economic enterprise. Possession of land, and not feudal title or ancient lineage as such, carried with it the right to govern people living on it.

At the same time, the internal organization of each fief, at least since the thirteenth century, was subject to an agreement or covenant (*communion* or *pactum*) between the baron and the settlers, specifying the rights and duties of each. The same covenantal arrangements applied to the territorial jurisdiction of ecclesiastical lords, though their legal claims to lordship differed from those of parliamentary barons. The agreement, which became known as the "Pact of the Land" or the "Chapters of the Land," was stipulated with minor exceptions in the language common to the contracting parties "for precaution, certitude or firmness" (from a 1482 agreement, quoted in Garufi 1947, 25). It represented the constitution of individual lands or settlements. Its foundation rested on its "stickiness" or congruency to the *metis* of Sicilians, which include the "skills, culture, norms, and conventions, which are shaped by the experiences of the individual" (Boettke, Coyne, and Leeson 2008, 338)—what earlier the Romans called *mos maiorum*.

A baron could sell the fief to someone else but the charter of the village remained customarily in force and the basic rights of villagers could not be changed without the consent of all the family heads. Civil disputes between barons and villagers were adjudicated by the judicial branch of the Patrimony, as chapters of the land were generally endorsed by the viceroy. Thus, the meaning of the manorial system in Sicily had reference to the rights and duties that each baron enjoyed under the constitution of each fief. Territorial jurisdiction of a baron was constrained by the constitution of each fief and by the conventions (*consuetudines*) that surrounded such arrangements (see also LaMantia 1993; Romano 1993).

To be sure, the earliest covenantal arrangements, generally involving an exchange of protection and long-term employment for labor services, had many of the master-servant relationships of villainage (Peri 1965). The need to have the consent of both contracting parties in order to alter the decision making capabilities assigned under a village charter also set limits upon the development of a new charter to meet the changing economic situation. In turn, settlers faced the critical problem of trying both to insure the integrity of the mutually agreed terms and conditions and to prevent unilateral changes in the contractual arrangements at the same time when, given the particular division of labor and the inequalities of conditions, they were in a markedly asymmetrical system of interdependence with the baron.

Yet the practice of grounding the constitution of settlements upon the consent of the barons and the settlers, and, correlatively, the practice of assigning the conduct of communal affairs to local residents acted not only as a constraint to baronial despotism but also as an incentive for the barons and settlers alike to sustain mutually productive relationships (Genuardi 1911, 43; Verdirame 1905, 45–46). It became not uncommon for barons and local residents to come to the aid of each other in times of distress. For example, in 1559 all the family heads of a town under the lordship of the marquis of Geraci, assembled as the "regular parliament" or civic council, agreed to levy additional imposts upon themselves in order to rescue the young marquis from heavy debts contracted by his deceased father as ambassador to Spain (Cancila 1974: 15–16, see also Cancila 2001, 2009). In other instances, barons came to the rescue of their tenants by shouldering or canceling payment of their taxes during bad harvest or drought years (Titone 1961, 35–40). Moreover, whenever communal officials were involved in renegotiating the terms and conditions of the contractual arrangement on behalf of the villagers and whenever villagers revolted en masse against their barons for levying what seemed intolerable increases in imposts, the protestors justified their acts of resistance or civil disobedience, and appealed for the resolution of conflict, on the necessity to realize their joint advantages with the lord (Ferrigno 1915–1916, 118–46; Guarnieri 1889, 293–314; Pupillo-Barrese 1903, 38, 64). The positive aspects of covenantal arrangements also entered in many ways into the pattern of local life to become an important feature of the Sicilian political tradition and culture.[5]

Villainage had disappeared by the thirteenth century though tenant farmers, as a general rule, were still subject to restrictions such as bringing their wheat to the lord's mill and grapes to the lord's wine press. The realization of joint advantages between barons and villagers and the gradual transformation of the chapters of the land were also facilitated by the scarcity of labor resulting from the eviction of Muslims in the thirteenth century as well as by recurrent plagues, internal migration of workers in search of more favorable employment opportunities, the growth of the market economy and the increasing use of money as the medium of exchange. By the sixteenth century under "pressures generated by self-interest," (Salvioli 1902, 390) master-servant relationships gave way to relationships between large landlords, on the one hand, and tenant sharecroppers, wage earners and small independent farmers or copyholders (*burgisi*) on the other brought many baronial houses into bankruptcy while baronial towns became depopulated and, in some cases, disappeared (Salvioli 1902, 390). By the end of the sixteenth century, a special parliamentary commission called the Deputation of States was set up to administer and, in some cases, sell bankrupt or depopulated baronies (see Tricoli 1966).

At the same time, however, the availability of capital resulting from the new economic situation, the increasing demands for Sicilian wheat and other products in Europe, the growth of population stimulated, in part, by the influx of Greek and Albanian refugees[6] from the Turkish empire and the relatively open entry rule for becoming a parliamentary baron joined together to make the seventeenth century "the golden age of baronial jurisdiction" and, at the same time, to sustain Sicily's integrated domestic market and its strong links with foreign markets. In the course of this century, old and new barons risked enormous sums of money to reorganize bankrupt fiefs and to establish new ones—in essence, to develop economically and politically the Sicilian interior. In turn, this "frontier movement" had the effect of renewing and strengthening the number, position, and title of parliamentary barons at the very time when, as a result of bankrupt or depopulated fiefs, bearers of ancient titles were losing standing as associates of the sovereign and when, as a result of the sale of regalian rights, the inflated number of titled Sicilians was eroding the prestige attached to titles of nobility. While the ecclesiastical and the domanial houses of parliament continued to have not more than 63 and 43 members respectively, the baronial house increased its membership from 72 in 1556 to 277 by 1800. Some barons represented as many as twenty fiefs.

The critical part played by old and new barons in the colonization of the Sicilian interior and in its economic development has led different historians of different ideological persuasions to refer to these Sicilians as "bold and courageous agrarian capitalists" (Pontieri 1943, 52–55; Renda 1963, 18–25; Titone 1955). Yet, barons were not the only bold and courageous entrepreneurs. Though we know less about the settlers, in part because of the assumption of self-sufficiency has led many researchers to neglect the capital requirements of frontier settlements, they were also engaged in the task of creating capital (see also Bauer 2000, 11). Scattered evidence in several works suggests that many of the settlers were able to outfit themselves with their own resources, literally taking their capital equipment with them (see Garufi 1922; Gattuso 1976; Testa 1973). In any case, it seems irrefragable that the colonization and development of the Sicilian interior led both barons and settlers to contract or covenant consciously with one another to create new communities and economies.

THE CONSTITUTION OF FIEFS AS ECONOMIC AND POLITICAL ENTERPRISES

It is difficult to know the precise number of fiefs either resettled or built anew. Data which may be subject to considerable inaccuracy suggest that from 1583 to 1650, some 120 cultivated fiefs were settled; from 1573 to 1652, another 88 were added; from 1653 to 1714 some 20 more fiefs became feudal towns (Garufi 1947, 59–64; Titone 1955, 51–52). This frontier movement continued, albeit, with less vigor, until 1790. Moreover, the chapters of the land varied from settlement to settlement. Yet though no two Sicilian settlements were constituted and governed in exactly the same way, there was an underlying similarity. The essential rights and duties of the baron and the villagers were usually the same in each constitution. The articles of each charter dealt with the baron's feudal rights, the villagers' feudal rights, property rights and the organization of village life.

At the beginning of each settlement, the baron gave land for the erection of the village and for the private use of each settler. Within the first two or three years of the establishment of the settlement, each settler was obliged to begin construction of his house. For a period that varied from two to ten years, the villagers were free of feudal obligations toward the baron and of local imposts for the parliamentary donatives. After that period, the baron claimed and the settlers were obliged to provide the following: (1) services without remuneration (yearly *angaria*) such as taking one load of hay to the manor and presenting the lord with a chicken on a specific feast day; (2) services with remuneration (yearly *perangaria*) such as the sale of hens and capons first to the lord and the lord's use of settlers' mules and donkeys especially during harvest time on payment of a daily fee; and (3) "special services" ranging from none at all to some services such as a small contribution to the "ransom fund of the baron" on the birth of the first son of a settler family. The proportion of imposts paid by local residents varied from settlement to settlement. Since baronial and domanial towns were assigned an equal share of the parliamentary donatives, the steady increase in the number of baronial towns had the effect of lightening disproportionately the fiscal burden of people living under baronial jurisdiction.

In turn, each villager enjoyed the rights specified under the village charter. These rights included the following liberties: (1) control, use and exchange of one's possessions in and beyond the village; (2) any male settler over the age of majority had the right to be a public official; (3) liberty of movement; and (4) no claim could be made on a villager beyond those specified in the chapters of the land.

The division of the fief's natural resources was generally between the private property of the baron and the villagers, and the commons—collective resources or civic usufruct rights—that each family member had under the chapters of the land. The collective resource (originally known as *communio pro indiviso*) were inherent in the *jura civitatis* and in part for this reason villagers were also known as "communists." In the course of time the sharing of the same collective resources such as trees gave rise to a complex configurations of uses.[7]

Like feudal rights and duties, the division and cultivation of land varied according to the competitive pressures of peopling fiefs. In addition to the feudal and tax exemptions, some barons attracted settlers by granting them strips of land around the village as private property. As a general rule, however, the principal form of settlers' rural private property was the long leasehold, the emphyteusis or copyhold contract (the *enfiteusi*), granted in exchange for a fixed annual rent. Under the emphyteusis the land could not be taken away from the cultivator as long as he, his family or his heirs cultivated it. It was this particular long-term lease that gave rise to the small landowning class in Sicily: the *burgisi*. A system of sharecropping was the common method of working the baron's land. The baron generally supplied the land, the seed and the fertilizer while the peasant supplied his labor and animals. The produce was often shared equally between the two. The decision of what to cultivate was arrived at between the landowner or his agent and the cultivator. This contract lasted several years.

Sicilian jurisprudence and convention had come to regard civic usufructs as essential rights that no prince or parliament could take away without the unanimous consent of villagers. Thus each "communist" enjoyed, subject to the specifications issued by local officials (the *baiulus*) for the maintenance and protection of a safe yield, the following civic usufruct or common property rights: (1) grazing rights (*ius pascendi* or *compascendi*); (2) wood rights, including the gathering of dead wood for fuel, of *disa* to make brooms, or *giunchi* to make chairs and baskets; (3) "fruit" rights, including the gathering of acorn to feed animals, and "wild herbs" such as mushrooms, cicorie, asparagus and liquorice; (4) water rights for water to be used for animals and humans, as well as irrigation; (5) "extractive" rights to quarry stones and gypsum; and (6) *ristoppiare* and *spigolare*, the gathering of hay and stalks of wheat at harvest time. The extent of these rights varied, however, according to the constitution of each fief. As a general rule, the larger the civic usufructs enjoyed, the greater the likelihood for yearly *angarie* and *perangarie*. Thus, for example, the "communists" of Roccapalumba in the Palermo hinterland enjoyed relatively few common property rights but were not burdened with yearly *angarie* and *perangarie* (Garufi 1922; also see Santamaria 1881, 318–21; cf. Bulgarelli Lukacs 2011).

FACILITIES FOR DETERMINING, ENFORCING AND ALTERING CHAPTERS OF THE LAND

The prerogatives to determine and enforce these rights were assigned to a board of local public officials appointed by the baron and chosen among villagers with at least one year of residence. The number of officials varied according to the size of the community. A board of local officials generally included a captain in charge of peace and security on the fief, a judge who presided over the seigneurial court, a notary public who acted as secretary, the *bagli* who supervised the use of "common property" resources and at least three jurors who, among others, dealt with matters of public interest and collected revenues on behalf of the baron and the vice-regal administration. The decision of what to tax rested with each baron, while the proportion of the parliamentary donatives paid by each community was calculated by the Deputation of the Realm on the basis of the census data, the famous *riveli*.

A second body, the civic council, known at times as "the regular parliament" or "general assembly," was composed of all the townsfolk. It was convened by the baron to decide on matters of importance. While the entire population did not elect its municipal officials, it maintained through the civic council "a watching brief" over the conduct of local officials; jurors often had to justify their acts to both the baron and "the regular parliament" (Diecidue 1966, 89–151; Verdirame 1905, 47–54). Thus community life in the new settlements was characterized by specialization and jointness of efforts between barons and settlers, including the sharing, in various degrees, of the residual claims to the earnings of baronial jurisdiction as an economic enterprise.

By the eighteenth century, the basic rights and duties of villagers and barons and the facilities to determine, enforce and alter them had become so widespread and recognized that some fiefs were peopled without written agreements. Also by that time, some inherent weaknesses in the constitution of established fiefs had reached staggering proportions.

SOURCES OF INSTITUTIONAL WEAKNESS AND FAILURE

The extent to which baronial jurisdiction functioned according to its design and performance criteria depended, in part, upon the willingness or interest of each baron to exercise his (or her) residual claimancy and control over the management of the fief so as to constrain those who found it to their advantage to shirk their efforts and function as free riders in the production process (Cancila 2007, 2008; for a more general treatment, Salter 2015). Yet there are at least two reasons why some barons had incentives to shirk these very responsibilities and to turn over the management of their estates to rentiers in exchange for a constant share of the estate earnings. First, while first-born sons stood to inherit baronies, they did not have sole claims to baronial earnings. Their brothers and sisters were entitled to receive at least one-third of those earnings without, however, shouldering any responsibility or risk for the economic productivity of the estate. Second, some barons found it difficult to resist the attraction provided by the tax-free position of Palermo and, thus, tended to abandon their fiefs to establish themselves in the capital city.

There thus developed a situation by the eighteenth century whereby many barons could not, in the words of the Sicilian economist Abbé Paolo Balsamo, "be persuaded that without the necessary attention, labor bestowed, and prudence, their forefathers could neither have acquired, nor bequeathed that to their descendants which secures them from the chilling hand of poverty" (Balsamo 1809 [1811], 13). In turn, leasing estates for a very short period helped barons to keep abreast of inflation but also discouraged rentiers (the *gabelloti*) from managing the estates as if they were their own (cf. for Lombardy, Greenfield 1934, 19–26). As Abbé Balsamo warned the prince of Fitalia, an absentee lord who had devised plans to improve land management and cultivation of his estate, such plans "would never be thoroughly completed until proprietors paraded less with expensive carriages and horses on (fashionable drives in Palermo), but were oftener in the saddle to visit their rich and capable estates" (Balsamo 1809 [1811], 10–11).

In such circumstances, shirking and free riding became widespread and, in certain cases, assumed major proportions. Some barons unilaterally canceled *enfiteusi* contracts when they found their fixed income sharply reduced by inflation. Baronial agents left to themselves were prone to do the same. In order to make quick returns, both rentiers and cultivators often underinvested in the factors of production (Sergio 1777 [1962], 7–9). Some boards of local officials became self-perpetuating local oligarchies operating with immunity from barons and villagers alike (e.g., Li Vecchi 1975). Villagers found that recourse to the vice-regal administration to command the services of impartial officials or to sustain existing agreements against new demands and unilateral cancellations of contracts was neither always readily available nor always impartial (Guarnieri 1892, 145).

In 1752, the Spanish Bourbon monarch ratified the arbitrary abrogation of *enfiteusi* by barons without any compensation to dispossessed cultivators in exchange for baronial support—further eroding the integrity of the Patrimony. In addition, as new knowledge and technological innovation expanded, attempts to alter authority assigned under the charters of settlements so as to take into account new possibilities proved to be difficult and costly undertakings for both village representatives and barons (for protracted efforts to modify by mutual consent original agreements, e.g., Battaglia 1895).

Thus the extent to which the manorial system in Sicily did not function "as it should" was due not only to a lack of baronial willingness or interest to exercise residual authority and control over the management of fiefs but also due to the failure of vice-regal administration to provide the supporting infrastructures for the (re)formulation and maintenance of chapters of the land. Only exposure to the competitive pressures existing in the "frontier movement" and in the wheat market served as effective means to bias or rig the structure of individual and family incentives toward a consideration of a wider community of interests and a longer time horizon.

FUNDAMENTAL CHANGES IN THE CONSTITUTION OF THE REALM

By the 1770s, a concern for the failings of Sicilian government and the consequences that these were having upon Sicilian life and economy was becoming widespread among members of the baronial class. This concern was stimulated by the writings of publicists who, as ecclesiastics, noblemen, or jurists, had already special interests in economics, education and law. The study of Sicilian history, coupled with the discovery of Blackstone, Hume and Adam Smith, led the great majority of Sicilian publicists to conclude that governmental reforms advantageous to all could be introduced in accordance with the Sicilian political tradition.

A concern for the failings of Sicilian government, filtered through the Neapolitan political tradition, led Bourbon officials to antithetical conclusions. In order to repair those failings, they reasoned, it was necessary to bring down the entire edifice of Sicilian government—in effect, to extend absolutist rule over the island. In the past, such attempts had been incidental to royal or imperial financial policies. Monarchs had been less concerned with the suppression of parliament, baronial jurisdiction and local laws and privileges—known as "freedoms"—than in making money out of them. Now, royal reforms intended to sweep away the very *Capitula regni Siciliae*. Neapolitan remedial policy was thus unprecedented in both intent and scope.

The marquis Domenico Caracciolo of Villamaina appeared to the Bourbon court as the best Neapolitan official to possess the skills and the knowledge necessary to effect basic changes in Sicily. As the Neapolitan envoy in Paris for more than a decade, the 66-year-old former magistrate had developed an admiration for the ability with which successive French monarchs had curtailed seigneurial jurisdiction and centralized the organization of the French state. The study of French political practices and ideas thus led the marquis of Villamaina to conclude that in order to repair Sicilian government and economy it was necessary "to liquidate the heredity of the past" (Pontieri 1943, 164). No intermediate power, secondary organizations or deliberative assemblies should stand in between the monarch and the Sicilian people. Caracciolo became viceroy in 1781.

As soon as he reached Sicily, the new viceroy confounded in indiscriminate hatred all things Sicilian (Renda 1974, 91–93)—both the worst and what was best in the Sicilian political tradition. He attempted to check baronial abuses but also to undermine the political covenant between the monarch and the barons. He sought to reduce the gross inequalities in parliamentary taxation and the accumulated immunities of local corporations but also to erase representative and secondary institutions. He tried to break down class distinctions but also to suppress the political rights and liberties of both the aristocracy and the lowest classes. Like the French he admired and the Neapolitans he served, the marquis of Villamaina could envisage political equality and free trade but could not envisage political liberty and free institutions. By declaring himself the enemy at once of Sicilian barons and Sicilian institutions, Caracciolo transformed baronial opposition to tax reforms into a defense of the *Capitula regni Siciliae*. As a result, baronial pressures on Sicilian officials in Naples to have the Bourbon court recall the viceroy received the support of the very same people Caracciolo thought needed to be delivered from bondage. If the marquis of Villamaina failed "to liquidate the heredity of the past," he did, however, introduce several reforms that, among others, strengthened the reach of vice-regal administration and brought baronial jurisdiction back to better performance levels.

At the same time, before leaving Sicily in 1786 Caracciolo prevailed upon King Ferdinand to force the royal courts to reinterpret the thirteenth-century laws *Si Aliquem* and *Volentes* that had become the legal basis of baronial jurisdiction. In 1788, the Bourbon monarch issued a pragmatic sanction or royal decree to the effect that *Volentes* (which allowed for fiefs to be sold in the open market) had made no fundamental change in feudal obligations. The original Norman barons had been feudatories and comrades-in-arms of Count Roger as Sicilian jurisprudence claimed. The fiefs were held in return for duties performed and could not be bequeathed or alienated like allodial property. Royal confirmation and a special payment were needed before they could be inherited. Without proper succession and entitlement, the fiefs should revert to the crown.

Events associated with the French revolution introduced critical variations in the conflict situation between the Bourbon crown and the Sicilian aristocracy. First, war compelled the royal family and court to seek refuge in Sicily and to depend upon money voted by the Sicilian parliament. Second, the Bourbon's flight to Sicily occurred at a time when, in part as a result of Caracciolo's reforms, most barons had acquired a new awareness of their constitutional rights. The parliamentary barons supported, financially and without stint, the Bourbon crown against revolutionary France. But they, and the ecclesiastical lords, resented the Neapolitans' failure to acknowledge fully the existence of a separate Sicilian nation and identity; they equally opposed the crown's claim that only the support of the royally hand-picked domanial house was sufficient to vote supply. Third, the British "occupation" of Sicily in 1806 not only strengthened Sicilian defense against French invasion from the Calabrian coast and furnished the Bourbon king with much-needed subsidies from the British government, but also gave Sicilian noblemen and publicists like the prince of Castelnuovo and Abbé Balsamo an opportunity to renew their ties with Britain considered as "Sicily's sister island."

In 1810, the 125th parliament met to hear a speech from the throne extolling the *Capitula regni Siciliae*—"institutions lost by other nations for lack of public spirit and national energy and preserved only in the two most famous islands in the world, Great Britain and Sicily" (quoted in Rosselli 1956, 14). This doffing of the hat to Sicilian political tradition was accompanied by a call for an extraordinary donative of 360,000 ounces of gold a year and a new distribution of taxes. The barons, led by the prince of Belmonte, the prince of Castelnuovo and the prince of Cassaro and supported by the ecclesiastical lords, reduced the royal request to half and presented a counterplan for taxation which went beyond the very tax reforms they or previous barons had bitterly opposed during Caracciolo's viceroyalty. Their counterplan did away with the eighteen different donatives as too cumbersome to collect and called for a single tax of 5 percent on the income of all the real estate outside of Palermo, including the barons' as well as the king's.

Rather than face the baronial challenge or turn to more British subsidies, the Bourbon monarch now tried to increase his revenues without parliamentary consent. A majority of peers requested the king to withdraw the non-parliamentary taxation and to trust to the bounty of parliament for the supply of his wants. King Ferdinand responded by ordering the arrest and exile of the leaders of the protesting lords. At this point the British minister plenipotentiary and commander of the British army in Sicily, the Whig nobleman William Bentinck, intervened in the struggle between the court and parliament. Sympathetic to what was to become known as "the constitutionalist party" and fearful lest the Sicilians should seek support from the French, Bentinck successfully pressured King Ferdinand to set free the imprisoned barons, to withdraw the extra-parliamentary taxes, and to replace the Neapolitan ministry with a Sicilian ministry. While Lord Bentinck became, in effect, the viceroy of Sicily, the new ministry, now made up of three of the five imprisoned barons, called parliament together in June 1812. The barons, led by Belmonte and Castelnuovo and aided by Balsamo, turned to the British constitution and the very terminology of British politics to deal once and for all with Neapolitan designs over Sicily and to adapt the medieval Sicilian constitution to modern conditions.

"The 1812 Anglo-Sicilian constitution" swept away baronial jurisdiction and feudal dues and privileges. The meaning of fiefs changed from a bundle of rights enjoyed by barons and villagers alike to private property enjoyed by the barons alone. The three houses of parliament were replaced by a House of Commons and a House of Lords. Money bills were to originate only in the Commons. The power of making laws resided in parliament while the king retained executive authority, including the right to dissolve parliament. The administration of justice was entrusted to a body of independent judges; everyone was equal before the law and no one could be imprisoned without due process. While Sicily was divided into 23 districts, municipal institutions were recast upon principles of local self-government. The realm of Sicily was declared independent of the realm of Naples and of every other country or dominion.

In Sicilian historiography the abolition of feudalism has often been interpreted as follows: "The 1812 parliament claimed to have freed a population from serfdom when, in fact, it was already free. . . . The truth is that Sicilian barons took away that freedom and, in return, gave nothing to the population" (Salvioli 1902, 339). It is true that the abolition of the commons (or civic usufruct rights) countervened the long—standing canon in Sicilian jurisprudence that no prince or assembly could take away such rights from villagers without their consent, transformed fiefs into allodial or private properties and gave barons extensive proprietary authority over natural resources. But the abolition of feudal laws and privileges also gave barons very limited scope and domain of authority over the local population under two conditions. A free labor market together with the reconstituted communal government and parliament could, potentially, if acted upon, represent a serious "devaluation"[8] of the rural proprietorship of large landowners as a determinant of authority and power among Sicilians. But these conditions did not have time to materialize. Hence, more than the abolition of feudalism as such, it was the chain of events that culminated in the destruction of Sicilian self-government that undermined or thwarted what is often referred to, mistakenly, as "the failure of rise of the Western world" in Sicily.

Before the Anglo-Sicilian constitution took effect, critical policy differences emerged between Belmonte, who could be compared to "a great Whig nobleman," and Castelnuovo, who drew inspiration from Republican Rome and America (Roselli 1956, 71). Soon after the election of the first reform parliament in 1813, both Belmonte and Castelnuovo faced *at once* all the problems that had accompanied the British unreformed parliament between 1604 and 1832 and that were to accompany the British reformed parliament after the abolition of "rotten" and "pocket" boroughs in 1832. As a result, they experienced serious difficulties in checking King Ferdinand's efforts to wreck the constitution, in establishing and following the principle of collective cabinet responsibility and in maintaining parliamentary support for their ministry in the face of an emerging "Jacobin party" in the Commons and a resurgent "*status quo ante Caracciolo*" party in the Lords. By 1814, constitutional barons could neither make use of parliament nor manage public affairs without it. What they needed was a longer time span in order to work out or solve the accumulation of governmental issues and problems generated by the constitutional reform experiment; but time they did not have.

Lord Bentinck's intervention in Sicilian affairs had given Belmonte and Castelnuovo hope that British support would serve to maintain conditions favorable to the long-term survival of the Anglo-Sicilian constitution. It was, however, an ill—founded hope. British policy in Italy, anchored as it was to Austria, ran precisely against the very survival of the Sicilian experiment in constitutional economy. By 1814, with the specter of Napoleonic domination of Europe receding in the background, the same military exigencies that had earlier led British foreign minister Castelreagh to support Bentinck's efforts now led him to do the opposite. Bentinck was dismissed and replaced with a minister who had the same regard for the 1812 constitution as King Ferdinand. Thus Sicily's experiment in constitutional economy was ultimately decided not at Palermo but at the Congress of Vienna.

In December 1816 the Bourbon king ceased to be designated as Ferdinand the Fourth of Naples and Third of Sicily and became known as Ferdinand I of the new kingdom of the Two Sicilies. The Sicilian parliament was abolished, as was the Sicilian flag. The Napoleonic code and the system of French administration imposed on the Neapolitan provinces during the French occupation were now found to be useful instruments to extend absolutist rule over Sicily. Seven Sicilian provinces were created and administered by provincial intendants and non-elected communal councils.

While the very abolition of feudalism served to pry Sicily loose from her political tradition, it took the Congress of Vienna to make of Sicily, in the famous words of a contemporary historian, Luigi Blanch, "a posthumous conquest of Napoleon" (quoted in Roselli 1956, 71). The enforcement of regulations issued from Naples became, however, subject to serious institutional weakness and failure. At the same time, control over agricultural resources now gave Sicilian barons and their agents a political power they never had before. By the 1870s, the situation had changed little. As Sidney Sonnino, a traveling companion of Leopoldo Franchetti, concluded his classic study of Sicilian rural conditions in 1876:

> The situation we found in 1860 persists today. . . . We have legalized the existing oppression and are assuring the impunity of the oppressors. In modern societies, tyranny of the law is restrained by fears of remedies outside the law. In Sicily, with our institutions patterned on liberal formalism rather than informed by a true spirit of liberty, we have furnished the oppressing classes [with] the legal means to defend their oppression and to take over all the public positions by the use and abuse of power (*forza*) that was and continues to be in their hands. We are now strengthening the oppressors' hands by reassuring them that, no matter how far they push their oppression, we will not tolerate any kind of illegal remedy, while there can be no legal remedy, for they have legality on their side. (1877 [1925], 39)

As a result, Sicilian peasants found themselves locked in what Sonnino called "an iron circle," or the many-person analogue to the prisoner's dilemma of modern game theory (on Franchetti and Sonnino, see Sabetti 1996). On one hand, they suffered labor contracts imposed by the monopoly of large landowners or their agents and supported by the arms of the State; on the other, they bore the cost of government, without voice and with little benefit. The reconstitution of agricultural and communal activities as a function of the new structure of centralized authority exposed the great majority of the Sicilian people to conditions of life devoid of opportunities and remedies for enhancing their long-term welfare potential. But the same reconstitution also failed over time to bring private rates of return on economic activities into parity with social returns and, ultimately, thwarted economic growth altogether. Thus, in the end, Sicilian landowners as well became locked into Sonnino's "iron circle."

The full emergence of private property in land (of former fiefs) and a free labor market could not, by themselves, assure and sustain modern economic and political development in Sicily largely because the creation of a legal-rational monocentric order à la Max Weber in 1816 reiterated the rule of the few over the many. This way the modern political and legal order represented a breakdown and not the beginning of "modernization" (see also Sabetti 2000, Chapters 2–3; 2002, Chapters 4–6). The creation of a united Italy reaffirmed and extended the legal-rational monocentric order on an unwilling people so that it continued to be a poorly understood source of weakness and failure.

CONCLUSION

This chapter suggests that the struggle to constitute and sustain productive orders over the course of more than 700 years of Sicilian history is a complex one, not subject to sweeping generalizations. But there are still some conclusions that can be offered. First, it is possible to remove the shadows and false lights that have, for so a long time, obscured an appreciation of the struggle of people to constitute and sustain productive orders in Sicily. Second, the island in its long history was a veritable laboratory of collective undertakings. The success and failure, the resilience and weakness, of these efforts remain to be fully explored but there is no denying the capacity of successive generations of people to engage in the struggle to undertake various forms of collective efforts to advance human welfare and economic growth. Third, the political and economic entrepreneurship sketched in the chapter may not entirely fit Israel Kirzner's characterization, but entrepreneurship and innovation have a long history in Sicily, if we are willing to pursue the path opened by the research of the late Stephan Epstein (1992; and see also 2000). The enormous investment of time and archival work by Epstein shows that it is possible to diligently uncover complex configurations of productive economic activities throughout the island in premodern times.

A fourth implication of the analysis is that, with our empiricist epistemology, we need to resist a positivist and unproblematic view of the monopoly of state powers and come to appreciate what Sonnino observed in 1876 (also echoed in Santi Romano's analysis of Sardinia [1959] and, more broadly by James C. Scott's research in Southeast Asia [2009]). The prevailing wisdom about the basic problem in Sicily, as in the South, is that with the making of a united Italy centralized government and administration did not go far enough in Sicily. We suggest instead that the basic problem was the opposite: the arms of the state tried to reach too far in the lives of an unwilling and subject people to make many people worse off.

Finally, a more general conclusion follows. We should be more sensitive to an important lesson from the Ostrom research agenda: that people, in some basic sense, build their own social and political realities and opportunities, and what officialdom in the formal regime may do is only part of the story. If some concepts or institutions do not work, or are rigged against them, ordinary people will make their own adaptations and these may become rather perverse when officialdom thinks it can govern but people go their own way.

NOTES

1. The Sicilian parliament was made up of three houses: the military or baronial, the ecclesiastical and the domanial. The domanial house contained representatives from towns which remained, at least in theory, under royal jurisdiction. There were seldom more than forty-five such towns and in part for this reason the domanial house never developed into a house of commons before 1812. The baronial house was the most important and the most powerful of the three.

2. H. G. Koeningsberger's *The Government of Sicily under Philip II of Spain: A Study in the Practice of Empire* (1951) is perhaps the single best source for this period. See also Corrao 1991.

3. This topic has not received the attention it merits, but the research of Adelaide Baviera Albanese (1974) and of Epstein (1992) remains a good starting point. The entrepreneurial activities required to start and sustain successfully, over several centuries, the sugar and silk industries and what made the Val Demone region (Messina and surrounding areas) as the most economically advanced area of Sicily until about the eighteenth century are yet to be fully investigated and remain not well understood.

4. The only restriction for a female lord—and there were many (and not just the queen who was entitled to rule over, thorough her household and local representatives and agents, her own economic and political enterprises composing the so-called *camera reginale*) who either inherited or bought fiefs—was that she could not sit in person in the baronial or military house of parliament. See Santoro 2003.

5. This was by no means confined to Sicily. See Castiglione 2005; Sabetti 2014.

6. Titone (1955, 81) speculates that for these settlers the establishment of new baronial communities "became that which the American colonies came to mean for rebels and refugees of so many European countries."

7. The complexity of users' rights in trees is effectively portrayed, albeit from a Roman law jurisprudence, by the now classic work of Camillo Giardina (1941). Giardina's work merits attention by those interested in a history of governing the commons.

8. Brian Loveman's framework of analysis (1973) on this point is still a worthy introduction.

REFERENCES

Albanese, Adelaide Baviera. 1974. *In Sicilia nel sec. XVI: Verso una rivoluzione industriale?* Caltanissetta: Salvatore Sciascia.

Alchian, Armen A. 1965. "Some Economics of Property Rights." *Il Politico* 30: 816–29.

Arnolfini, G. A. [1962] 1768. *Giornale di viaggio e questioni sull'economia siciliana.* Caltanissetta: Salvatore Sciascia.

Backman, Clifford R. 1995. *The Decline and Fall of Medieval Sicily Politics, Religion, and Economics in the Reign of Frederick III, 1296–1337.* Cambridge: Cambridge University Press.

Balsamo, Paolo. 1811. *A View of the Present State of Sicily: Its Rural Economy, Population, and Produce, Particularly in the County of Modica, English ed.* London: Gale & Curtis.

Battaglia, Aristide. 1895. *L'evoluzione sociale in rapporto alla proprieta fondiaria in Sicilia.* Palermo: Libreria Carlo Clauden di Alberto Reber.

Boettke, Peter, Christopher Coyne and Peter Leeson. 2008. "Institutional Stickiness and the New Development Economics." *American Journal of Economics and Sociology* 67: 331–58.

Brancato, Francesco. 1946–47. "Il Commercio dei grani nel settecento in Sicilia," *Archivio Storico Siciliano*, 3rd series: 255–65.

Bulgarelli Luckacs, Alessandra. 2011. "La gestione delle risorse collettive nel regno di Napoli in eta' moderna: un percorso comparativo," in Guido Alfani and Riccardo Rao, eds., *La gestione delle risorse collettive. Italia settentrionale, secoli XII–XVIII.* Milan: FrancoAngeli, 227–45.

Cancila, Orazio. 1974. *Gabelloti e contadini in un comune rurale (secc. XVIII–XIX).* Caltanissetta: Salvatore Sciascia.

Cancila, Orazio. 2001. *La terra di Cerere.* Caltanissetta: Sciascia Editore.

Cancila, Rossella. 2007. *Gli occhi del principe. Castelvetrano:uno stato feudale nella Sicilia moderna.* Rome: Viella editore.

Cancila, Rossella. 2008. "*Merum et mixtum imperium* nella Sicilia feudale." *Mediterranea* XIV (December): 469–504.

Cancila, Rossella. 2009. "Per una retta Amministrazione della giustizia: la giustizia dei baroni nella Sicilia moderna." *Mediterranea* XVII (August): 315–52.

Castiglione, Caroline. 2005. *Patrons and Adversaries. Nobles and Villagers in Italian Politics 1640–1760.* New York: Oxford University Press.

Cattaneo, Carlo. [1861] 2002. *Intelligence [Human Thought] as a Principle of Public Economy*, ed. by Marco Vitale. Lanham: Lexington Books.

Corrao, Pietro. 1991. *Governare un regno. Potere, societa, e istituzioni in Sicilia tra il Trecento e Quattrocento.* Naples: Liguori Editore.

Diecidue, Gianni.1966. "I consigli civici a Castelvetrano nei secoli XVI–XVIII," *Archivio Storico Siciliano* 16: 89–151.

Epstein, Stephan R. 1992. *An Island for Itself: Economic Development and Social Change in Late Medieval Sicily.* New York: Cambridge University Press.

Epstein, Stephan R. 2000. *Freedom and Growth. The rise of states and markets in Europe, 1300–1750.* London: Routledge.

Ferrigno, Giovanni Battista. 1915–1916. "Un contratto di pace tra donna Antonina Contessa d'Aragona e l'Universita di Terranova nel 1516," *Archivio Storico Siciliano* 40:118–46.

Garufi, Carlo Alberto. 1947. "Patti agrari e comuni di nuova fondazione in Sicilia: dallo scorcio del secolo XI agli arbori del settecento." *Archivio Storico Siciliano* 2, 3rd Series: 59–64.

Garufi, Carlo Alberto. 1922. *Roccapalumba dal feudo alla abolizione de la Feudalità.* Palermo: Stabilimento E. Priulla.

Gattuso, Ignazio. 1976. *Economia e societa in un comune rurale della Sicilia (Secoli XVI—XIX).* Palermo: Tumminelli.

Genuardi, Luigi. 1911. *Terre Comuni ed usi civici in Sicilia prima dell'Abolizione della Feudalità.* Palermo: Scuola Tip.

Giardina, Camillo. 1941. "La cosidetta proprieta' degli alberi separata da quella del suolo in Italia." *Atti della Reale Accademia di Scienze, Lettere e Arti di Palermo* 4 serie: 203–80.

Greenfield, Kent R. 1948. *Economics and Liberalism in the Risorgimento: A Study of Nationalism in Lombardy 1814–1848.* Baltimore: The Johns Hopkins University Press.

Guarnieri, Andrea. 1892. "Alcune notizie sovra la gestione d'una casa baronale e sull'amministrazione della giustizia in Sicilia verso la fine del secolo XVIII," *Archivio Storico Siciliano* 17: 145.
Guarnieri, Andrea. 1889. "Un diploma di grazie e privilegi municipale concessi nel 1393 dai magnifici Conti di Peralta," *Archivio Storico Siciliano* 14: 293–314.
Hayek, F. A. 1937. "Economics and Knowledge." *Economica* 4: 33–54.
Koenigsberger, H. G. 1951. *The Government of Sicily Under Philip II of Spain: A Study in the Practice of Empire*. London: Staples Press.
Koenigsberger, H. G. 1971. *Estate and Revolutions: Essays in Early Modern European History*. Ithaca: Cornell University Press.
Li Vecchi, Alfredo. 1975. *Caltanissetta feudale*. Caltanissetta: Sciascia.
Loveman, Brian. 1976. *Struggle in the Countryside: Politics and. Rural Labor in Chile, 1919–1973*. Bloomington: Indiana University Press.
Mack Smith, Denis. 1988. *A History of Sicily: Medieval Sicily 800–1713*. New York: Dorset Press.
Ostrom, Elinor. 1990. *Governing the Commons. The Evolution of Institutions for Collective Action*. New York: Cambridge University Press.
Ostrom, Vincent. 1980. "Artisanship and Artifact." *Public Administration Review* 40 (July/August): 309–17.
Ostrom, Vincent. 1997. *The Meaning of Democracy and the Vulnerability of Democracies*. Ann Arbor: University of Michigan Press.
Peri, Illuminato. 1965. *Il villanaggio in Sicilia*. Palermo: Manfredi.
Petino, Antonio. 1946. *La Questione del Commercio dei Grani in Sicilia nel Settecento*. Catania,
Pontieri, Ernesto. 1943. *Il tramonto del baronaggio siciliano*. Florence: Sansoni.
Pupillo-Barrese, Antonio. 1903. *Gli usi civici in Sicilia: Ricerche di storia del diritto*. Catania: Giannotta Editore.
Renda, Francesco. 1974. *Baroni e riformatori in Sicilia sotti in ministero* Caracciolo *(1786–1789)*. Messina: Editrice La Libra.
Renda, Francesco. 1963. *L'emigrazione in Sicilia*. Palermo: Edizioni Sicilia al Lavoro.
Romano, Andrea. 1993. "Vito La Mantia e le fonti della Legislazione cittadina Siciliana medievale." *Antiche consuetudini delle Citta' di Sicilia*, V. La Mantia, v–lxxxviii. Palermo: Intilla Editore.
Romano, Santi. [1917] 1946. *Ordinamento giuridico*. Florence: Sansoni Editore.
Rosselli, John. 1956. *Lord William Bentinck and the British Occupation of Sicily: 1811–1814*. New York: Cambridge University Press.
Sabetti, Filippo. 1996. "Path Dependency and Civic Culture. Some Lessons from Italy about Interpreting Social Experiments." *Politics and Society* 24 (March): 19–44.
Sabetti, Filippo. 2000. *The Search for Good Government. Understanding the Paradox of Italian Democracy*. Montreal: McGill-Queen's University Press.
Sabetti, Filippo. 2002. *Village Politics and the Mafia in Sicily, 2nd Ed*. Montreal: McGill-Queen's University Press.
Sabetti, Filippo. 2010. *Civilization and Self-Government: The Political Thought of Carlo Cattaneo*. Lanham: Lexington Books.

Sabetti, Filippo. 2014. "Artisans of the Common Life. Building a Public Science of Civics." In *Civic Studies*, edited by Peter Levine and Karol E. Sołtan, 23–32. Washington, D.C.: Bringing Theory to Practice.
Salter, Alexander W. 2015. "Rights to the Realm: Reconsidering Western Political Development." *American Political Science Review* 109 (November): 725–34.
Salvioli, Giuseppe. 1902. "Il Villanaggio in Sicilia e la sua abolizione," *Rivista Italiana di Sociologia*: 371–401.
Santamaria, Nicola. 1881. *I feudi, il diritto feudale e la loro storia nell'Italia meridionale*. Naples: Ricc. Marghieri di Gius Editore.
Santoro, Daniela. 2003. *Messina l'indomita.* Caltanissetta: Sciascia Editore.
Scott, James C. 2009. *The Art of Not Being Governed: An Anarchist History of Upland Southeast Asia.* New Haven: Yale University Press.
Sergio, Vincenzo E. 1962. "Lettera sulla pulizia delle pubbliche strade di Sicilia (1777)," in *Un Secolo di politica stradale in Sicilia*, edited by C. Trasselli, pp. 1–30. Caltanissetta: Sciascia.
Simon, Herbert. 1981. *The Ultimate Resource*. Princeton: Princeton University Press.
Sołtan, Karol. 2016. "Civic Theory, Bloomington, and a Republican Renewal." Chapter in this book.
Sonnino, Sidney. 1877. *La Sicilia nel 1876: I Contadini,* nuova edizione. Florence, 1925.
Sproule-Jones, Mark, B. Allen and F. Sabetti, eds. 2008. *The Struggle to constitute and sustain productive orders. Vincent Ostrom's Quest to understand human affairs.* Lanham: Lexington Books.
Testa, Giuseppe. 1973. *Il Principato di Campofranco nel feudo 'Fontana di li Rosi.'* Agrigento: Tipografia Primavera.
Titone, Virgilio. 1955. *La Sicilia dalla Dominazione Spagnola all'Unita d'Italia.* Bologna: Zanichelli,
Titone, Virgilio. 1961. *Origini della Questione Meridionale: Riveli e platee del Regno di Sicilia.* Milan: Feltrinelli.
Tocqueville, Alexis de. [1859] 1956. *The Old Regime and the French Revolution.* Garden City, NY: Doubleday Anchor Books.
Tricoli, Giuseppe. 1966. *La Deputazione degli Stati e la Crisi dle Baronaggio Siciliano.* Palermo: Fondazione Culturale 'Lauro Chiazzese.'
Verdirame, Gaetano. 1905. "Le istituzione sociali e politiche di alcuni municipi della Sicilia orientale nei secoli XVI, XVII, XVIII: Imposte e tasse." *Archivio Storico Siciliano* 2: 19–60.

Chapter 9

Public Goods and the Diagnosis of Counter-intentional Policy Outcomes

Michael A. Fotos, III

This chapter responds to Vincent Ostrom's challenge to work out "patterns of counterintentionality and counterintuitivity" in policy analysis.[1] As Ostrom describes the problem,

> If inferences do not hold, then one might conjecture that patterns of counterintentionality and counterintuivity or both are at work, requiring elaboration in a political science. Working out patterns of counterintentionality and counterintuitivity, then, would require reference to classificatory schema and the conceptual logics at work. (V. Ostrom 2012 [1991], 254)

The first part of the chapter elaborates on the conceptual logic of the Ostrom typology of goods, developing a policy theory that relates the realized or unrealized intentionality of policy outcomes to the adequacy of rules for solving problems of exclusion and use regulation. The second part describes a typology of outcomes ordered according to true intentionality and three forms of counterintentionality and provides illustrative examples corresponding to each of the four outcome types. The third part of the chapter advances a conceptual logic of policy design based on a synthesis of policy theory and the outcome typology that is achieved by relating the design requirements and design objectives of exclusion and use rules to the logical components of those rules. The discussion of design logic locates inferred rule components in relation to the IAD framework and by invoking the concept of nested levels of choice, relates the proposed logic of design to the problem of problem definition, policy theory and implementation scenarios, rent-seeking and the consequences of constitutional rules. The fourth and final part of the chapter elaborates on intentionality, shared intentionality, and the analysis of political experiments. The discussion of intentionality addresses the presumed problem of operationalizing shared intentionality and offers a critical appraisal of axiomatic evaluative standards including efficiency and equity.

A CONCEPTUAL LOGIC LEADING TO ADEQUATE POLICY THEORY

Vincent and Elinor Ostrom (1977, 1991; E. Ostrom 2010) employ the concepts of exclusion, non-exclusion and joint and non-joint use as definitional attributes to construct a typology of economic goods shown in Figure 9.1, thereby making intelligible distinctions between public, private, and two newly-described, mixed goods: common pool resources and toll goods.

When re-stated as problems to be solved by policy design, non-exclusion and joint use explain cases of intentional and counterintentional policy outcomes. When situated with reference to the IAD framework, the conceptual logic of the Ostrom typology offers encompassing explanations of coproduction, implementation scenarios, rent-seeking, and policy causal theory.

All economic goods present certain problems of exclusion and joint use that define the type of good. Effective policies match exclusion and joint use rules to problems. For example, competitive free markets allocate private goods efficiently because enforceable property rights solve the producer's problem of excluding non-payers from using the good and the price mechanism provides information consumers need to "self-regulate" consumption of scarce goods. Markets do not efficiently allocate public goods because producers cannot exclude non-payers from consuming the goods they produce and the absence of effective price signals precludes consumer discovery of the good's scarcity (Munger 2000). Public policies such as licenses and

	Feasible exclusion	Infeasible exclusion
Non-joint use	Pure private goods	Common pool resources
Joint use	Toll goods/Club goods	Pure public goods

Figure 9.1 Typology of Goods: Feasibility of Exclusion Across; Jointness of Use Down.
Source: Based on Ostrom and Ostrom (1977, 12; 1991, 168).

permits address the problem of exclusion and taxes and fees imposed under conditions of fiscal equivalence address consumers' information problems.

Specifying the public goods components, that is, the latent problems of non-exclusion and joint use, of a policy or program enables the forward-looking analyst to design rules that assure any given policy or program will achieve intended outcomes. In retrospective, ex post analysis, discovering the unsolved but solvable problems of non-exclusion and joint use enables the analyst to diagnose causes and identify remedies for the rule-based causes of counterintentional policy outcomes.

Most public policies and programs provide for or deliver services aimed at producing complex packages of public, private, and mixed goods. For example, good public schools generate the non-excludable, jointly consumed public goods associated with societies of well-educated citizens and workers. Even so, graduates of good schools enjoy the individually appropriable, excludable and non-joint benefits of better career prospects and higher incomes. Delivering educational services entails implementation scenarios where the goods at stake have mixed attributes, feasible exclusion and joint use (e.g., the classroom) and infeasible exclusion and high subtractability (e.g., study carrels in the school library). By solving problems of exclusion and joint use successful public schools achieve their intended aims, which the analyst can conceptualize as a package of public, private, and mixed goods.

High quality education requires coproduction, where the consumer and the producer cooperate to produce the desired public good or service. Coproduction presumes a level of shared understanding between the consumer and producer. That shared understanding includes matters of technology or technique, for example, how to use computers or how to plan study time, but more importantly, it also refers to joint and individual expectations about present and future states of affairs, how much and what kind of cooperation is required, and the ultimate value of the benefits of cooperation. If students and teachers, consumers and producers respectively, expect their efforts to be suitably rewarded, then the level of coproduction effort is likely to be high. If not, then coproduction may be difficult to achieve. Coproduction depends on expectations about shared and joint strategies and about future states of affairs.

As noted in Figure 9.2 and described in more detail below, the design objective of exclusion rules with respect to public goods is to stabilize shared expectations concerning individual and collective choices of citizen consumers (or resource appropriators) and the future condition of the public good (or commonly held resource system) (Ostrom 1990, 2005; Ostrom et al. 1994). Well-conceived, contextually appropriate exclusion rules underwrite the coproduction of public goods by stabilizing participants' individual and shared expectations. Good schools stand for a large class of policies and programs.

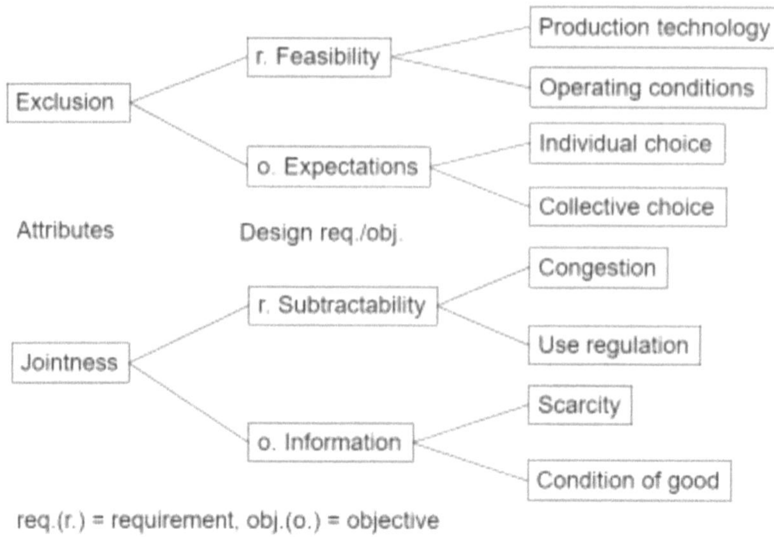

Figure 9.2 A Conceptual Logic of Policy Design. *Source*: Created by author.

THE TYPOLOGY OF OUTCOMES AS SEEN THROUGH THE CONCEPTUAL LOOKING GLASS

Vincent Ostrom (2008, 54–55; 2012 [1994], 334) describes three types of counterintentional outcomes, ambiguous (or no) effect at high cost, monopolization of public goods leading to the erosion of their public value, and unequivocally counterintentional results. The three types suggest a fourth type, successful policies that work as intended. Figure 9.3 presents a typology of outcomes that logically mirrors the typology of goods shown in Figure 9.1.

When intentionality and outcomes match, the analyst can presume that the policy adequately addresses problems of exclusion and joint use. When implementation procedures conform to policy requirements but policy outcomes are spurious, that is, when outcomes bear no apparent relation to the level of effort, the analyst can presume that rules for addressing exclusion are inadequate. When a single user, or a single class of users, dominates a public good, the analyst can presume that the rules relating to joint use are inadequate. Single-use dominance indicates that the exclusion problem has been solved but not which actor, the policy maker or the dominant user, solved it. And when the policy outcomes are perverse, when the reverse happens, the analyst can presume that the rules are inadequate with respect to exclusion and joint use. The policy examples described below and summarized in Table 9.1 illustrate the logic of classification.

	Exclusion rules work as intended.	Exclusion rules do not work as intended.
Joint use problems resolved	Intentionality and outcomes match.	Outcomes are spurious, effects of effort not apparent.
Joint use problems not resolved	Use monopolization, one user class dominates public good.	Unequivocal counter-intentionality, the reverse happened!

Figure 9.3 Typology of Outcomes Exclusion Rules Across; Joint Use Rules Down. *Source*: Classification scheme: by author, after Ostrom and Ostrom (1977, 1991).

Lobster Fishing in the Gulf of Maine: Intentionality Realized

As James Acheson (2003) explains, lobstermen and Maine state regulators have solved problems of exclusion by adopting territorial and limited-entry rules enforced by harbor gangs and zone management councils and they have solved key problems of use regulation by setting trap limits and imposing size and sex restrictions on harvested lobsters. By almost any measure, the Maine lobster fishery is a policy success story. According to the Maine Lobster Marketing Collaborative, in 2012, 5,900 licensed lobster fishers landed 126 million pounds of lobster worth over $338 million at dockside. In contrast, during the "lobster bust" of the 1930s when stocks were so low that biologists worried about the future of the species, about 2,900 lobstermen harvested between five and six million pounds of "bugs" (Acheson 2003, 17). Biologists studying the Gulf of Maine today worry that lobster numbers are too high for the health of the species (Dean 2011). Many factors explain the boom in lobster stocks but catching them in the manner prescribed by present rules has clearly not constrained their abundance. The successes of the Maine lobster fishery illustrate a policy design with exclusion and joint use rules adequate to the public goods produced. Acheson's (2003) examination of the fishery substantiates this claim.

The War on Drugs: Great Effort, Spurious Outcomes

The War on Drugs exemplifies the second category where despite incurring immense direct costs to public treasuries and unimaginably high human costs

Table 9.1 Summary of Policies and Outcomes

Case	*Public Goods*	*Exclusion Rules*	*Use Regulation*	*Outcome*	*Comments*
Maine Lobster Fishery	Natural resource based economic growth, biologically and economically viable fishing resources	Territorial rules, apprenticeship and licensing rules, zone management system [a]	Escape vents, double gauge rule, V-notch rule, conservation ethic [a]	Record harvests, healthy stocks, thousands of fishers making decent livings [b]	Politically well-organized fishing community works effectively at local, state and federal levels [a]
War on Drugs	Externalities from drug abuse or narcotics addictions	Criminal penalties for drug possession or trafficking and violating prescription rules	Prescription limits and reformulation for opioids, treatment for addiction	Direct costs for incarceration of drug users, dealers, etc. are $16.9bn. 2 percent of male workforce is in jail [c]	Enormous direct and indirect costs to society, little apparent effect on the problem or its causes
Atlantic Menhaden	Healthy oceanic food chain, sustainable recreational and commercial fisheries	Layers of permits required to fish commercially, state licensing of guides and recreational fishers	Limits on recreational and commercial harvest, no meaningful restriction on capture technology	Single processer accounts for 80 percent of the harvest. Stocks have declined across the entire range of the species [d]	Omega Protein is politically well-connected [e]. Recreational and bait fishers and wild predators are more numerous but less effective in setting policy
Flood Recovery & Relief	Safety from flood disasters, reduced property losses from flooding	Missing or perverse exclusion rules [g]	Some flood proofing required, subsidized flood insurance is available [f]	Building in flood zones accelerates in the aftermath of disasters [g]	Policy effectively suspends the price mechanism with respect to flood risk.

Sources: [a] Acheson (2003); [b] Maine Lobster Marketing Collaborative (2014); [c] Schmitt, Warner, and Gupta (2010); [d] Pew Environment Group (2013), ASMFC, Omega Protein; [e] Fairbrother (2012); [f] Sylves (2008); [g] Saulny (2007, Hiles (2012).

the intended outcome of reduced social harm from drug addiction bears little apparent relation to the level of public effort. In fact, the indirect human costs of the policy have risen in direct relation to implementation efforts.

> "We must now candidly recognize that the deliberate procedures embodied in present measures to control drug abuse are not sufficient in themselves. The problem has assumed the dimensions of a national emergency. I intend to take every step necessary to deal with this emergency. . ." President Richard M. Nixon, June 17, 1971. (*The New York Times* 1971)

When President Nixon defined drug abuse as a national policy problem, his statement was widely characterized as a declaration of "war on drugs." Nixon called for a national effort lasting three years with the possibility of a two-year further extension (*ibid.*). He proposed adding 325 positions and $45 million in additional budgetary authority to national drug enforcement activities and predicted that this extraordinary yet temporary effort would be sufficient to solve the problem (*ibid.*).

In FY 2011, the Drug Enforcement Agency had an annual budget of $2.2 billion and employed nearly 10,000 people, roughly half of whom are special agents charged with enforcing the nation's drug laws (US Drug Enforcement Administration 2011). According to *The New York Times*, total spending by the national government to prosecute the "war on drugs" runs about $25 billion annually (Cave and Schmidt 2012). In 2008, 2.3 million Americans, roughly 2 percent of the working age male population, were in jail, a quarter of them for nonviolent drug offenses (Schmitt et al. 2010). The direct cost to national, state, and local governments of the United States for incarcerating nonviolent drug offenders alone was approximately $16.9 billion (*ibid.*). The indirect costs in lost wages, foregone tax payments, unpaid child support, and so on are no doubt substantial.

The economic costs, great as they are, appear trivial in relation to the human consequences. Our "war on drugs" has become a literal war in Central and South America, involving the militaries of the United States, Mexico, Colombia, and other nations in battles with heavily-armed traffickers including some reputedly comprised of former military elements. In 2012, the widely-circulated estimate of murders attributed to narco-trafficking in Mexico in the present era was 50,000 (Keefe 2012, *The Telegraph* 2012). The number only rises as the trafficking continues.

Yet, the pharmacopeia and the public's appetite for self-medication seem little diminished.[2] Drug policy designs have focused on stabilizing a particular set of expectations, break the law and you go to jail. Unfortunately, rulemakers have not resolved the problem of infeasible exclusion. Law enforcement crackdowns on the supply or consumption of any particular intoxicant either create opportunities for new supply networks to arise or re-direct demand to more readily available substances (Cave and Schmidt 2012). Feasible exclusion remains an elusive goal; the boundaries between alternative forms of self-medication are porous. Users switch from hard-to-find or more costly drugs to other, more readily available substances. Addicts move back and forth between regulated and informal drug markets seemingly always several steps ahead of the law (Seelye 2013; 2014).

Atlantic Menhaden: A Single User Dominates

Shortcomings in marine fisheries regulation illustrate the third outcome category, when a single user or a single class of users monopolizes consumption of the public good, thusly eroding its public value. Under present rules, a single processor Omega Protein in Reedsville, Virginia captures approximately 80 percent of the entire commercial harvest of the Atlantic menhaden (Goodnough 2011; Pew Environment Group 2013; Plante 2013). The Atlantic Menhaden occupies an admirable, albeit unenviable position in the oceanic food chain. Many depend on it because seemingly everything wants to eat it. Ospreys, loons, and other sea birds fatten themselves and their young on the menhaden's oily, soft flesh. Bluefish, striped bass, and blue fin tuna hunt the menhaden along the US Atlantic coast because it is the most nutritious forage fish in this part of the ocean (Pew Environment Group 2013). Recreational anglers use live menhaden to troll for blues, stripers, and other game fish. Commercial fishers bait lobster traps, crab pots, and long lines with dead menhaden, accounting for approximately 20 percent of the commercial harvest. And finally, Omega Protein deploys a fleet of company-owned vessels that capture 80 percent of the commercial harvest, amounting to 183,085 metric tons of menhaden in 2013, for reduction to fertilizer, animal feed, and human dietary supplements (Pew Environment Group 2013; ASMFC; Omega Protein).

We have been catching menhaden on the Atlantic coast for a long time at rates faster than the fish can reproduce. The Atlantic States Marine Fisheries Commission (ASMFC) estimates that the remaining bunker population is about 8 percent of what an un-fished stock would be.[3] Commercial fishing for menhaden as bait once occurred in nearly all the Atlantic states. Now waters off the New Jersey coast and the Chesapeake Bay are the only places where the bait fishery exists at greater than de minimis levels (ASMFC). The Pew Environment Group estimates a dramatic impact on wildlife diets; bunker comprised 75 percent of the average osprey's diet in the 1980s, now they comprise 24 percent; 77 percent of the striped bass diet in the 1950s, now 7 percent; 42 percent of the weakfish diet in 1991, now 3.3 percent; and 41 percent of the bluefish diet in 1991, now 11.6 percent.

Notice in the introductory paragraph to this section how the numbers of users and relative shares of the commercial harvest form an inverted pyramid. Zero percent of the commercial harvest goes to the countless wild birds, animals, and fish that make no direct commercial use of menhaden but depend on them for survival. Twenty percent of the commercial harvest goes to the tens of thousands of recreational anglers and the thousands of commercial fishers for lobster, crab, and other marketable species. Eighty percent of the commercial harvest goes to a single processing plant. Omega Protein's highly efficient capture technology and its concentrated interest in a single point of consumption effectively dominate consumption of the resource, thus eroding its public value. Reduction of fish to beauty aids and nutrition supplements is clearly incompatible with feeding birds and catching other fish.[4]

Unequivocal Counterintentionality: The Reverse Happened!

Vincent Ostrom (2012 [1986]) introduces the fourth category, the unequivocally counterintentional result, by recounting the outcomes of Bolshevist-Stalinist political and economic experiments. He quotes Milovan Djilas,

> Everything happened differently in the U.S.S.R. and other Communist countries from what the leaders—even such prominent ones as Lenin, Stalin, Trotsky, and Bukharin—anticipated. They expected the state would rapidly wither away, that democracy would be strengthened. *The reverse happened* (*ibid.* 227, italics added by Ostrom)

As Ostrom, Djilas, and many others have noted, the unequivocally counterintentional outcomes of the successful Marxist revolution include the expansion, not the withering away, of the state, the replacement of the old oppressor class with a new, more oppressive class of oppressors, the decline, not the improvement of working class living standards, and the installation of an unresponsive autocracy when democracy was expected.

Life on the Mississippi: Perverse Policy Outcomes are Not Solely Soviet Affairs

Floods are a fact of life in all riverside communities. People living along the Mississippi River witnessed "great" floods in 1844, 1927, and 1951 that set the pattern and lent a name to the Great Midwest Flood of 1993. From May through September of 1993, heavy rains and snow melt in the Mississippi Watershed drove the great river and its tributaries to record heights, flooding 15 million acres of farmland, destroying over 10,000 homes, and taking 50 lives (Larson 1996). The Missouri and the Mississippi Rivers delivered a double blow to St. Charles, Missouri, the floodplain community located where the two streams join. St. Charles experienced 94 days when the Missouri was at flood stage or higher including a new record high of 14.5 feet above flood stage on August 1, 1993 (*ibid.*). Floodwaters forced 2,000 St. Charles County families from their homes and caused $160 million in property damage in the county (Sylves 2008).

The people of St. Charles and other flood-stricken locales did not go without help in their time of need. A generous and provident nation responded by expending over $5.5 billion in recovery assistance to repair or replace public facilities such as roads, bridges, and levees as well as private homes, businesses, and other personal property (Sylves 2008). Then something unexpected happened. The grateful beneficiaries of the public's largesse did not relocate their homes and businesses to higher ground as federal flood officials recommended. Rather, the people of St. Charles County and adjacent St. Louis County looked at the stronger, higher levees (built with the nation's money) and resettled the flood zone. In the decade after the flood, they constructed 28,000 new homes and thousands of acres of new commercial space "estimated to be worth more than $2.2 billion" *in the flood plain* (Saulny 2007; Hiles 2012, italics added).

The Mississippi and Missouri Rivers run high every year. Great floods recur periodically. Yet, national policies intended to repair and remediate flood damage make the people living there more, not less, exposed to losses from flooding. Policies intended to help a community recover from a flood causing $160 million in damages fostered conditions that place $2.2 billion worth of property in similar peril. *The reverse happened*!

This case contains evidence of design failures with respect to both exclusion and joint use rules. Local land use regulations may feasibly prevent building in hazardous areas, although in this case local authorities relaxed, rather than strengthened rules related to flood plain development (Hiles 2012). National flood relief places restrictions on how funds are used but national rules do not preempt local zoning for the most part (Sylves 2008). Therefore, the rules-in-use make exclusion from the flood zone infeasible. The delivery of publicly-funded flood relief, equal to or exceeding the value of the property lost, fosters individual and collective expectations that rebuilding or building anew in aid-eligible areas is free of flood-related financial risk.

Flooding is a public "bad" jointly consumed by flood plain residents and property owners. It is not entirely non-subtractable, patterns of settlement and flood dynamics interact to wipe out some while sparing others. Nonetheless, joint consumption rules fail by design at signaling the condition of the resource and the anticipated relative costs of building in different locations with respect to the river. Higher, stronger levees signal that flooding will occur less frequently. State and local subsidies for new flood plain building and generous national aid for recovery from past floods augment the power of that signal, reinforcing a rational expectation of minimal financial and safety risks among flood plain residents and investors.

A CONCEPTUAL LOGIC OF POLICY DESIGN

Figure 9.2 presents (in schematic form) the computational logic for relating the attributes of non-exclusion and joint use to the requirements and objectives of policy design. Design requirements are equivalent to performance standards. For example, structural engineers charged with bridge design would specify a deck capable of supporting a given weight load. Design objectives relate to purpose. Traffic engineers working on the same bridge project would locate the bridge and situate its access ramps to achieve an identified goal, such as reducing average travel time between two cities by a targeted number of minutes.

Rulemaking problems associated with non-exclusion and joint use are describable by reference to the design requirements and objectives of applicable rules. The design requirement for exclusion rules is that they make exclusion feasible. Feasible exclusion requires rules that adequately address production technology and the operating conditions encountered by producers and citizen/consumers with access to the good or resource (Ostrom 1990). As noted in the school example above, the design objective of exclusion rules is to stabilize shared expectations with respect to individual and joint strategies of students, parents, and teachers (Ostrom 1990, 2005; Ostrom et al. 1994).

Joint use rules must solve the problem of subtractability. No public good, except perhaps gravity, is perfectly non-subtractable (Ostrom and Ostrom 1977, 1991). So, joint use rules must address conditions of subtractability with reference to congestion (relative demand) and use regulation (the problem of incompatible uses). The objective of joint use rules is to provide information concerning the scarcity (relative to demand) and the condition of the public good (or commonly owned resource).

Relating the Examples to the Conceptual Logic

Lobster fishing rules have the intended effect of making a high level of fishing effort compatible with the long-term conservation of the species because they effectively address problems of exclusion (territoriality) and joint use (gear limits and size and sex restrictions). The War on Drugs has exacted enormous financial and social costs with spurious results because excluding suppliers and consumers from legal and illicit drug markets remains an insoluble law enforcement problem. Omega Protein and its trawlers dominate the Atlantic

Menhaden catch because the rules regulating use of the public resource do not account for the capture and processing technology they employ. National flood and disaster policy increases the public's exposure to harm by effectively reversing the price signal and encouraging the adoption of rules that invite rather than exclude development in flood prone areas. One can explain the outcomes noted above by relating particular rules to specifiable problems of exclusion and joint use.

As the reader well knows, four cases do not establish a general claim. The selected cases illustrate the conceptual logic put forth in this chapter and suggest that the systematic study of counterintentional policy outcomes is possible and potentially beneficial to the field of policy analysis. I note a few other examples that merit investigation.[5] The "No Child Left Behind" protocols of student testing and school performance rating have instead hollowed out learning and distorted teacher incentives (Ravitch 2010). A suite of urban policies makes cities less desirable places to live and work (Peterson 1981). Home finance policies intended to make homes more affordable and raise middle class living standards instead wipe out middle class savers while placing millions of families in homes they cannot afford to live in or to leave (Timiraos 2013; Desmond 2016). The US national surface mining law intended to protect natural landscapes instead incentivizes the leveling of entire mountain systems (Fotos 2000). Social welfare programs meant to safeguard the living standards of the most vulnerable among us instead trap their recipients in webs of geographic and social immobility. World-topping health care spending delivers mediocre health outcomes (Tavernise 2013). And food and nutrition policies assure that millions of Americans suffer simultaneously from food insecurity and chronic illnesses caused by over-eating, some of them literally "dying of food" (Hansen 2012). This is not easy to do. Perhaps, the most ironic and paradoxical counterintentional policy outcome involves the progress of American arms in the post-9/11 era. The United States fields the most lethal and operationally proficient armed forces the world has ever known. They prevail in nearly every tactical encounter and yet the nation loses the wars they fight on its behalf (Bolger 2014). Reformulating these policy problems and outcomes with reference to the encompassing logic of non-exclusion and joint use might illuminate the counterintuitive properties that explain the observed patterns of counterintentionality. As Elinor Ostrom (2005, 18) notes, "One cannot improve outcomes without knowing how the structure itself is produced."

Relating the Logic of Rule Design to the IAD Framework

The IAD framework is a heuristic device for systematically observing rule-ordered relationships among communities of people (Kiser and Ostrom 1982;

Ostrom 1990; 2005; 2010; Ostrom et al. 1994; Polski and Ostrom 1999; Aligica 2014; see also the chapters by Aligica and Sterpan by Polski in the book). The conceptual logic and outcome typology described above usefully elaborate on the IAD heuristic function by adding specificity to the nature and function of feedback from policy outcomes. The feedback loops (shown with dotted lines in Figure 9.4) originate in the outcomes box in the lower right and lead to the action arena in the central area and to the exogenous variables area on the left side of the diagram.

The proposed method of analysis with its focus on shared intentionality does not depend on or necessarily influence the evaluative criteria the participants apply to interactions and outcomes.

I refer again to Figure 9.2 for the purpose of relating the conceptual logic of rule design shown therein to the logic of processes represented by the IAD framework diagram shown in Figure 9.4. Figure 9.2 identifies the concepts of feasibility and subtractability as design requirements of exclusion and joint consumption, respectively. Their respective components, technology and operating conditions for feasibility and congestion and use regulation for jointness of consumption, are material facts. Figure 9.2 locates expectations and information as design objectives respectively of exclusion and jointness. Expectations of exclusion refer to individual and collective choice situations and information about joint use refers to scarcity and resource conditions.

The reader will notice a pattern of relationships between design requirements and objectives and the respective destinations of the feedback loops. Outcomes relating to design requirement components are primarily material in nature. Material consequences exert their effects on the exogenous variables. Outcomes relating to design objective components involve social processes or the transfer of information. They have no proximate material content but they do have potentially significant impacts on the knowledge, perceptions, and expectations of participants in the action arena. This

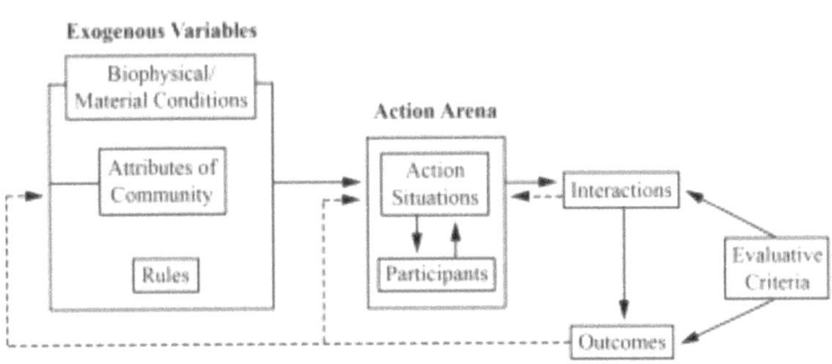

Figure 9.4 The Institutional Analysis and Development Framework. *Source*: E. Ostrom (2005, 15; Figure 1.2, used by permission).

observed relationship lends support to the proposed diagnostic method by showing a logical fit between the method and the framework it purports to support. This logical exercise also expands upon the heuristic uses of the IAD framework by specifying in greater detail how an observer might characterize relations among rule design, outcomes, and feedback loops in empirical settings.

Policy Problems, Policy Theory, Implementation, and the Design of Rules

Policy problems are "both real and socially constructed" (Greenhalgh 2003, 189). No one doubts the objective reality of drug addiction, poverty, environmental degradation, or any other societal affliction. Nonetheless, policy makers cannot act intelligently to ameliorate undesirable social conditions without first "imposing certain frames of reference on reality" (Dery 1984, 4). And moreover, even if communities agree on what is undesirable today, they may not agree on what future conditions are feasible and desirable or how to get there. Framing policy problems as goal setting opportunities, that is, clarifying collective intentions, enables communities to decide what they want and so defining the problem becomes a guide for meaningful action aimed at some future good (Dery 1984, 7–9). The confluence of problem definition and goal setting demonstrates the essential intentionality of policy choice and rule (or program) design (Bardach 2009).

Creative human artisans compose mental images of "the order of events and the relationships that occur" leading to future desired states of the world (Ostrom 1980, 311). In other words, the formulation of policy theory includes the visualization of implementation scenarios (Kellogg Foundation 2004 [1998]). The considerable body of implementation research that Pressman and Wildavsky (1973) initiated and that Paul Sabatier and his many collaborators and colleagues (Sabatier 1988, 1991; Weible et al. 2011) carried forward elaborates on this fundamental point; warrantable rule design considers the determinate causal ordering between activities and outputs and accounts for the "quasi-causal" ordering that accompanies the necessary reliance on fallible, self-favoring human agents to conduct and monitor prescribed activities and outputs (Ostrom 2008, 2). Visualizing implementation scenarios and accounting for the uncertain reliability of human agents leads rulemakers to impose administrative procedures aimed at assuring compliance with the policy directives of those who make the rules (McCubbins et al. 1987; 1989). To sum up, implementation is a normal and regular part of rule design and so anticipating implementation scenarios and problems of agency are encompassed by any adequate theory of rule design.[6] Or, as Elinor Ostrom (1992, 41) observes in a particular empirical context,

Crafting the institutions for the supply and use of irrigation systems is challenging and requires skill in understanding how rules, combined with particular physical, economic, and cultural environments, produce incentives and outcomes.

Rent-seeking and Deeper Levels of Choice

The potential to claim "economic rents offers the motivation" for virtually the entire range of human enterprise (Buchanan 1980, 5). Whether rent-seeking enhances social welfare, has no effect, or transforms into a negative sum game is a function of the constitution of the respective society or system (Krueger 1974; Rowley 1988; Tullock 1980; Ostrom et al. 1993). In a competitive market for private goods, rents flowing to producers tend to be eroded or dissipated due to the entry of new competitors or the introduction of new technologies or products but entry and competition among producers increase the consumer surplus, thusly enhancing social welfare (Buchanan 1980). The high level of fishing effort in the Maine lobster fishery, thousands of fishers fishing millions of traps, indicates a substantial potential for rent dissipation but the sustained productivity of the resource implies that social losses from rent-seeking are minimized. On the other hand, Omega Protein's domination of the menhaden fishery, accompanied as it is by high opportunity costs for wildlife and other fishers and the liquidation of menhaden stocks, suggests that rent-seeking in this fishery constitutes a negative sum game. In Maine, lobster fishers are well organized politically and as a consequence have successfully resisted the introduction of some ill-conceived regulations and non-selective fishing technologies (Acheson 2003). Omega Protein on the other hand has carved out exceptional catch allotments as a consequence of what some observers consider privileged access to national and state regulatory processes (Fairbrother 2012; Pew Environment Group 2013).

Rent-seeking is one element in a class of strategic or opportunistic behaviors that also includes free riding and corruption (Ostrom et al. 1993). Rent-seeking behavior is "particularly" associated with infeasible exclusion from funding or budget processes and, when conditions of fiscal equivalence are not met, rent-seeking is individually more profitable, less likely to generate effective, directed opposition, and therefore more likely to emerge as a systemic feature (Ostrom et al. 1993; Rowley 1988). With reference to the IAD framework, the emergence and consequences of opportunistic behavior at one level of choice are explained by reference to the next deeper level of choice. For example, at the level of operational choice, Maine lobster fishers are highly selective between "keepahs" and lobsters that are thrown back for reasons of size or sex (Acheson 2003). Allowable gear, approved at the collective choice level, makes selection easy and the constitutions of harbor-based marketing co-ops and social networks make mutual monitoring a daily fact of life (*ibid.*). The temptation to fish opportunistically never goes away but the options and incentives each fisher faces day-in and day-out are products of deeper levels of choice.

INTENTIONALITY, SHARED INTENTIONALITY, AND THE ANALYSIS OF POLITICAL EXPERIMENTS

John Searle (1998, 85) defines intentionality as "the general term for all the various forms by which the mind can be directed at, or be about, or of, objects and states of affairs in the world." When two or more people direct their minds at or about the same objects or affairs, then "I" intentionality takes the form of collective, or "we" intentionality (Searle 1998, 118). Michael Tomasello (2014) uses the modifier "shared" in place of "collective" when referring to this latter form of intentionality. Shared intentionality comprises two further forms, joint and collective. According to Tomasello (2014, 113), "Modern humans participate not only in joint intentionality with other individuals but also in collective intentionality with the entire cultural group." The uniquely human capacity for shared intentionality ". . .brings together in particularly intimate ways the workings of biology and culture" (Tomasello and Carpenter 2007, 124). Searle (1969) identifies language as the fundamental form of shared intentionality. Searle's claim connects contemporary philosophy and developmental psychology to the inquiries of earlier political philosophers, most notably Hobbes's (2011 [1651]) declaration that the faculty of language distinguishes humans from "all other living creatures." Elinor Ostrom draws the metaphorical threads of shared intentionality, language, and rulemaking together in this way,

> The stability of rule-ordered actions is dependent upon the shared meaning assigned to words used to formulate a set of rules and how they will be enforced. If no shared meaning exists when a rule is formulated, confusion will exist about what actions are required, permitted, or forbidden. (Ostrom 2005, 40)

Rulemakers act with intention and the outcomes they anticipate constitute their shared intentionality. Moreover, rulemaking requires rulemakers to engage in inferential reasoning, making "if/then" statements linking sentences of a particular form to anticipated changes of behavior among a particular group of actors with the further anticipation that the changed behavior will alter the state of the world in the intended way. The linking of words to actions and actions to outcomes constitutes the terms and conditions of a political experiment. Shared intentionality is therefore the scientifically sound evaluative standard of policy analysis.

Shared intentionality presents other proximate benefits to the practice of policy analysis. The intended results of rulemaking are always relevant as both matters of policy science and community values. The objects of a policy are plainly what policymakers and affected publics care about. Shared intentionality satisfies the requirement of objectivity because the intentionality of policy makers is formed and manifests itself by processes that operate independently of the analyst's preferred evaluative standards. Furthermore, the standard of intentionality enforces a stance of epistemic humility on the part of the analyst because interpreting the shared intentionality of rulemakers prevents the analyst from presuming to know, or know how to select, "the single best" option in any given situation. Not knowing beforehand what is best reinforces respect for institutional diversity, a beneficial corrective to the default position of mainstream policy analysis that presumes parliaments and bureaucracy are the "normative exemplar" of modern government (Ostrom 1994, 30) and that markets and states comprise the full complement of valid institutional arrangements for solving collective action problems (Ostrom 2010). And finally, paying attention to the terms and conditions of the political experiment at hand enables the analyst to observe with discrimination the process of hypothesis testing and by so doing attend to "the need for the development of theory as the basis of our discipline" (Ostrom 1982, 11) thereby helping "to develop a science of . . . institutional rules that individuals choose within their own communities" (Herzberg 2015, 100).

Operationalizing Shared Intentionality

Defining a concept and operationalizing (i.e., observing and measuring) it are two different things. In this section, I propose three ways of operationalizing shared intentionality, each reflecting one of three subjects central to policy analysis: policy purpose, policy problem, and policy causal theory. I begin by addressing the mechanics for achieving reliable and valid observation of the concept.

Operationalizing shared intentionality is first a problem of empathy. "And so for us this [specifying collective intentions] means that something like recursive mind-reading or inferring—still not adequately characterized, and in most instances fully implicit—has to be a part of the story of shared intentionality" (Tomasello 2014, 152). "Recursive mind-reading" so defined would potentially seem at odds with Hobbes's (2011 [1651]) conceptualization of the human capacity for empathy, that we can know the manner of a person's thoughts but not the object. The apparent contradiction is just that, apparent but not actual. Shared intentionality, as conceptualized by Tomasello, exhibits the properties of common knowledge as that concept is used in game theory (Ostrom et al. 1994). "From the individual's point of view, shared intentionality is simply experienced as a sharing, but its underlying structure, reflecting its evolution, is that each participant in an interaction can potentially take the perspective of others taking her perspective taking their perspective, and so forth for at least a few levels." (Tomasello 2014, 152) And so, the claim that shared intentionality is specifiable and observable requires only that people engaged in rulemaking possess a modicum of mutual self-awareness and that the analyst possess a reasonable capacity for observation and empathetic reasoning.

The observational task is surmountable, to say the least. Rational politicians trumpet their attachments to public-spirited purposes. When we suspect them of sincerity, the stated intentionality of policy makers is easily discovered.[7] The Preamble to the US Constitution of 1787 is a statement of shared intentionality rightly admired for its high-minded and elegant presentation of The Framers' aims.

> We the People of the United States, in Order to form a more perfect Union, establish Justice, insure domestic Tranquility, provide for the common defence, promote the general Welfare, and secure the Blessings of Liberty to ourselves and our Posterity, do ordain and establish this Constitution for the United States of America.

The terms and conditions of the political experiment are contained in the 7 articles and 27 subsequent amendments that follow.

The US Constitution's manner of expressing the shared intentionality of its authors is far from unique among written laws. Virtually all public acts begin with a statement of purpose and, absent evidence to the contrary, analysts seeking objective standards of evaluation can accept them at face value. For example, the *Kyoto Protocol to the United Nations Framework Convention on Climate Change* ("the *Kyoto Protocol*"), which served from 1998 to 2015 as the only globally sanctioned, international agreement on greenhouse gas emissions, states that the signatory nations are "In pursuit of the ultimate objective of the Convention. . ." later listed (in part) as "achieving its quantified emission limitation and reduction commitments. . ." (United Nations 1998). Presumably, a stated, quantified commitment constitutes an objective standard for evaluating the *Kyoto Protocol* as a political experiment.

Alternatives to Intentionality: Axiomatic Evaluative Standards

Shafqat Hussain (2014) makes the keen observation that biologists working on problems of global biodiversity perceive the people living among the animals they study as occupants of a "culture" and themselves, the biologists, as occupants of a realm of science and objectivity that is universal and "outside culture." Policy analysts who stake their evaluations of policy outcomes on the supposedly objective criteria of efficiency and equity do likewise.

By subscribing to axiomatic (i.e., self-evident) normative standards and discounting the intentionality of policy makers, they reduce analysis to a rating of outcomes rather than a quest to understand rulemaking. They risk ignoring the simple fact that, "The design of a tool is always a function of what it is designed to do" (Ostrom 1980, 310). To evaluate the skills of any rule makers, attention must be given to their intentions and the terms and conditions of the political experiments embedded in the rules they enact.

A warrantable science of rules contains explanations of why particular policies, when applied in specifiable circumstances, either work or do not work as intended. No chemist or biologist would report the results of an experiment without first specifying the hypothesis the experiment is intended to test. Why then would anyone report the outcomes of any policy or program (i.e., any political experiment) without making reference to the hypotheses embedded in the terms and conditions of the experiment? Standards that are self-evident to the analyst may not be relevant to the community of practitioners in any given situation. Efficiency, equity, accountability, adaptability, transparency, and other high-minded concepts are undeniably desirable properties but their unexamined use embeds scientific and pragmatic errors in the analytic process. Axiomatic standards cannot be objective because their selection depends on the subjective judgment of the analyst. Moreover, they fail the test of practicality because people engaged in collective rulemaking do not seek abstractions, they seek outcomes.

Measuring progress toward collectively intended outcomes and relating that progress to the terms and conditions of the experiment is scientific because its subjective relevance to the experimenter makes it objectively relevant to investigation. Analysis that frames experimental results in terms of progress toward normative properties selected by the analyst reveals the analyst's values but by foregoing to test the hypotheses embedded in the policies analyzed, analysis contributes little to advancing the science of rules and rulemaking. Normative evaluation is not equivalent to explanation derived from a process of hypothesis testing. Policy analysis is not a beauty contest conducted by econometricians.

A Further Critique of Efficiency and Equity

Conventional policy analysis based on neoclassical economics focuses analytic attention on the efficiency effects of policy (Weimer and Vining 1992; Stokey and Zeckhauser 1978). The competent analyst can tell whether a policy is good or bad by its effect on Pareto optimality. Properly employed, the Pareto standard is a useful gauge for evaluating the effect of a policy on conditions of scarcity and net social product, but alas, it represents only one aspect of what are almost always complex packages of public, private, and mixed goods.

The public nature of policy raises problems of quantifying the net benefits of goods with no market-based equivalents, weighing the relative social benefits of incommensurable events, and measuring goods or services with low "packageability." Conventional measures of efficiency, expressed as units of a common currency, may simply be inapplicable. Currency-based measures may further compromise analysis because the conventions of measuring economic activity count some forms of consumption, such as the liquidation of natural capital when a forest is cut, as net additions to GDP. Efficiency, as an evaluative standard in policy analysis, has the benefit of being a well-established concept but its apparent solidity belies the many acts of interpretation required to apply it operationally.

Equity is an equally problematic gauge of policy effect. Michael Munger (2000) describes three forms of equity (or justice): market, Marxian, and simple fairness. A fourth form, intergenerational equity incorporates the dimension of time and the property of sustainability. Crafting just policies is intrinsically dilemmatic. Satisfying one form of justice requires shortchanging others. Market justice, shares according to product, requires that some citizens receive higher shares than others, violating the justice principle of simple fairness. Marxian justice rewards the recognized needs of some citizens at a cost to all others. Intergenerational equity requires a reduced standard of consumption among those living today regardless of product or need to provide for those who are not yet born.

Policies are the product of politics. Politics makes winners of some and losers of others. Without exception, laws of general application favor some citizens over others. In other words, all policies require that some citizens suffer some form of injustice. Who is qualified to evaluate the trade-offs inherent in every policy choice? In a democracy, the people decide. They pick the winners and losers. The people, or their elected representatives, not the professional policy analyst, rightfully weigh competing claims and decide what trade-offs to make. The public's collective intentionality by right sets the evaluative standard, not the analyst's own notions of public morality. Moreover, axiomatic standards such as efficiency and equity are descriptive measures useful for normative evaluation not explanation. When the analyst evaluates a policy on axiomatic grounds, explaining policy outcomes requires further searching for theories of the policy problem, additional evidence, or other methods of inquiry.

CONCLUSION

This chapter extends the application of the Ostrom typology of goods (Ostrom and Ostrom 1977, 1991) by relating intentionality to the conceptual logic differentiating private, public, and mixed goods. The result is an ordered set of inferences capable of explaining policy outcomes. When outcomes line up with intentionality one can infer that the rules satisfy conditions of feasible exclusion and adequate use regulation. Spurious outcomes infer unsolved problems of exclusion. Use domination infers unsolved problems of incompatible uses, congestion, or use regulation. Complete perversity, *the reverse happened*, infers problems with exclusion and use regulation.

As noted above, these inferences require reformulation as hypotheses amenable and subjected to testing in empirical settings but regardless of their empirical validity, the logic of the set constitutes an epistemic contribution to the craft of policy analysis. Their formulation and accompanying discussion show that the conceptual logic of the Ostrom typology contains the elements of an encompassing theory of policy outcomes, one capable of replacing shoulder shrugs and invocations of "the law of unintended consequences" with investigatory strategies that promise explanations of "outcomes that are foreseeable but unanticipated." By relating policy outcomes to intentionality and the design logic of rules, analysis premised on explanation advances the quest for a science of rulemaking, a central goal of Vincent and Elinor Ostrom and of the many scholars they trained or influenced.

NOTES

1. This essay is a substantially revised and rewritten treatment of a working paper prepared for presentation at the F. A. Hayek Program for Advanced Study in Philosophy, Politics, and Economics of the Mercatus Center at George Mason University, 24 March 2014. The author gratefully acknowledges Peter Boettke and Paul Dragos Aligica for their support of and feedback on the original paper and the editors of this book for their generous and insightful comments on several intermediate drafts.

2. The longest running surveys of illicit drug use ask young people about "past month use" of marijuana. After a spike in the late 1970s and a decline in the 1980s, usage rates of this drug among young people have varied little in recent decades (Substance Abuse and Mental Health Services Administration 2011).

3. The ASMFC is a compact of 15 Atlantic coast states that regulates the menhaden fishery under authority granted by the US Congress (P.L. 539 as amended by P.L. 721, August 19, 1950).

4. For a mainstream policy analyst, Omega Protein's catch share offers evidence of regulatory capture and a sign that national and state fisheries regulators lack the political will to crack down on a well-connected corporate operator (Fairbrother 2012). In other words, mainstream analysis attributes counterintentionality in this case to human weakness, implying the existence of prospectively effective but as-yet untried rules that address the human condition. My experience with fishers, fisheries regulation and regulators indicate that while the latter explanation offers emotional

satisfaction, explanation in terms of problems related to joint use and the regulation of incompatible uses offers greater analytic traction.

5. For an examination of the epistemic choices associated with these examples, see Fotos (2015).

6. Skillful and properly resourced implementation does not overcome or remediate inadequate policy design. For example, fisheries management that targets the biggest, oldest fish will derange oceanic food webs and the health of surviving stocks no matter how skillfully the policy is implemented (Apollonio 2002, 2010). As the drug policy example indicates, when the policy criminalizes mental health impairments, energetic implementation generates additional social pathologies. Therefore, one can reasonably claim that the proposed framework for policy design and outcome diagnosis encompasses theories of implementation.

7. One may acknowledge that rational politicians are also capable of strategic, opportunistic behavior and so stated intentions may differ from true ones. As with rent-seeking (described above), the occurrences and consequences of strategic or opportunistic behavior are products of rules made at deeper levels of choice.

REFERENCES

Acheson J. 2003. *Capturing the Commons: devising institutions to manage the Maine lobster industry*. Hanover & London: University Press of New England.

Aligica PD. 2014. *Institutional Diversity and Political Economy: The Ostroms and Beyond*. New York: Oxford University Press.

Apollonio S. 2002. *Hierarchical Perspectives on Marine Complexities: Searching for systems in the Gulf of Maine*. New York: Columbia University Press.

Apollonio S. 2010. "A Testable Hypothesis for Ecosystem-Based Fisheries Management." *Reviews in Fisheries Science* 18 (2): 183–88.

Atlantic States Marine Fisheries Commission. (no date). Atlantic Menhaden. Accessed 1 August 2016. Available at http://www.asmfc.org/species/atlantic-menhaden.

Bardach E. 2009. *A Practical Guide to Policy Analysis* (3rd edition). Washington: CQ Press.

Bolger D. 2014. *Why We Lost: A General's Inside Account of Why We Lost in Iraq and Afghanistan*. New York: Houghton-Mifflin Harcourt.

Buchanan J. M. 1980. "Rent Seeking and Profit Seeking," in *Toward a Theory of the Rent-Seeking Society*, edited by Buchanan J. M. et al., 3–15. College Station: Texas A&M Press.

Cave D. and Schmidt M. S. 2012. "Rise in Pill Abuse Forces New Look at U.S. Drug Fight." *The New York Times*, July 16. Accessed July 17 2012. http://www.nytimes.com/2012/07/17/world/americas/us-priority-on-illegal-drugs-debated-as-abuse-rises.html?smid=pl-share.

Dean C. 2011. "Lobsters Find Utopia Where Biologists see Trouble." *The New York Times*, August 23. Accessed March 20 2014. http://www.nytimes.com/2011/08/23/science/23lobster.html?_r=0&gwt=regi.

Dery D. 1984. *Problem Definition in Policy Analysis*. Lawrence KS: University Press of Kansas.

Desmond M. 2016. *Evicted: Poverty and Profit in the American City*. New York: Crown Publishing Group.

Fairbrother A. 2012. "The Secretive Fishery Management Agency that Regulates Your Fish." (October 22). Accessed January 23, 2013. http://publictrustproject.org/blog/environment/2012/the-secretive-fishery-management-agency-that-regulates-the-fish-on-your-table/.

Fotos M. A. 2000. "Organized Interests and the Implementation of Environmental Policy." PhD diss., Bloomington IN: Indiana University.

Fotos M. A. 2015. "Vincent Ostrom's Revolutionary Science of Association." *Public Choice: The Journal of the Public Choice Society* 163 (1–2): 67–83.

Goodnough A. 2011. "Panel Votes to Reduce a Forage Fish Catch." *The New York Times*, November 9. Accessed June 18, 2013. http://www.nytimes.com/2011/11/10/us/menhaden-catch-reduction-is-approved.html?_r=0.

Greenhalgh S. 2003. "Science, Modernity, and the Making of China's One-Child Policy." *Population Development and Review* 29 (2) (June): 163–96.

Hansen S. 2012. "What Can Mississippi Learn from Iran?" *The New York Times Magazine*, July 27. Accessed January 22 2013. Available at: http://www.nytimes.com/2012/07/29/magazine/what-can-mississippis-health-care-system-learn-from-iran.html?smid=pl-share.

Herzberg R. Q. 2015. "Governing their Commons: Elinor and Vincent Ostrom and the Bloomington School." *Public Choice: the Journal of the Public Choice Society* 163 (1–2): 95–109.

Hiles S. (aka Shipley S.) 2012. *Blog*, February 2. Accessed June 27, 2012. http://sarashipleyhiles.com/2012/02/02/a-flood-of-development-10-years-later/?utm_source=rss&utm_medium=rss&utm_campaign=a-flood-of-development-10-years-later.

Hobbes T. [1651] 2011. *Leviathan: Revised Edition edited by A. P. Martinich and Brian Battiste*. Peterborough, Ontario: Broadview Press.

Hussain S. 2014. "Global Dimension of Human-Wildlife Conflict in Northern Pakistan." Lecture presented at Trinity College Hartford CT, February 18.

Johnson W. R. 2011. "Doctrine for Irregular Warfare: Déjà vu all over again?" *Marine Corps University Journal* 2-1 (Spring): 34–64.

Keefe P. R. 2012. "Cocaine Incorporated." *The New York Times*, June 15. Accessed August 23, 2012. http://www.nytimes.com/2012/06/17/magazine/how-a-mexican-drug-cartel-makes-its-billions.html?smid=pl-share.

Kellogg Foundation W. K. [1998] 2004. *Logic Model Development Guide: Using Logic Models to Bring Together Planning, Evaluation, and Action*. Battle Creek: W. K. Kellogg Foundation.

Kiser L. L. and Ostrom E. 1982. "The Three Worlds of Action: A Metatheoretical Synthesis of Institutional Approaches," in *Strategies of Political Inquiry*, edited by Ostrom E., 179–222. Beverly Hills: Sage Publications.

Krueger A. O. [1974] 1980. "The Political Economy of the Rent-Seeking Society," in *Toward a Theory of the Rent-Seeking Society*, edited by Buchanan J. M. et al., 51–70. College Station: Texas A&M Press.

Larson L. W. 1996. "The Great USA Flood of 1993." Paper Presented at IAHS Conference, June 24–28, Accessed June 27, 2012. *Destructive Water:*

Water-Caused Natural Disasters-Their Abatement and Control, Anaheim CA. http://www.nwrfc.noaa.gov/floods/papers/oh_2/great.htm.
Maine Lobster Marketing Collaborative. 2014. Accessed March 17, 2014. http://www.lobsterfrommaine.com/about-lobster.aspx.
McCubbins M., Noll R. and Weingast B. 1987. "Administrative Procedures as Instruments as Instruments of Political Control." *Journal of Law, Economics, and Organization* 3: 243–77.
McCubbins M., Noll R. and Weingast B. 1989. "Structure and Process: Administrative Arrangements and the Political Control of Agencies." *Virginia Law Review* 75: 431–82.
Munger M. 2000. *Analyzing Policy: Choices, Conflicts, and Practices.* New York: WW Norton.
Omega Protein. (no date). Available at: http://omegaprotein.com/.
Ostrom E. ed. 1982. *Strategies of Political Inquiry.* Beverly Hills: Sage Publications.
Ostrom E. 1990. *Governing the Commons: The Evolution of Institutions for Collective Action.* New York: Cambridge University Press.
Ostrom E. 1992. *Crafting Institutions for Self-Governing Irrigation Systems.* San Francisco: ICS Press.
Ostrom E. 2005. *Understanding Institutional Diversity.* Princeton NJ: Princeton University Press.
Ostrom E. 2010. "Beyond Markets and States: Polycentric Governance of Complex Economic Systems." *American Economic Review* 100 (3) (June): 641–72.
Ostrom E., Gardner R. and Walker J.M. and Agrawal A. et al. 1994. *Rules, Games, and Common Pool Resources.* Ann Arbor: University of Michigan Press.
Ostrom E., Schroeder L. and Wynne S. 1993. *Institutional Incentives and Sustainable Development: Infrastructure Policies in Perspective.* Boulder CO: Westview Press.
Ostrom V. 1980. "Artisanship and Artifact." *Public Administration Review* 40 (4) (July-August): 309–17.
Ostrom V. 1991. *The Meaning of American Federalism: Constituting a Self-Governing Society.* San Francisco: ICS Press.
Ostrom V. 2008. *The Intellectual Crisis in American Public Administration (3rd edition) foreword by Barbara Allen.* Tuscaloosa: University of Alabama Press.
Ostrom V. [1991] 2012. "Some Ontological and Epistemological Puzzles in Policy Analysis." Paper prepared for presentation to the American Political Science Association meeting panel on "The Future of Policy Analysis" (August 30 1991) at the Brookings Institution, WP 91–6, July 8.
Ostrom V. 2012 [1986]. "Culture, Liberation Movements, and Human Development," in *The Quest to Understand Human Affairs: Essays on Collective, Constitutional, and Epistemic Choice (volume 2)*, edited by Ostrom V., Allen B.; foreword by Ostrom E., Lanham, MD: Lexington Books, pp. 219–52
Ostrom V. 2012 [1994]. "Great experiments and the welfare state: basic paradigmatic challenges." In *The quest to understand human affairs: essays on collective, constitutional, and epistemic choice (volume 2)*, edited by Ostrom V., Allen B.; foreword by Ostrom E., Lanham, MD: Lexington Book, pp. 323–53.
Ostrom V. and Ostrom E. 1977, 1991. "Public Goods and Public Choices: The Emergence of Public Economies and Industry Structures," in *Alternatives for*

Delivering Public Services: Towards Improved Performance, edited by Savas E. S. 1977. Boulder CO: Westview Press; reprinted in Ostrom V. 1991. *The Meaning of American Federalism: Constituting a Self-Governing Society*. San Francisco: ICS Press, pp. 163–97.

Pew Environment Group. 2013. *Atlantic Menhaden Campaign*. Accessed January 23, 2013. http://www.pewenvironment.org/campaigns/atlantic-menhaden-campaign/id/85899364506.

Peterson P. E. 1981. *City Limits*. Chicago & London: University of Chicago Press.

Plante J. M. 2013. "Menhaden Quotas in Place for 2013; 1% Set Aside for NE 'Episodic' Events." *Commercial Fisheries News*, July 16–17. Accessed June 25, 2013. http://cfn.epubxp.com/i/137027.

Polski M. and Ostrom E. 1999. "An Institutional Framework for Policy Analysis and Design." Bloomington: The Vincent and Elinor Ostrom Workshop in Political Theory and Policy Analysis Indiana University Bloomington. WP 98–27 (15 June).

Pressman J. and Wildavsky A. 1973. *Implementation*. Berkeley: University of California Press.

Ravitch D. 2010. *The Death and Life of the Great American School System: How Testing and Choice Are Undermining Education*. New York: Basic Books.

Rowley CK. 1988. "Rent-Seeking in Constitutional Perspective," in *The Political Economy of Rent-Seeking*, edited by Rowley C. K. et al., 447–64. Boston: Kluwer Academic Publishers.

Sabatier P. A. 1988. "An Advocacy Coalition Framework of Policy Change and the Role of Policy-Oriented Learning Therein." *Policy Sciences* 21 (2/3): 129–168. http://www.jstor.org/stable/4532139.

Sabatier P. A. 1991. "Toward Better Theories of the Policy Process." *Political Science and Politics* 24 (2) (June): 147–56. http://www.jstor.org/stable/419923.

Saulny S. 2007. "Development Rises on St. Louis Area Floodplains." *The New York Times*, 15 May 15. Accessed June 27, 2012. http://www.nytimes.com/2007/05/15/us/15flood.html?_r=1.

Schmitt J, Warner K. and Gupta S. 2010. "The High Budgetary Cost of Incarceration." (June) accessed July 5, 2012. Washington DC: Center for Economic and Policy Research. http://www.cepr.net/documents/publications/incarceration-2010–06.pdf.

Searle J. 1969. *Speech Acts: An Essay in the Philosophy of Language*. Cambridge: Cambridge University Press.

Searle J. 1998. *Mind, Language, and Society: Philosophy in the Real World*. New York: Basic Books.

Seelye K. Q. 2013. "Heroin in New England, More Abundant and Deadly." *The New York Times*, July 18. Accessed March 20, 2014. http://www.nytimes.com/2013/07/19/us/heroin-in-new-england-more-abundant-and-deadly.html?smid=pl-share&gwt=regi.

Seelye K. Q. 2014. "Heroin Scourge Overtakes a 'Quaint' Vermont Town." *The New York Times*, March 5. Accessed March 20, 2014. http://www.nytimes.com/2014/03/06/us/bulwark-in-revolutionary-war-town-in-vermont-faces-heroin-scourge.html?smid=pl-share.

Stokey E. and Zeckhauser R. 1978. *A primer for policy analysis*. New York: WW Norton.

Substance Abuse and Mental Health Services Administration. 2011. Accessed November 14 2015. *Results from the 2010 National Survey on Drug Use and Health: Summary of National Findings*. NSDUH Series H-41, HHS Publication No. (SMA) 11–4658. Rockville MD: Substance Abuse and Mental Health Services Administration. http://archive.samhsa.gov/data/NSDUH/2k10NSDUH/2k10Results.htm#Fig8–4.

Sylves R. 2008. *Disaster Policy & Politics: Emergency Management and Homeland Security*. Washington: CQ Press.

Tavernise S. 2013. "For Americans Under 50, Stark Findings on Health." *The New York Times*, January 9.

The New York Times. 1971. "Excerpts from President's Message on Drug Abuse Control." "ProQuest Historical Newspapers." *The New York Times* (1857–2001) June 18: 22.

The Telegraph. 2012. "Mexico Drug War Has Claimed 47,500 Victims in Five Years." *The Telegraph*, January 12. Accessed August 23, 2012. http://www.telegraph.co.uk/news/worldnews/centralamericaandthecaribbean/mexico/9009574/Mexico-drug-war-has-claimed-47500-victims-in-five-years.html.

Timiraos N. 2013. "Number of 'Underwater' Borrowers Drops Below 10 Million." *The Wall Street Journal*, June 12, (blog).

Tomasello M. 2014. *A Natural History of Human Thinking*. Cambridge and London: Harvard University Press.

Tomasello M. and Carpenter M. 2007. "Shared Intentionality." *Developmental Science* 10 (1): 121–25.

Tullock G. 1980. "Rent Seeking as a Negative-Sum Game," in *Toward a Theory of the Rent-Seeking Society*, edited by Buchanan J. M. et al., 16–36. College Station: Texas A&M Press.

United Nations. 1998. *Kyoto Protocol to United Nations Framework Convention on Climate Change*. Accessed October 27, 2015. http://unfccc.int/resource/docs/convkp/kpeng.pdf.

US Drug Enforcement Administration. 2011. *DEA Fact Sheet*. Available at: http://www.justice.gov/dea/1112_fact-sheet.pdf.

Weible C. M., Sabatier P. A., Jenkins-Smith H. C., Nohrstedt, D., Henry A. D., and deLeon P. 2011. "A Quarter Century of the Advocacy Coalition Framework: An Introduction to the Special Issue." *Policy Studies Journal* 39 (3) (August): 349–60.

Weimer D. L. and Vining A. R. 1992. *Policy Analysis: Concepts and Practice* (2nd edition). Englewood Cliffs NJ: Prentice Hall.

Chapter 10

Moving toward Sustainability

Integrating Generational Equity into Institutional Analysis

Abigail Sullivan, Abigail York, and Scott Yabiku

Over the past four decades, Workshop scholars developed and utilized the IAD framework (Ostrom et al. 1994) to understand governance of the world around us, but the IAD framework has not been operationalized to fully capture the breadth of sustainability (Cole et al. 2014). Sustainability has been defined myriad ways, but often has been conceptualized with the "triple bottom line diagram," where the intersection of environment, economy, and equity is characterized as achieving sustainability (Hansmann et al. 2012). We argue that although the institutional literature has made significant contributions to our understanding of the environment and economy, scholars frequently fail to incorporate or consider the third component of sustainability, equity (Barnaud and Van Paassen 2013). In this chapter, we unpack the attributes of the community to explore equity in community forestry membership within a case study of 21 forests in Chitwan, Nepal. We then present a richer conceptualization and integration of equity within the IAD framework.

Community forestry is a type of locally governed, decentralized forest governance. There can be numerous social benefits to community forest membership (Adhikari et al. 2007), but the primary benefit is arguably increased access to natural resources, including non-timber forest products and, to a lesser extent, timber. The relationship between household wealth and income and natural resource use is diverse; even within small, rural communities there may be differences in resource use among households within the same income level, and poorer households do not always extract the most natural resources (Cavendish 2000). However, often as household wealth and income increase, reliance on and benefit from natural resources decreases relative to lower income households (Turner et al. 2007). The relationship between household socioeconomic status and environmental degradation is complex and in some cases reinvestment and intensification of agriculture by higher income households may lead to increased resource extraction (Scherr 2000). Both in urbanizing regions (such as parts of Chitwan) and more isolated rural communities, markets for products and labor are critical to understanding natural resource governance; yet global labor markets and flows of remittances are often overlooked. We explicitly explore the impact of globalization through labor markets that allow Chitwan residents to work abroad and send remittances, changing household structures, livelihood strategies, and natural resource use. This critical teleconnection affects and connects the developing world and in turn influences the ability of communities to sustainably manage natural resources for future generations.

In Nepal, the 1993 Community Forestry Act granted communities use and management rights of forests, while the national government retained official ownership of the land. The government designated areas with land available for community management, such as those adjacent to the Chitwan National Park, known as the Buffer Zone, and communities organized and registered with the government prior to gaining official recognition and access to the land and forestry resources. All of our case study forests fall within the Buffer Zone of Chitwan National Park; the National Park oversees management plans, fiscal accounts, and forestry conditions. The community forests in our study were officially recognized by the government five years ago, on average, but there was great variability with some of the forests recognized in 1993. Households do not live within the community forests, but rather live nearby; eligible member households live within a catchment area, designated wards within the local level of government, called the Village Development Committee. These catchment area boundaries were established by the government in order to limit harvesting pressure on any particular forest, fitting one of Ostrom's (2005) Design Principles establishing clear boundaries for user groups. Each community forest in Chitwan is governed by a community forest governance committee, elected by its members who establish management plans. Governance committees enforce the management plans including rules regarding resource collection and use and they collect any fees or fines. They additionally provide welfare programs such as discounted firewood for impoverished households, and provide various economic development, educational, and environmental programs for the benefit of the community and forest. To become a member of a community forest, households pay a membership fee; some community forests also require other fees, or purchase of tickets, for collection of resources like grasses, thatch, and firewood. A few of the community forests offer timber sales to member households, but these sales are typically irregular for most Chitwan community forests because of the ecological conditions. Community forestry in Nepal has been widely hailed as a global model because of the locally created management plans, with their associated rules and boundaries, graduated sanctions, and nested governance structure which has reduced forest degradation while promoting development within the community (see Gilmour (2003) for an overview of community forestry in Nepal more generally). This success mirrors many of the Design Principles for successful common pool resource management (Ostrom 2005), but less attention has been paid to issues associated with intra and intergenerational equity.

Padilla (2002) clearly articulated the linkages between intra and intergenerational equity whereby inequity among the current generation (intra-generational inequity) may exacerbate intergenerational equity (recognition of the rights of future generations to natural resources) via overharvesting of natural resources to mediate poverty. Efforts to reduce intra-generational inequity may increase tension in management of the resources for biodiversity or economic development. Yet there is also evidence that better management of natural resources increases the ability of elites to capture rents, which may enhance the economy in the aggregate and the resource base, but increases inequity (Persha and Andersson 2014). As Padilla (2002) points out efforts to sustainably manage resources inherently must recognize persistent inequality and poverty of the current generation. Because studies of intra-generational equity within community forestry largely focus on member households they may fail to address a more fundamental intra-generational equity question: who has access to community forest resources in Chitwan via household membership? Community forestry has often been recognized as a means to both increase forest health, but also to improve livelihoods, yet who is being left behind?

Our work is building upon new institutional scholarship examining community forestry governance and common pool resource management (see Ostrom 2005). Within this literature, there is a recognition that the first step in understanding equity for sustainable resource management is an assessment of who has rights to access (Ostrom 2005), yet there is a dearth of literature that actually examines this question empirically. In this chapter, we will develop a multi-level model that will explore who has access to natural resources by unpacking the factors that influence community forest membership in Chitwan.

The Action Arena, gray area in Figure 10.1, of the IAD framework is relatively well studied and understood (Ostrom 2005), but there is a need to better understand how community attributes (such as sociodemographics and livelihoods) affect membership and heterogeneity among resource users (Varughese and Ostrom 2001). Extending this, we model how community and household attributes affect household membership in order to understand how heterogeneity of members may be related to inequity and intra-generational sustainability.

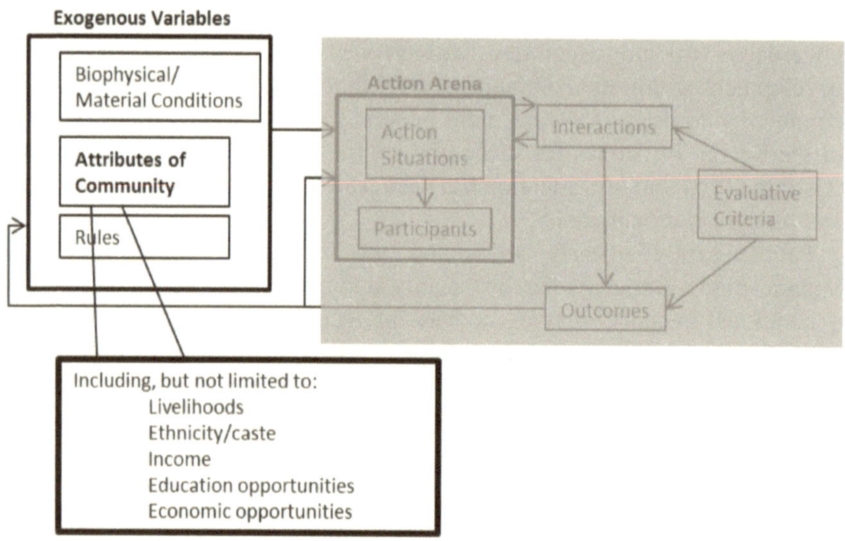

Figure 10.1 Unpacking Attributes of Community in the IAD Framework. *Source*: Created by author.

SUSTAINABILITY, COMMUNITY FORESTRY, AND EQUITY

Community forestry includes diverse programs that incorporate local governance and management of forest resources. Research on community forestry has examined how to sustainably manage a common pool resource (Charnley and Poe 2007); this work largely reinforces the Design Principles that Elinor Ostrom (1990, 2005) developed. The Nepalese community forestry program has been hailed as one of the world's most successful (Acharya 2002) and by many measures has achieved its initial goals of providing community access to resources while simultaneously reducing forest degradation through overharvesting (Bhattarai and Ojha 2001). The community forestry program in Nepal has provided natural resources that are indispensable to a predominantly agricultural workforce (Baral and Subedi 2000; Rai and Scarborough 2014). In this sense, the economic and ecological aspects of community forestry, two elements of sustainability, have been widely considered. However it is not clear whether the third aspect of sustainability, equity, has been achieved; partially this is due to more limited scholarly activity (Agarwal 2013). Thus to achieve sustainability, researchers and practitioners need to not only understand how community forestry has impacted rural development and forest conditions, but also equitability of resource distribution and access.

Understanding who has access to natural resources is an important issue globally, but it is a particularly vital issue in the context of developing countries. Historical and social processes have ensured that specific ethnic groups in developing countries are disproportionately disadvantaged in educational and economic opportunities. In Nepal in particular, historical displacement of indigenous groups and a caste system influenced the social structure and unequal relationships between ethnic groups that persist in many present situations (Jha 2014).

Income inequality is another important indicator of inequality, which is frequently measured with the Gini coefficient, a measure of statistical dispersion producing a ratio that was developed to assess national income inequality (Deininger and Squire 1996). The ratio ranges from 0 to 1, with 1 representing complete inequality (e.g., all income is controlled by one person) and 0 representing a completely equal distribution of income (Kennedy et al. 1996). One critique of the Gini coefficient is that it is an oversimplified and relative measure, which is often incorrectly used and misinterpreted (Cobham and Sumner 2013). Thus, it is important to keep in mind that the Gini coefficient does not provide information on absolute changes in income, as we may be interested in for economic development, so it should be used in tandem with other measures, including qualitative context. Within Nepal, it has been used to assess income inequality between community forest member households (Sharma 2009).

Community forest membership is often an important indicator of the resources eligible households have access to, yet few previous studies have explicitly considered how community forestry membership mediates access to natural resources. Coulibaly-Lingani et al. (2011) explored factors that influenced established community forest members' access to forest products in Burkina Faso. Maskey et al. (2006) examined factors that influenced the level of participation in community forest management decisions. Because much of the research on community forestry bounds the study with members, it is unclear what factors influence the decision to become a member in contexts where households must register and pay a fee to join. How access to common pool resources is determined represents both a key to sustainably managing the resource, and preventing over-harvesting (Ostrom 1990), but also an important determination of sustainability writ large if exclusion is exacerbating inequity within the community. Thus, this study presents an opportunity to begin with a fundamental examination of who joins and who is excluded from a community-managed common-pool resource critical to livelihoods within in a developing country context.

CASE STUDY

In our case, not all households are members of community forests. In this western Chitwan area, 34 percent of the survey sample consisted of nonmember households. A household may be a nonmember by purposeful choice, or a household may be a nonmember through a barrier it cannot overcome. In Chitwan, all of the community forests have some sort of barrier to entry; these are rules regarding where a household is located, as well as fees. The fees vary across the forests, although very few nonmembers (3 percent) cited fees as being problematic. Rather the most common reasons nonmember households cited for not joining include distance to the forest (i.e., a household is too far away from the resource for it to be useful, which is by far the most common reason for nonmembership) and disagreement with a community forest governance committee's policies. Our goal is to better understand additional household attributes that may drive the decision to join a community forest.

MODEL DEVELOPMENT

Household Level

Technology: Ownership of Dairy Animals and Use of Firewood

We hypothesize that a household's reliance on natural resources, which they expect will be available via obtaining community forest membership, will increase the likelihood of becoming a community forest member. Agricultural households are more likely to need access to forest resources than non-agricultural households (Adhikari et al. 2004). Specifically, households that own dairy animals (such as buffalo, cows, sheep, and goats) need access to grasses and fodder to care for these animals. Without membership, agricultural households have limited legal access to forest resources such as grasses and fodder; the only remaining access to these products is to purchase on the market, gather along the roads or small public areas such as schoolyards, or own extensive lands to provide fodder (which is very uncommon). While agricultural households without farmland rely on access to forest grasses and fodder, they do not rely on these forests to the same extent for firewood and timber resources. Many of the Chitwan Buffer Zone community forests provide limited timber resources to members, often due to lack of timber ready for harvest. Buffer Zone households have other ways of accessing and collecting firewood for cooking and heating; thus, while this resource is important to consider and could be a significant influence on membership in many other regions, we do not hypothesize that a household's use of firewood will be an important indicator of community forestry membership in Chitwan because most community forests limit access to firewood for members due to the ecological conditions.

We code dairy animals as a continuous variable representing the number of dairy animals the household owns. Firewood usage is a binary variable that is coded 1 if the household uses firewood for cooking, and 0 otherwise.

Income

The literature contains mixed evidence regarding the influence of household income on use of community forest resources. For instance, lower income households might be less able to join a community forest if the fees are too high and lower income groups have been found to receive fewer benefits from community forestry in many instances (Adhikari 2005). Higher income households are often better positioned to take advantage of intermediate forest resources (Acharya 2005) while very high-income households may not need forest products and may opt not to become members.

Income was measured as total household income from all sources in the past year, including wages, salaries, pensions, income from selling crops, animals, or goods, income from renting houses, land or equipment, business income, or income from gifts or other payments. This was coded as an ordinal variable representing seven income categories of Nepali rupees.

Ethnicity/Caste

Nepal has a complex social structure with castes and ethnicity historically playing a role in access to resources and livelihood strategies (Pokharel 2011). Since the mid-twentieth century, Chitwan has been the site of extensive internal migration within Nepal; minority households from the Hills have moved to access land and economic opportunities (Shrestha 1989). In Nepal, the Bramin and Chhetri are religious castes of higher status, the Newar is a middle caste associated with trade and shop-keeping, the Hill Janajati and Terai Janajati are indigenous groups with a historically lower socioeconomic status, and Dalit are a religious caste with historically lower socioeconomic status (Stash and Hannum 2001). Minority households are classified into four dummy variables, with the nonminority ethnicity (Bramin/Chhetri) serving as the reference case. The variables represent the Hill Janajati (indigenous ethnicity historically from the mountains and hills in Nepal), Dalit, Newar, and Terai Janajati (indigenous ethnicity from the Terai, which includes Chitwan). In many cases, minority access to locally governed natural resources is underrepresented (Gilmour et al. 2004). We anticipate that minority households may be underrepresented in community forest memberships.

Receipt of Remittances from Household Members Abroad

Both migration into the region and the temporary absence of individuals to work abroad are very common in Chitwan (Bohra and Massey 2009). Households that are receiving remittances from family members abroad tend to have higher incomes than strictly agricultural households. Increased income combined with increasing market access in Chitwan provides some households the opportunity to reduce their dependence on agriculture and the need to harvest their own natural resources (Acharya 2011). Thus, remittances may reduce the need to access natural resources and decrease the likelihood of joining a community forest. Household remittances were coded as the number of household members currently away who sent remittances in the past year.

Household Size

Most of the households in Chitwan are agricultural (over 80 percent). It follows that households with more individuals require increased natural resources to support their lifestyle. We anticipate that larger households will have a higher rate of community forest membership in an effort to access these resources. Household size is coded as the number of household members.

Household Distance from Community Forest Center

In the Chitwan household survey, 179 nonmember households (51 percent) identified distance to the forest as a barrier to membership. Previous studies have found that distance to other natural resources influences access and usage, especially when human-wildlife or armed conflicts are present (Stites et al. 2010). We propose that distance to the community forest will influence a household's ability to regularly access the forest resources, and thus the likelihood they will join. Distance was calculated as the kilometers between the interviewed household and the center of the community forest.

Community Level

At the community forest level, community forests with higher levels of income inequality may have lower membership rates. We employ the Gini coefficient to assess the level of income inequality within 21 community forests in Chitwan and explore whether potential heterogeneity between the community forests impacts membership decisions.

METHODS

Our analysis utilizes a sub-set of a 2014 survey consisting of 1041 households in the catchment area of 21 community forests located in the buffer zone in Chitwan (194 households surveyed outside the community forest catchment area were excluded, because these households were ineligible for community forest membership based on their location). The survey was implemented in 2014 with a response rate of 98.6 percent. Using this robust dataset, we develop a multilevel model to explore the factors influencing community forest membership, as a lens to examine equity in access to forest resources. Multilevel models are useful for accounting for group effects in a dataset (Steele 2008). Not accounting for group effects in grouped data will likely violate the assumption of independence in an ordinary least squares (OLS) regression. While there are ways of accounting for group effects in OLS regression, such as using dummy variables to represent groups, such approaches risk over fitting the model when there are a large number of groups (Steele 2008). Here, our data are structured in terms of households (level 1) within community forest catchment areas (level 2).

As our dependent variable (membership) is binary, we fit a binary logistic model. Member and nonmember households are present across the 21 community forest catchment areas. Table 10.1 presents this breakdown in detail. Overall, about two-thirds (690/1041) of eligible households have joined a community forest, but this varies from a low of 38 percent to a high of 93 percent.

The independent variables included in our specification are presented in Table 10.2. The model was implemented in R (version 3.1.2) using the lme4 package (version 1.1–9).

Table 10.1 Membership Dependent Variable Categories by Community Forest

Community Forest	*Nonmember HHs*	*Member HHs*	*Total*
1	18	33	51
2	5	39	44
3	11	35	46
4	27	34	61
5	15	34	49
6	14	34	48
7	16	33	49
8	22	28	50
9	10	39	49
10	15	35	50
11	33	31	64
12	20	32	52
13	3	38	41
14	36	22	58
15	13	34	47
16	12	27	39
17	12	33	45
18	14	33	47
19	10	33	43
20	36	28	64
21	9	35	44
Total	**351**	**690**	**1041**

Table 10.2 Multilevel Membership Model Variables

Variable	*Type*	*Description*
Dairy_animals	Continuous	Number of dairy animals owned by a household
Ethnicity_2	Binary	Ethnicity of the head of household; coded 1 if Hill Janajati
Ethnicity_3	Binary	Ethnicity of the head of household; coded 1 if Dalit
Ethnicity_4	Binary	Ethnicity of the head of household; coded 1 if Newar
Ethnicity_5	Binary	Ethnicity of the head of household; coded 1 if Terai Janajati
Use_firewood	Binary	Household use of firewood; coded 1 if the household uses firewood
HH_size	Continuous	Number of individuals in a household
HH_remittances	Continuous	Number of individuals abroad sending remittances to a household
Income	Categorical	Household income, categorized into seven ascending categories based on survey
HH_dist_CF	Continuous	The distance (in kilometers) of a household from the center of the closest community forest
CF_gini	Continuous	The Gini index of a community forest, based on household income

RESULTS

We find that ownership of dairy animals and household size are positively correlated with being a community forest member and that belonging to the Hill Janajati or Dalit ethnicities, income, and a household's distance to the closest community forest are negatively correlated with being a community forest member (Table 10.3). These results are consistent with previous literature and our hypotheses. We also find that belonging to the Terai Janajati minority ethnicity, household use of firewood, a household's receipt of remittances from household members abroad, and a community forest-level measure of income inequality are not significantly correlated with community forest membership. We discuss the potential reasons for these findings next.

DISCUSSION

Our results highlight two important themes that influence access to natural resources: social structure and livelihood transitions. We unpack each of these, as well as examine the role of distance from a community forest and the potential role of community forest-level income inequality, in order to understand these important indicators of access to resources and equity in locally governed common pool resource systems.

Table 10.3 Multilevel Membership Model Regression Results

Level 1 (HH)	*Estimate*	*Standard Error*
Intercept	1.07566	2.09252
Dairy_animals	0.16319***	0.02898
Ethnicity_2 (Hill Janajati)	–1.04440***	0.23224
Ethnicity_3 (Dalit)	–0.71965***	0.25293
Ethnicity_4(Newar)	–0.15315	0.39821
Ethnicity_5 (Terai Janajati)	–0.38262	0.25627
Use_firewood	–0.05036	0.18111
HH_size	0.08630***	0.03735
HH_remittances	0.03512	0.10683
Income	–0.06680**	0.03179
HH_dist_CF	–0.51833***	0.13358
Level 2 (CF)		
CF_gini	0.48778	4.07159

Significance: $p < 0.001$ '***' $p < 0.01$ '**'; N = 1041 HH, 21 CFs.

Social Structure Matters

There is local debate regarding how caste and demographics affect community forest membership, which largely centers on whether lower castes, many of which are indigenous groups, were stripped of access via formalization of the community forests and creation of local user groups to manage these forests. The evidence is decidedly mixed depending on where the research is done and how the lower castes and socioeconomic classes are defined, yet it clearly remains a concern within the nation via policies that implement ethnicity quotas in community forest management.

In our case it does appear that Bramin/Chhetri are more likely to be members of a community forest than Dalit; additionally, all of the community forest presidents are also Bramin/Chhetri, which echoes prior work such as Yadav et al. (2015). But our survey demonstrates that the fees set in Chitwan forests are not cost prohibitive with only 3 percent of nonmembers reporting that high fees were a reason for not joining, indicating that there are more complex reasons for these decisions. Thus, a significantly lower likelihood of membership among lower caste groups, like the Hill Janajati and Dalit in our analysis, may be more reflective of social differences as opposed to income. It is possible the relatively high number of nonmembers expressing concern about forest policies, which are largely written by higher caste Bramin and Chhetri management committees, may indicate the tension between the ethnic and caste groups. Nepal has changed numerous institutions regarding castes (Lawoti 2007), but these structures have evolved over centuries, so it may take time for differences in access to be understood and recognized, but more importantly for their influence on access and economic opportunity to decline.

Unpacking the Influence of Ethnicity in Chitwan

The historic roots of the caste system and the migration of indigenous ethnicities continue to influence community forest membership today. Members of the Terai indigenous population, which is from Chitwan and nearby districts in southern Nepal, are just as likely to be a community forest member as a Bramin/Chhetri individual. This is likely influenced by a unique feature of the Chitwan region; in comparison to the remainder of Nepal, there is substantially more government oversight of community forests due to their proximity to the jewel of Chitwan National Park. Government oversight in the Terai includes recent policy efforts to increase the participation of the indigenous Terai Janajati population in Chitwan community forests. Community forest governance committees in the Terai region were encouraged to provide membership/fill quotas related to this indigenous group. In contrast, the indigenous population that emigrated to Chitwan from the hills, the Hill Janajati, is significantly less likely to be a member than the Bramin/Chhetri and similar policy efforts do not exist in the Terai region for this indigenous group.

Livelihood Transitions: The Shift from Agriculture

The negative correlation of income with community forest membership indicates that our model may have captured some households shifting out of agriculture. Although households with higher income are often better positioned to take advantage of intermediate forest products provided by many community forests (Acharya 2005), some higher income households in Chitwan are receiving income from nonagricultural sources and this correlation indicates that they may have become less dependent on forest resources. One of the most common sources of nonagricultural income in Chitwan is the receipt of remittances from family members working abroad. Although receipt of remittances is not significant in our model, this is an important area for future research and further ethnographic work may aid our understanding of the relationship between remittances, livelihoods, and community forestry. It appears that the more critical element in determining membership is overall income level, which is likely related to other sources of nonagricultural income. For instance, the increasing urbanization of the region has afforded some households opportunities to work in industries such as tourism, hospitality, and industry, facilitated by a household's proximity to the highway and the nearest city (Narayangarh). Future modeling efforts will incorporate related variables to assess their possible influence and better understand the linkage between household income and community forestry.

The ownership of dairy animals is one of the most direct linkages between households and natural resource use, as they require grasses and fodder for feeding and bedding. These resources are sometimes obtained from an individual's farmland, but farmland is typically utilized for other crops for both subsistence and market. Households with dairy animals are reinforcing resource ties to the community forests.

Relatedly, we found that the farther from the nearest community forest a household is located, the less likely they are to become a member. This could be an indicator that distance is a physical barrier to access to community forest membership, but typically in Chitwan households farther from the community forests are nonagricultural and dependent on some of the alternative income sources mentioned above, such as tourism, hospitality, or other market opportunities. It member households relatively close distance to the forests and longer distance to urban areas creates a barrier for shifting to alternative livelihood opportunities, which is an important area for further study.

The Potential Importance of Community Forest-Level Income Inequality

Populations eligible for community forest membership with higher levels of income inequality are theoretically more likely to have lower membership rates (Adhikari 2004; Bhattarai and Ojha 2001), but in our case there are two factors that limit the effects of income inequality on membership. First, there is very little variation in the level of income inequality among the 21 community forests. Second, as noted earlier 97 percent of nonmember households did not indicate that fees were obstacles to membership. Similar to the impact of household level income on membership, the fact that membership fees were not identified as an issue for low income households indicates that even with an increase in community forest-level income inequality, there may not be a significant difference in Chitwan community forest membership. Importantly, these relationships between income, income inequality, and membership may not hold if community forest membership fees are increased enough that they become burdensome to lower income households in the future. As the prior results in ethnicity make clear, it may be important for us to investigate how community level ethnic heterogeneity affects membership. Our results indicate that the relationships between sociodemographics and equity in terms of community forest access are complex.

Implications of Incorporating Equity in Institutional Analysis

Incorporating equity of access within Ostrom's body of work more explicitly extends the IAD framework in a manner, which we believe, she would have strongly supported. Increasing equal access to resources strengthens natural resource management efforts (e.g., some development work notes that inequality in access to natural resources is a catalyst for violence and other issues (Jensen and Halle 2013)). Including equity in institutional analysis will not necessarily alter important theoretical findings, such as the Design Principles, but rather it allows researchers to understand obstacles to common pool resource management, impediments to collective action, and provides relevant scholarship for community members and policymakers advocating for justice in cases of inequity.

Resource management can be achieved under circumstances of inequality (Baland et al. 2007), but equity in resource access will shift communities toward sustainable resource management. Within Chitwan, there is evidence that households that perceive greater equity in their community forest resource distribution are more likely to engage in collective management (Sullivan et al. 2016). Some institutional literature has considered equity (e.g., Clement 2009), but we hope that extending equity considerations to fundamental aspects of membership and access in addition to resource distribution and management will facilitate sustainable management of common pool resources. This usage of the IAD framework enables researchers to systematically understand under what conditions equity contributes to sustainable resource management and the institutions that engender equity.

CONCLUSIONS

In this chapter, we analyzed community forest membership as a starting point for investigating equity of natural resource access. We recognize that this is but one aspect of equity. In the future, we would like to examine elite capture, or the control of resources primarily by elite groups (Persha and Andersson 2014), in more detail. In the case of Chitwan, we find that certain minority ethnic groups are as likely as elite groups to have access to community forest resources via membership, while others are more likely to be excluded. Through our fieldwork we know that most forests are led by elites. Thus, while our results support equitable access for some indigenous groups, it is unclear how this translates to tangible resource collection or perhaps more importantly to forest policies that affect the overall economic development trajectory of the community. While our findings are situated in Chitwan community forests in the Chitwan National Park Buffer Zone, we believe they point toward the importance of studying and understanding membership decisions in natural resource user groups as a way to explore equality in access to natural resources throughout the world.

Studies informed by institutional perspectives and theory consistently consider economic and environmental components of natural resource governance, but institutional studies explicitly incorporating equity are infrequent. We believe that examining the attributes of a community within the IAD framework will naturally aid in revealing characteristics where inequalities have manifested within a system (Figure 10.1). Coupling a more detailed understanding of community attributes (and revealed inequalities) with an understanding of biophysical conditions and rules will position researchers to holistically understand of the sustainability of a system, which is ultimately necessary to maintain and design sustainable social-ecological systems (Ostrom 2007, 2009).

REFERENCES

Acharya, K. P. 2002. "Twenty-Four Years of Community Forestry in Nepal." *International Forestry Review* 4 (2): 149–56. doi:10.1505/IFOR.4.2.149.17447.

Acharya, Umesh Prasad. 2011. "Livelihood Strategy of Bote Community: A Case Study of Bote Community of Patihani VDC of Chitwan." *Dhaulagiri Journal of Sociology and Anthropology* 4 (0) pages. doi:10.3126/dsaj.v4i0.4524.

Adhikari, Bhim. 2004. "Community Forestry in Nepal." http://www.academia.edu/2597059/Community_Forestry_in_Nepal.

Adhikari, Bhim. 2005. "Poverty, Property Rights and Collective Action: Understanding the Distributive Aspects of Common Property Resource Management." *Environment and Development Economics* 10 (01): 7–31. doi:10.1017/S1355770X04001755.

Adhikari, Bhim, Salvatore Di Falco, and Jon C. Lovett. 2004. "Household Characteristics and Forest Dependency: Evidence from Common Property Forest Management in Nepal." *Ecological Economics* 48 (2): 245–57. doi:10.1016/j.ecolecon.2003.08.008.

Adhikari, Bhim, Frances Williams, and Jon C. Lovett. 2007. "Local Benefits from Community Forests in the Middle Hills of Nepal." *Forest Policy and Economics* 9 (5): 464–78.

Agarwal, Bina. 2013. *Gender and Green Governance: The Political Economy of Women's Presence Within and Beyond Community Forestry*. Reprint edition. Oxford University Press.

Baral, J. C., and B. R. Subedi. 2000. "Some Community Forestry Issues in the Terai, Nepal: Where Do We Go from Here?" *Forests, Trees and People Newsletter* 42: 20–25.

Barnaud, Cecile, and Annemarie Van Paassen. 2013. "Equity, Power Games, and Legitimacy: Dilemmas of Participatory Natural Resource Management." *Ecology and Society* 18 (2). pages

Bhattarai, Basundhara, and Hemant R. Ojha. 2001. "Distributional Impact of Community Forestry: Who Is Benefiting from Nepal's Community Forests?" http://agris.fao.org/agris-search/search.do?recordID=GB2013202900.

Bohra, Pratikshya, and Douglas S. Massey. 2009. "Processes of Internal and International Migration from Chitwan, Nepal." *The International Migration Review* 43 (3): 621–51.

Cavendish, William. 2000. "Empirical Regularities in the Poverty-Environment Relationship of Rural Households: Evidence from Zimbabwe." *World Development* 28 (11): 1979–2003.

Charnley, Susan and Melissa R. Poe. 2007. "Community Forestry in Theory and Practice: Where Are We Now?" *Annual Review of Anthropology* 36 (January): 301–36.

Cole, Daniel H., Graham Epstein, and Michael D. McGinnis. 2014. "Toward a New Institutional Analysis of Social-Ecological Systems (NIASES): Combining Elinor Ostrom's IAD and SES Frameworks." SSRN Scholarly Paper ID 2490999. Rochester, NY: Social Science Research Network. http://papers.ssrn.com/abstract=2490999.

Coulibaly-Lingani, Pascaline, Patrice Savadogo, Mulualem Tigabu, and Per-Christer Oden. 2011. "Factors Influencing People's Participation in the Forest Management Program in Burkina Faso, West Africa." *Forest Policy and Economics* 13 (4): 292–302.

Deininger, Klaus and Lyn Squire. 1996. "A New Data Set Measuring Income Inequality." *The World Bank Economic Review* 10 (3): 565–91. doi:10.1093/wber/10.3.565.

Gilmour, Don. 2003. "Retrospective and Prospective View of Community Forestry in Nepal." *Journal of Forest and Livelihood* 2 (2): 5–7.

Gilmour, Don, Yam Malla, and Mike Nurse. 2004. "Linkages between Community Forestry and Poverty." *Bangkok: Regional Community Forestry Center for Asia and the Pacific*. http://www.recoftc.org/site/uploads/content/pdf/Community_forestry_and_poverty_69.pdf.

Hansmann, Ralph, Harald A. Mieg, and Peter Frischknecht. 2012. "Principal Sustainability Components: Empirical Analysis of Synergies between the Three Pillars of Sustainability." *International Journal of Sustainable Development & World Ecology* 19 (5): 451–59. doi:10.1080/13504509.2012.696220.

Jensen, David and Halle, Silja. 2013. "Women and Natural Resources: Unlocking the peacebuilding potential." United Nations Environment Programme Reports. HYPERLINK "https://urldefense.proofpoint.com/v2/url?u=http-3A__www.undp.org_content_dam_undp_library_crisis-2520prevention_WomenNaturalResourcesPBreport2013.pdf&d=CwMFaQ&c=AGbYxfJbXK67KfXyGqyv2Ejiz41FqQuZFk4A-1IxfAU&r=H3P_V4ANXsuasWzeQA_aJME3VUECcFW9uGEixpy1nKo&m=NzOYB6tHkVo6miMqaTVou4AmTRvHiwHmKXftql5ArCg&s=IbRhUKUYnvXddxbrMMkEGD2q9pplS6N8CGMCI_amgo4&e="; http://www.undp.org/content/dam/undp/library/crisis%20prevention/WomenNaturalResourcesPBreport2013.pdf.

Jha, Prashant. 2014. *Battles of the New Republic: A Contemporary History of Nepal*. New Delhi: Aleph Book Company.

Kennedy, B. P., I. Kawachi, and D. Prothrow-Stith. 1996. "Income Distribution and Mortality: Cross Sectional Ecological Study of the Robin Hood Index in the United States." *BMJ* 312 (7037): 1004–7. doi:10.1136/bmj.312.7037.1004.

Lawoti, Mahendra. 2007. *Looking Back, Looking Forward: Centralization, Multiple Conflicts, and Democratic State Building in Nepal*. Washington, DC: East-West Center. http://scholarspace.manoa.hawaii.edu/handle/10125/5480.

Maskey, Vishakha, Tesfa G. Gebremedhin, and Timothy J. Dalton. 2006. "Social and Cultural Determinants of Collective Management of Community Forest in Nepal." *Journal of Forest Economics* 11 (4): 261–74. doi:10.1016/j.jfe.2005.10.004.
Ostrom, Elinor. 2005. *Understanding Institutional Diversity*. Princeton University Press.
Ostrom, Elinor. 2007. "A Diagnostic Approach for Going beyond Panaceas." *Proceedings of the National Academy of Sciences* 104 (39): 15181–87. doi:10.1073/pnas.0702288104.
Ostrom, Elinor. 2009. "A General Framework for Analyzing Sustainability of Social-Ecological Systems." *Science* 325 (5939): 419–22. doi:10.1126/science.1172133.
Ostrom, Elinor, Roy Gardner, and James Walker. 1994. *Rules, Games, and Common-Pool Resources*. University of Michigan Press.
Padilla, Emilio. 2002. "Intergenerational equity and sustainability." *Ecological Economics* 41 (1): 69–83.
Persha, Lauren and Krister Andersson. 2014. "Elite Capture Risk and Mitigation in Decentralized Forest Governance Regimes." *Global Environmental Change* 24 (January): 265–76. doi:10.1016/j.gloenvcha.2013.12.005.
Pokharel, Ramesh. "Politics and Problematics of the Definition and Categorization of Ethnicity in Nepal." *Bodhi: An Interdisciplinary Journal* 5.1 (2013): 1–15.
Rai, Rajesh K., and Helen Scarborough. 2014. "Understanding the Effects of the Invasive Plants on Rural Forest-Dependent Communities." *Small-Scale Forestry*, August, 1–14. doi:10.1007/s11842–014–9273–7.
Scherr, Sara J. 2000. "A Downward Spiral? Research Evidence on the Relationship between Poverty and Natural Resource Degradation." *Food Policy* 25 (4): 479–98.
Sharma, Anuja Raj. 2009. "Impact of Community Forestry on Income Distribution in Nepal." Text. http://www.forestrynepal.org/publications/thesis/4664.
Shrestha, N. R. 1989. "Frontier Settlement and Landlessness among Hill Migrants in Nepal Tarai." *Annals of the Association of American Geographers* 79 (3): 370–89.
Stash, Sharon and Emily Hannum. 2001. "Who Goes to School? Educational Stratification by Gender, Caste, and Ethnicity in Nepal." *Comparative Education Review* 45 (3): 354–78.
Sullivan, A., A. York, L. An, S. Yabiku, and S. Hall. "How Does Perception at Multiple Levels Influence Collective Action in the Commons?" Unpublished Manuscript.
Turner, R. A., A. Cakacaka, N. A. J. Graham, N. V. C. Polunin, M. S. Pratchett, S. M. Stead, and S. K. Wilson. 2007. "Declining Reliance on Marine Resources in Remote South Pacific Societies: Ecological versus Socio-Economic Drivers." *Coral Reefs* 26 (4): 997–1008.
Varughese, George, and Elinor Ostrom. 2001. "The Contested Role of Heterogeneity in Collective Action: Some Evidence from Community Forestry in Nepal." *World Development* 29 (5): 747–65. doi:10.1016/S0305–750X(01)00012–2.
Yadav, B. D., Bigsby, H., & MacDonald, I. (2015). How can poor and disadvantaged households get an opportunity to become a leader in community forestry in Nepal? *Forest Policy and Economics* 52: 27–38.

Index

Note: Page references for figures and tables are italicized

About the Contributors

Paul Dragos Aligica is a Senior Research Fellow at the F. A. Hayek Program for Advanced Study in Philosophy, Politics, and Economics, Mercatus Center, George Mason University where he teaches in the graduate program of the Economics Department. He is the author and coauthor of five books—including *Institutional Diversity and Political Economy. The Ostroms and Beyond*, Oxford University Press, 2014—and of numerous academic articles on political economy and institutional theory.

Rosolino Candela is a PhD Candidate in Economics at George Mason University and a Graduate Research Fellow in the F. A. Hayek Program for Advanced Study in Philosophy, Politics, and Economics at the Mercatus Center at George Mason University. He holds a BA in History from St. John's University and an MA in Economics and International Political Economy from Fordham University. Previously, he was also a Visiting PhD Student in the Department of Political and Social Sciences at the European University Institute and a Charles G. Koch PhD Fellow at Suffolk University, where he was also a Koch Summer Fellow. Among his research interests are Austrian Economics, Public Choice, and New Institutional Economics.

Dario Castiglione teaches Political Theory at the University of Exeter. His main research interests are in theories of democracy and constitutionalism, with particular reference to the European Union, and the history of political thought. His publications as either author or coeditor include *The Handbook of Social Capital* (Oxford University Press, 2008); *Constitutional Politics in the EU* (Palgrave, 2007); *The Language Question in Europe and Diverse Societies*, (Hart Publishers, 2007), *The Making of European Citizens* (Palgrave, 2006); *The History of Political Thought in National Context*,

(Cambridge University Press, 2001); *The Constitution in Transformation: European and Theoretical Perspectives*, (Blackwell, 1996).

Michael A. Fotos, III is, since 2007, a Lecturer in Political Science at Yale University. He is also, since 2000, a Visiting Assistant Professor in the graduate public policy program at Trinity College in Hartford, CT. He is the author of "Vincent Ostrom's Revolutionary Science of Association," published in 2015 in *Public Choice: the Journal of the Public Choice Society* (163(1–2), 67–83). His research and teaching focus on institutional, political, and policy theory with particular reference to the research program of the Bloomington School. Areas of subject matter expertise include coal mining regulation, voter turnout, ecosystem services, marine fisheries management, and military doctrine and strategy. Dr. Fotos is a mid-career academic with previous work experience in energy sales and marketing, West Virginia state government, and environmental NGO management. He is a 1978 graduate of Yale College, holds an MPA from Harvard University, and a PhD in Political Science from Indiana University. Dr. Fotos serves as a volunteer director of Warrior-Scholar Project and Connecticut Farmland Trust.

Anas Malik is Associate Professor of Political Science at Xavier University, Cincinnati, and Affiliated Faculty, The Ostrom Workshop, Indiana University, Bloomington. He received his Ph.D. in Political Science and his Master's in Economics from Indiana University, Bloomington. Malik is the author of *Political Survival in Pakistan* (Routledge, 2011), *The Polycentric Islamic Polity* (Lexington, forthcoming), and *Islamic Interreligious Covenants* (Palgrave, forthcoming). His research program explores institutional potentials for facilitating collective action and sustainability in the Middle East and South Asia.

Ronald J. Oakerson is Davidson Distinguished Professor of Social Science and Professor of Political Science at Houghton College, where he has served on the faculty since 1992, serving as academic vice president and dean of college from 1999 to 2006. Previously he taught at Marshall University (1974–1979 and 1982–1985). He received his PhD in political science at Indiana University in 1978, where Vincent Ostrom was his dissertation chair, followed by a two-year postdoc at the Workshop in Political Theory and Policy Analysis in Bloomington. He served as a member of the Panel on Common Property Resource Management of the National Academy of Sciences (1983–1985) and was a senior analyst at the US Advisory Commission on Intergovernmental Relations (1985–1988), where he directed the Commission's metropolitan area studies. As a member of the research faculty at the Ostrom Workshop (1988–1992), he began a series of consultancies with the US Agency for International Development in Cameroon and later with the Africa Bureau in Washington. His professional service has included the first executive council of the International Association for the Study of the Commons (1989–1991), the National Rural Studies Committee (1987–1997), and the Task Force on Civic Education for the Twenty-First Century of the American Political Science Association (1996–2000). His published research has dealt mainly with issues of metropolitan governance, publishing *Governing Local Public Economies: Creating the Civic Metropolis* in 1999. Most recently, he has been engaged in collaborative research with students dealing with the urban commons in Buffalo, NY, and decentralization, village organization, and customary land tenure in Sierra Leone.

Margaret M. Polski is a researcher in the field of national security policymaking, strategic planning, and operational design. She serves as a research analyst with the Center for Naval Analyses (CNA); an affiliate research fellow in the Krasnow Institute for Advanced Study; a consultant to the National Academy of Sciences; a panel member for the National Science Foundation; and supports the US Department of State in public diplomacy. Dr. Polski has a PhD from Indiana University in Political Science; an MPA from Harvard University in Business Economics and Policy; and a Bachelor's in Elected Studies from the University of Minnesota.

Filippo Sabetti is a Professor of Political Science at McGill University, Montreal, Quebec, Canada, and a Senior Research Fellow at the Ostrom Workshop, Indiana University. He works on a range of issues across history, comparative politics and political theory seeking to uncover the mechanisms that enable social cooperation to emerge and to show why centralization need not be inevitable in democracy. His most recent publications include Vincenzo Cuoco's *Historical Essay on the Neapolitan Revolution* (2nd edition of 1806) coedited with Bruce Haddock (University of Toronto Press, 2014), and *Choice, Rules and Collective Action: The Ostroms on the Study of Institutions and Governance* coedited with Paul Dragos Aligica (ECPR Press, 2014).

Karol Edward Sołtan teaches in the Department of Government and Politics at the University of Maryland, where he has also taught in the Law School. He has held positions in the Department of Economics at University of Warsaw and in the National School of Public Administration (Warsaw). In 2000 he was Deputy Director of the Office of Political, Constitutional and Electoral Affairs in the United Nations Transitional Administration for East Timor, and Acting Cabinet Member in the Transitional Government of East Timor. He is Cofounder and Codirector of the Summer Institute of Civic

Studies at Tufts University and the European Summer Institute of Civic Studies at the University of Augsburg. His most recent book (coedited with Peter Levine) is *Civic Studies.*

Ion Sterpan is an Economics PhD student at George Mason University and a graduate fellow at Mercatus Center's F. A. Hayek Program. He studied philosophy at Central European University in Budapest and at the University of Bucharest and worked in Bucharest with the Center for Institutional Analysis and Development. His research is on polycentric institutional systems which he approaches from an Austrian and Virginian Political Economy perspective.

Abigail Sullivan is an interdisciplinarily trained scholar studying social-ecological systems from an institutional perspective. She received her PhD in Environmental Social Science from Arizona State University in 2016 and holds a master's in Ecology and Environmental Science from the University of Maine. She is broadly interested in understanding factors influencing collective action; collective action processes at multiple scales; and modeling techniques to explore difficult to observe aspects of institutions, like long-term changes in social norms.

Scott Yabiku is a Professor of Sociology at The Pennsylvania State University. His research asks questions about human and ecological systems, migration, substance use, and family. Although initially trained as a sociologist and demographer, Yabiku's research is now characterized by diverse collaborations across disciplines. This interdisciplinary research on how human and natural systems affect each other spans the social and natural sciences. Yabiku's research is also international in scope with data collections or field work in the United States, Mexico, Mozambique, China, and Nepal.

Abigail York is an Associate Professor of Public Policy and Governance at Arizona State University where she directs the Environmental Social Science PhD Program. She has a PhD in public policy from Indiana University chaired by Elinor Ostrom. York's work examines the dynamics of collective action and institutional change within social-ecological systems. She works on diverse empirical projects in historical and contemporary contexts, USA and internationally to better understand impacts and drivers of institutional change. Throughout her career, York has focused on how institutions affect and are affected by urbanization and environmental change, while more recently she has begun to examine theoretical questions surrounding power, equity and environmental justice in the provisioning of public services and goods.

Albert Weale is Emeritus Professor of Political Theory and Public Policy at University College London. His research and publications have been concentrated on issues of political theory and public policy, especially the theory of justice and the theory of democracy, health policy and comparative environmental policy. His principal publications include *Equality and Social Policy* (Routledge and Kegan Paul, 1978), *Political Theory and Social Policy* (Macmillan, 1983), *The New Politics of Pollution* (Manchester University Press, 1992), *Democracy* (Macmillan, 1999 and 2007 revised), *Democratic Citizenship and the European Union* (Manchester University Press, 2005), *Democratic Justice and the Social Contract* (Oxford University Press, 2013) and, with others, *The Theory of Choice* (Blackwell, 1992) and *Environmental Governance in Europe* (Oxford University Press, 2000) as well as a number of edited books, journal paper and chapters.

He is currently working on a monograph on modern social contract theory which examines the principal variants of social contract theory since 1950.

www.ingramcontent.com/pod-product-compliance
Lightning Source LLC
Chambersburg PA
CBHW051253200926
51612CB00001B/34
* 9 7 8 1 4 9 8 5 2 7 6 7 5 *